About the Author

Mike Rees was educated at Newbridge Grammar School and is a history graduate of UCW Aberystwyth where he was awarded both BA and MA degrees. He also studied at Leeds Polytechnic and Goldsmiths College, University of London. Mike worked as an administrator in the National Health Service before spending thirty years as a teacher. He retired as Deputy Head of West Monmouth School, Pontypool in 2012. Mike now regularly gives talks to local history groups and serves as treasurer to the Gwent Branch of the Western Front Association. When he is not reading his many history, sport or music books, strumming his guitar or following, from the comfort of an armchair, all the major sporting events, Mike enjoys spending time with his family. He lives in Newport and is married with two children, and two young grandsons. This is his second book.

WHERE SKILL AND COURAGE COUNT

The Experiences and Sacrifices of Sportsmen in World War Two

MIKE REES

WHERE SKILL AND COURAGE COUNT

The Experiences and Sacrifices of Sportsmen
in World War Two

Vanguard Press

VANGUARD PAPERBACK

© Copyright 2023
Mike Rees

The right of Mike Rees to be identified as author of
this work has been asserted by him in accordance with the
Copyright, Designs and Patents Act 1988.

A CIP catalogue record for this title is
available from the British Library.

ISBN 978 1 80016 389 8

*Vanguard Press is an imprint of
Pegasus Elliot Mackenzie Publishers Ltd.*
www.pegasuspublishers.com

First Published in 2023

**Vanguard Press
Sheraton House Castle Park
Cambridge England**

Printed & Bound in Great Britain

To my wonderful wife, Hilary; to my beautiful family and to all those sportsmen and women who sacrificed so much during six years of war. May their contribution never be forgotten.

Acknowledgements

The writing of this book has, as much as anything, confirmed that a person is never too old to learn. On re-reading my first book, 'Men Who Played the Game': Sportsmen who gave their lives in the Great War, I reflected on my conclusion. Quite properly I had emphasised the extent of the price paid by many sportsmen of the early years of the twentieth century, their bravery and self-sacrifice, as well as the distress felt by the families that many of them left behind. What also leapt out from the final pages however was the rather dismissive way in which I referred to their successors who, in 1939, took up arms in the fight against fascism. I decided that many had become physical training instructors charged with improving fitness and raising morale. Not for them the brave, ultimate sacrifices of my World War 1 heroes, at that time being rightly recognised for their bravery during the centenary commemorations.

As time went on this niggled at me. I had heard some stories first hand from my father who had served as a wireless operator in India and the Far East and from my uncle who had flown Lancaster bombers over Germany and Italy throughout the war. Both had recently passed on. Typically, neither had said very much about their own contribution but, as a student of modern history who had taught the subject for more than thirty years, my printed comments made me uncomfortable. Had I been far too cavalier in my assumption? I felt the need to correct the record, if indeed it needed correction.

So began the task of writing this current book, a work which I hope does justice to those sports stars who gave so much to the war effort whether on the Home Front or in the many theatres of warfare, from Western Europe to North Africa, from the Mediterranean to the Far East. Many of the participants were reluctant to discuss their contributions during their lifetime, no doubt eager to return to a more normal existence. The result of this reluctance is that their war service has often been overlooked, a secondary, even irrelevant story, when set against glittering careers on the sports field. It is time for their more complete stories to be told and I hope that I have made a small contribution to achieving this.

Of course, one cannot succeed in this without enormous help and I thank Pegasus Publishers for giving me this opportunity. With so much competition it is still a great thrill to see your book in the market place and I am very grateful for this opportunity. During my research I made great use of Cardiff City library, especially their online service which allowed me access to all past copies of the Times newspaper relevant to the period. Many secondary sources were also available to me through the use of both Newport and Cardiff libraries, the extent of which is made clear in the bibliography. Libraries remain the single most important means of research and they must continue to be supported. Several sports clubs were also able to point me in the right direction and special mention must be made of Worcestershire, Essex, Kent and Glamorgan County Cricket Clubs, Blackheath and Bath Rugby Clubs and Luton, Southampton and Arsenal Football Clubs. Glamorgan Cricket Archives were particularly generous in allowing Pegasus to reproduce the images of Maurice Turnbull. Indeed, Glamorgan Cricket Archives Heritage and Education Co-ordinator and Maurice Turnbull's biographer, Dr Andrew Hignell, took the time to read the relevant chapter and offer advice concerning some of the detail. I am very grateful to him for his help.

The support of those much nearer to home has been crucial to my endeavours. Sadly, both my mother, Pam, and sister, Helen, passed away during the writing of this book but those family who remain are a constant source of encouragement. Since I set out to complete this book, I have become the proud grandfather of two beautiful grandsons, Charlie and Joey, and I hope that one day in the future both will have sufficient interest in history and sport to want to pick up this book and read it. I know that their mother, my daughter Hannah, will encourage them as she, and husband Gareth, are supportive of all my 'retirement' activities. My son Tom shares my interest in sport and history and I am confident that he too will enjoy reading his dad's latest project. My pride in both my children knows no bounds.

My greatest debt, however, lies elsewhere. One Spring evening in 1991, following an afternoon of watching rugby, I made my way to a small dinner party in the South Wales valleys near my childhood home. There, besides the three married couples I was expecting to find, I was introduced to Hilary, a young lady far away from her Hampshire roots. No steps that I have taken before or since have proved to be as important as those I took that Saturday evening. Within eight months we were married and throughout the subsequent years Hilary has been my greatest supporter and inspiration. Regarding this book Hilary has made observations and suggestions even to the extent of proof reading every page. This book, like anything that I have been fortunate enough to achieve, would not have been possible without her.

Contents

INTRODUCTION
FRIDAY 1ST SEPTEMBER 1939

On Friday 1st September 1939, with the English summer drifting towards an inevitable close, Yorkshire County Cricket Club secured its 21st County championship title with a dramatic victory over Sussex at Hove. The great England left arm spinner, Hedley Verity, ensured this win with the astounding return of 7 wickets for the cost of 9 runs, amazing figures even for this remarkable bowler. Supporting him in this sensational display of bowling was Yorkshire's fast bowler and England teammate Bill Bowes, fresh from achieving his best ever test figures of 6/33 against the touring West Indies at Manchester. Victory should have ensured that it was a wonderful day in the history of Yorkshire cricket. Yet all was not as it seemed. The other two County Championship matches due to finish that day had already been abandoned, at Leicester and at Old Trafford, the former, allegedly, due to the state of the Leicestershire pitch. The game at Hove, crucial though it proved to be, was, Bowes tells us, played in a "strained atmosphere" where spectators watched the game with their minds on matters other than cricket. Bowes was of the opinion that the game was only concluded because it was the testimonial for the very popular Sussex batsman, Jim Parks. The importance of the game in deciding the title had suddenly become of secondary importance.

What was it that was occupying the thoughts of even 'cricket mad' supporters as the season reached its annual climax? The Lancashire fixture against Surrey had been abandoned after two days due to a quickly developing international crisis and it was the global political situation that was dominating discussion throughout the country. Europe was once again on the brink of war and players and supporters alike were as aware as anybody of the gravity of the situation. Even at the moment of their triumph, Yorkshire's finest were debating the effect that this crisis would have on their futures. Bowes tells us of his team's journey home on that September evening, where in order to return to Yorkshire, the team had to hire a char-à-banc. All of England was blanked out, he tells us, and the championship winning team were forced to halt their journey at Leicester. There the players had their last dinner together, with Champagne and oysters. Verity and Bowes discussed the future, safe in the knowledge that they had been first and second respectively in the national bowling averages that year. Possibly England's two finest bowlers with several more summers ahead during which they could add to their numerous triumphs for both Yorkshire and England on the cricket field. But the onset of war would soon put paid to that. Little did they know that Bowes would be one of 20,000 British soldiers captured at Tobruk Aerodrome and spend the following three years as a German prisoner of war, returning home weighing four and a half stone less than when he joined the forces. Verity would never return. England's greatest spin bowler was killed in the Italian campaign of 1943. As in 1914, the Sussex v Yorkshire fixture played at Hove was the last first-class cricket match to be completed before the outbreak of a world war. Sportsmen and women throughout the country were, along with the rest of the country, about to experience its 'darkest hour'.

"This is not peace. It is an armistice for 20 years." So said the perceptive Marshall Foch, Supreme Allied Commander of the Allied Forces during World War 1 on the conclusion of the Paris Peace Conference in June 1919. Twenty years and sixty-five days later, this grim analysis came to dreadful, costly fruition with the onset of the most devastating war in human history. On September 1st, 1939, a German warship opened fire on the Polish garrison in the special area reserved for them within the Free City of Danzig, now known as Gdansk. Events moved at breathtaking speed. France immediately declared war against Germany, with Britain following two days later. At 11.00 a.m. on 3rd September, Prime Minister, Neville Chamberlain, spoke to the British people using the now popular and much listened to radio.

"This morning the British Ambassador in Berlin handed the German Government a final note stating that unless we heard from them by eleven o'clock that they were prepared at once to withdraw their troops from Poland, a state of war would exist between us. I have to tell you that no such understanding has been received and that consequently this country is at war with Germany."

This was, without doubt, the most dramatic statement made by a British Prime Minister during the whole of the twentieth century. The remainder of Chamberlain's address is often overlooked, yet his words set out only too clearly the sacrifices that would be necessary in this 'total war'. He talked of the many ways in which the British people would need to contribute. He spoke solemnly of the work needed in order to maintain the life of the people, in factories, in public utilities, maintaining transport and in supplying the essentials of everyday life. Chamberlain stressed the importance that people carry on with their jobs as best they could. Total war involved everybody. Fighting fascism directly on the battlefield would only be part of the story.

Chamberlain, who remembered only too well the horrors of the Great War twenty-five years before, was right to be fearful. At Munich, eleven months earlier, he had believed, at least briefly, that war could still be avoided. The subsequent occupation of the rest of western Czechoslovakia in March 1939, the Nazi-Soviet Pact concluded in August and the invasion of Poland on 1st September ensured that this was a forlorn hope and left the British Prime Minister's reputation in tatters. This war was a 'total war' like no other. The historian John Campbell has written that whatever measurement we use, whether it be geographic extent, the scale of military and economic mobilisation, the impact on non-combatants, the toll of casualties, the disruption of civilian lives or the dislocation of the world economy, this war affected more people directly than any other war before or since. Campbell correctly concludes that World War Two was "the overwhelming experience of the twentieth century."

The scale of casualties, backs Campbell's argument. It is impossible to give precise figures regarding deaths and estimates vary greatly from 50 million to around 80 million. These figures include up to 25 million military deaths, including around 5 million deaths in captivity and up to 55 million civilian deaths, around 28 million of these being from war-related disease and famine. It has been generally accepted that military deaths numbered around 7 million in the Soviet Union, 3.5 million in Germany, 1.2 million in Japan, 300,000 in the USA and 250,000 in Britain. Civilian casualties resulting from the relatively recent use of bombing have been recorded as 300,000 in Germany, 500,000 in Japan and, according to CN Truman in "Civilian Casualties of World War Two", 60,000 in the UK. Gerhard Weinburg tells us that 33,000 were killed by bombers alone in Britain bringing to horrid fruition the notion present throughout the 1930s that 'the bomber would always get through'. Add to this the genocide of the European Jews and the full horror of this war becomes apparent.

When counting casualties, there is also the debate around when the war actually began. Japan had struck in China as early as 1937 and the conflict continued as part of World War Two until 1945, while Japan and the Soviet Union had been fighting on the borders of their respective puppet states since May 1939. More recently, since the collapse of the Soviet Union, many countries in Eastern Europe have begun to revise the figures. It barely seems possible but it could be that historians have underestimated the scale of loss.

Nevertheless, however often these figures are repeated and revised, it is almost impossible to absorb the scale of this cataclysmic event. The effect of World War Two on international relations is also difficult to quantify. It left a scar on both Germany and Japan that, notwithstanding the economic success of the post-war years enjoyed by both countries, has been difficult to erase. For Britain, success in 1945 disguised the inevitability of reduced British influence in the second half of the twentieth century while the USA was boosted by the impression of limitless power and of having responsibility for the protection of freedom and democracy throughout the world. Meanwhile events left the Soviet Union with a feeling of distrust and a determination that it would never be invaded again. The dropping of the atom bomb perhaps made the Cold War of the post-war years inevitable while the guilt experienced by Europe over the Holocaust has affected the politics of Israel and the Middle East to the present day. Not that the social upheaval created by the war was all bad. Women, at least in some countries, gained more opportunities for independence while some social rigidities were loosened. There was excitement as well as tragedy, heroism as well as cruelty, while some participants discovered a new sense of purpose, despite the periods of futility and tedium that inevitably come from such a conflict.

From the outset there was a very different mood to that of 1914. There was no jingoistic notion of 'teaching the Hun a lesson' or excitement of going to war. This war was very unlikely to be over by Christmas. Rather, there was a feeling that this was a necessary war, one in which Britain had to defend democracy and defeat the fascist dictators. The mood was one of apprehension coupled with a resigned acceptance that there was a job to do. In both Britain and France, Hitler was seen as waging a war of conquest by launching an unprovoked attack on Poland. According to Nicholas Stargardt in his ground-breaking book *The German War*, Germans saw the war very differently. When war broke out it was deeply unpopular in Germany but there was no great soul searching as to why it had happened. The German people saw it as more of a war of national defence.

There were some in Britain of course who did find the idea of war exciting. Lieutenant Dick Caldwell, a surgeon in the Royal Navy, tells us that his fellow officers felt that they would now earn their keep and that they were well prepared for the ordeal ahead. Their Admiral even called his officers together to propose a toast, calling for "damnation to Hitler." Although there was conscription some men joined up from the start and many were optimistic of the outcome even believing that stories of a large German army were greatly exaggerated. Rumours took hold that some tanks known to have been on parade in Northern Germany had been made of cardboard. Others were less hopeful. Ex-soldier Eric Doe had no illusions about what war would mean. He had fought in the recent Spanish Civil War and realised that, despite conscription, Britain had insufficient kit and men. His verdict was "we just weren't ready." Moreover, the fear of air raids was very real. The Great War had given the population a taste of what was possible as they recalled Zeppelins coming down over Elstree. Older people, remembering the horrors of 1914-18, feared that the civilian population would be gassed. Gas masks appeared almost immediately, much to the amusement of children, and air-raid shelters appeared in gardens. The whole atmosphere was what Max Arthur called one of "fear and anticipation." Lady Anne Chichester, living in Hampshire, remembers this mood clearly in the early days of September 1939.

"On that fateful day of Sunday, 3rd September at 11.00 in the morning, we all sat round the radio and we heard Neville Chamberlain's speech with the horrific news that we were actually, from that moment, at war with Germany. Everybody was extremely shattered, and by an extraordinary coincidence, within ten minutes of the announcement, all the sirens went off. We really did think at that very moment the bombers were about to arrive. But it was only a false alarm, and the all-clear went — but it was a very strange time. We really thought that we were going to be bombed."

During the coming years, Britain mobilised in a way unmatched by other countries. By June 1944, as the Allies prepared to reoccupy France, 55% of Britons were either serving in the armed forces or were involved in civilian war work. Employment in 'war industries' increased at the expense of civilian needs and labour was diverted into engineering, chemical industry and other work connected with munitions. Women, in particular, were used in these ways more than in any other country. By 1943 it was almost impossible for any woman under 40 to avoid 'war work' and by 1944, 48% of civil service jobs were done by women. The percentage of women in engineering and vehicle building rose from 9% to 34% in the war years while those involved in agriculture more than doubled. A recent visit to Bletchley Park, the top-secret home of the World War Two codebreakers, confirmed that 75% of those employed there by the end of the war were women.

Perhaps the best way to appreciate the full effect of the war is by examining the human stories that emerge. In recent years, historians have examined in detail the sacrifice made by sportsmen during the Great War. It now seems entirely appropriate to examine the contribution made by sportsmen and, in some instances, women to

World War Two. It is a major regret that the role of sportsmen and sportswomen in the years 1939-1945 remains largely unexplored and is still an area requiring further research. It is likely that the sports stars of 1939 lacked the innocence of their predecessors of 1914 and it is entirely understandable if they were filled with trepidation at the future that awaited them. Yet none of this detracts from their value as a group in helping us to understand the impact of World War Two. As in 1914–18, the importance of their contribution, often played down by the participants themselves, is worthy of study.

Although a relatively small number of well-known international sportsmen were, like Hedley Verity, killed in the war, the sporting careers of hundreds of top sportsmen were affected. A total of 14 players who took part in the last Test match played before the war, England v West Indies at the Oval in August 1939, never played international cricket again. Ted Drake, the prolific Arsenal centre forward, scored 4 goals in his team's 5–2 victory over Sunderland on that final Saturday before the war but this 27-year-old, despite surviving the war, had played his last top-class match. The 19-year-old Tommy Lawton scored twice for Everton against Bolton that same afternoon but, although he later became something of a household name and successful England striker, the first, possibly most productive, half of his career was lost. At least Drake and Lawton were able to survive the war. A total of 80 footballers, 14 of whom played in the top flight, did not. Rugby internationals, too, fell in significant numbers. A total of 40 international players from the British Isles were killed, many in training accidents, but in active service nonetheless.

Just as in the Great War, the contribution made by sportsmen was significant. Yet it appears that, to an even greater extent than in the earlier war, their contribution as a group has been largely unrecognised. By 1939, as we shall see, sport was playing an increasing role in the fabric of people's lives, the way in which much of the world communicated with one another. Young boys enthusiastically collected player cigarette cards whenever they could. They gathered around the radio, which by now most families owned, with their fathers, and sometimes mothers too, to listen to the major sporting events. These would include FA Cup Finals, world championship boxing, cricket Test matches and rugby internationals. British Pathé newsreels shown in the cinema brought sport further to life in the imaginations of a sports-mad population. Yet when we delve into the sporting history books there is little mention of the sacrifice made by our sportsmen. The contribution made in maintaining morale through wartime fixtures is well-documented. The authorities were, more than ever, keen to stress the value of sport in raising morale, both of the soldiers and of the general population. As a result, during the war people played more sport than ever before. Central and Local Government made sure that this was so, unlike 1914 when men such as Lord Baden-Powell, Sir Arthur Conan Doyle and Lord Derby ridiculed men who played sport when there was a war to fight. Sportsmen were seen to have the qualities of teamwork and loyalty that were crucial attributes for those on the battlefield and those trying to cope at home in the most difficult of circumstances. But the extent of the losses to sport in World War Two, with the notable exception of the cricketer's bible, Wisden, is almost ignored and certainly underplayed in sports history books. One or two sentences appears to suffice. Even the obituaries of sportsmen who survived the war make few references to their war record. On those occasions that it is mentioned it is often to retell a humorous anecdote, glossing over the significant contribution that they may have made.

It is time that this wrong was put to rights. As in World War One, sportsmen and women made great sacrifices, and in many cases, the ultimate sacrifice. Throughout the 1930s, sportsmen and women had shown what was possible and gave hope to people trying to escape the economic woes of the Depression. Along with the Hollywood film stars, sportsmen and women provided a form of escapism during those most challenging years. Heroes in their communities yet still, in a way largely impossible today, a part of that community sharing in the challenges of one of the most difficult decades of the twentieth century. Their stories and wartime experiences, which so often reflected or in many cases exceeded, the heroism shown on the sports field, deserve, finally, to be heard.

CHAPTER 1
INCREASED COVERAGE AND PROPAGANDA:
SPORT IN THE INTERWAR YEARS

During the years immediately following the Great War sport began the task of rebuilding after four and a half years of intense warfare which had left the country exhausted and irrevocably weakened. This applied to sport as much as to any other facet of life. The years before 1914 had seen both the playing, and particularly the watching of sport, become central to people's lives. With increased leisure time and improved public transport, the Edwardian Age had seen spectator sports thrive. Cricket had begun the twentieth century as the number-one sport and national figures like WG Grace were as recognisable as any politician. Test matches, still most often played against Australia, were very popular, although they still took second place to a very competitive County Championship. By the 1920s there had been a significant shift. Football was catching up quickly and by the 1920s was well established as the national sport. In 1923, when the FA Cup Final was played at Wembley for the first time, there was clear evidence of this. The ground capacity was stated to be 125,000 and official figures confirm the ground as being full for the Bolton Wanderers v West Ham, north versus south showdown. This was the cup final of 'The White Horse' where newsreels from the time show a white horse driving overenthusiastic spectators from the pitch. Including the numbers still locked outside, more recent estimates put the attendance figure at nearer 300,000. Impossible to confirm, no doubt, but evidence that football was well and truly increasing in popularity.

The footballers themselves, by now almost totally professional, were beneficiaries. Although the maximum wage for footballers remained in place until 1961, the true superstars knew how to make their fame pay. David Jack, scorer of Bolton's first goal in their 2-0 victory over West Ham, was transferred to Arsenal in 1928 for a world record £10,000. Duncan Hamilton, in his book *For the Glory*, the excellent biography of Olympic champion and Scottish rugby international, Eric Liddell, reminds us that this sum was enough to buy a plush property in Park Lane and employ staff to run it. Jack himself earned £468 a year from his job as Arsenal's inside forward but made much more from various bonuses. Jack Hobbs, still during the 1920s England's premier cricketer, advertised everything from suits to cereals, cigarettes and drinks. Hobbs was able to earn around £1500 a year, £500 more than a doctor or solicitor and approximately £1000 more than a head teacher. Sport in the 1920s was bigger than ever and not just in Britain. In the USA, sporting figures such as golfer Walter Hagen, tennis champion Bill Tilden, world champion heavyweight boxer Jack Dempsey and baseball's leading figure Babe Ruth earned huge sums.

The public's growing appetite for sport was increasingly satisfied by the advent of radio. In Britain by 1922 there were 36,000 radio licenses but by 1927 this figure had exploded to around 2,000,000. The growth continued through the 1930s so that by 1939, on the eve of war, three quarters of British households, 9,000,000 in total, possessed a licence. Nevertheless, as Mihir Bose in his book *The Spirit of the Game* tells us, Britain was slow off the mark when compared to the USA. Here, in what Bose describes as a 'free-for-all industry', sport relied on commercial advertising and sponsorship. This allowed them to broadcast big boxing fights from 1921. Britain, who with the BBC had gone down the road of a monopoly service, had got off to a slow start. Bose suggests that the BBC was more concerned with accuracy whereas in the USA they opted for entertainment. Not that the BBC were always accurate. In 1926, the commentator of the Derby could not clarify the result and had to guess the winner. However, with Teddy Wakelam, George Allison and Raymond Glendenning at the helm at the BBC, rugby and football at least improved considerably while Howard Marshall and John Snagge successfully brought cricket and rowing respectively into millions of homes. Yet it was 1934 before there was live radio commentary of Test match cricket in England, fully ten years after such an innovation had been introduced in Australia. It was felt that cricket's tempo was too slow to make entertaining listening, a view that presumably changed after the 'Bodyline' series. This first live radio commentary, done by Howard Marshall at Lords, was carried out from a space in the Tavern rented from the MCC for 20 guineas.

Radio was not alone in bringing sport even more into people's lives. Television was still a new, largely minority luxury. The BBC did not begin its service until November 1936, although by September 1939, they had transmitted 2 FA Cup Finals, Test Match Cricket, International Rugby and 2 Oxford/Cambridge Varsity Boat Races. The first television coverage of Test match cricket was the Lord's Ashes test of 1938 when pictures were provided by three cameras and the experienced radio commentator Teddy Wakelam acted as commentator. Viewers were confined to the London area but the response was positive, so much so that the Oval Test of that year was also covered. Only 25,000 televisions had been sold before the war as each TV set would have cost the equivalent of £3000 in today's money. Newsreels, however, were much more accessible. They had first appeared before the Great War and became very popular during the interwar years. Indeed, sports coverage totals around one fifth of all surviving newsreel. Their popularity remained high despite some of the action only being shown weeks after the events had taken place. The roots of today's total 24-hour sports coverage, emerges here. However, there was controversy, for example Newcastle United's controversial goal in the 1932 FA Cup Final, and much hype as the regular showing of Prince Alexander Obolensky's tries that defeated the 1936 All Blacks confirms. The positive and upbeat voice of Alan Howland of British Movietone News became a very important part of the weekly trip to the cinema. The fact that there was little or no commentary or analysis did not matter at all. Indeed, after receiving an update on the major sports stories it was quite possible that cinemagoers would settle down to watch a feature film that had sport at its heart. Films were made about sports stars such as Babe Ruth and footballer Billy Meredith while Alfred Hitchcock made a film, *The Ring*, about boxing. In 1939 Leslie Banks starred in the popular film *The Arsenal Stadium Mystery*, the plot of which concerns the murder of a footballer at Highbury Stadium. Sporting idols such as Johnny Weissmuller, Esther Williams and Glen

Morris even went into films themselves. Sport and the cinema, the most popular pastime of British families, were comfortable bedfellows.

What was the effect of these important developments on the print media? The introduction of both the radio and television coverage was warmly received by many players who saw this medium as an improvement on newspaper reports. Simon Wilde, in his history of English cricket, *England: The Biography*, argues that radio and television was seen "as more reverential in tone than newspapers, whose sales had long depended on the vigorous airing of opinions." Bob Wyatt, the experienced England test batsman and former captain, complained in a letter how he was treated by newspapers in the 1934 Ashes series. Wilde tells us that Wyatt "was given a rough ride by the cheap press without a real knowledge of the game and always looking for a sensation." In the 1930s at least, radio and television did not suffer this criticism. Newspapers realised the need to change significantly, not least in the way in which they made much greater use of photographs, a direct response to the pictures seen in the newsreels.

One result of this was that sports stars were now far more recognisable to the public. In Victorian times, with the exception of WG Grace, supporters would be hard-pressed to recognise the leading players unless they had seen them in action. Now the faces of the most successful were instantly recognisable. Newspapers themselves recruited 'big name' reporters; often ex-players able to give more detailed analysis without the charge that they lacked sufficient expertise. It became common for forthcoming rugby internationals to be discussed and analysed on the day before, or morning of, the big game. In the lead-up to the game, team selection also came more under the spotlight. Cricket continued to be well reported in the newspapers, both local and national. County matches were covered each day as they had been before the Great War but now Test matches were given more attention. Comments were published in the press expressing opinions of test selection by England, particularly when playing at home.

The biggest change was probably in the quality newspapers such as *The Times*, *Manchester Guardian* and *Daily Telegraph*, especially to their coverage of football. Before the Great War, football had definitely been seen as the poor relation, a sport of lesser importance. Games were rarely reported in these newspapers with only the result, not the scorers, being given. Local newspapers did give greater coverage to football but, before 1914, the FA Cup had been largely ignored by the quality press, certainly until the Final. During the 1930s the competition was given full coverage. A full preview of the top league and cup games was published on the day of the game and details of scorers and, often a match report, appeared the following day. This was a very significant change but, unlike today, newspapers kept well clear of commenting on the private lives of the players. One example of this concerned Wally Hammond, future England cricket captain and England's most prolific batsman of the interwar period. Hammond, a known ladies' man, missed the whole of the 1926 season following a winter tour to the West Indies. David Foot, a well-respected chronicler and writer on county cricket, has since argued that he had contracted syphilis or a related sexually transmitted disease, so that today's public, or at least those with a fascination for all things cricket-related, are now aware of the rumours that had been circulating for years. There was never any chance of this gossip being published at the time. If the leader of the Liberal Party and ex-prime minister, David Lloyd George, was able to keep his mistress and their daughter under wraps, then Walter Hammond could sleep easy at night. The public weren't even being given the full story of the biggest sporting controversy of the period, the Bodyline Ashes tour to Australia in 1932/33 where the tensions were serious enough to merit discussion in the Cabinet. Even in the USA, where film stars gave many juicy stories to the gossip columns, it was not widely known exactly how unpopular Babe Ruth was with his teammates.

With this growth of interest in sport and the much-improved coverage, it was inevitable that sportsmen would become more and more influential in their communities. With the arrival of the 1930s, football increased in popularity to the extent that the FA Cup Final was pretty much guaranteed a gate of 100,000 at Wembley. The game was also becoming far more international. In 1919, FIFA could point to 24 members. By 1939 this number had risen to 56, helped, no doubt, by the success of the 1930 World Cup where 80,000 spectators watched host country Uruguay defeat Argentina 4–2. It was decided that the following day be declared a Bank Holiday. Having won the Olympic title both in 1924 and 1928, Uruguay were leading the way, although only 4 European nations had taken part in this particular tournament. But by 1934, European countries had caught up with victory, once again, going to the host nation, Italy. In an action of 'tit for tat', only Brazil and Argentina were there to represent South America, and on this occasion, it was Italy who triumphed, as they did once again four years later, under the shrewd management of Vittorio Pozzo. As for England, they were slow to catch this particular bug, refusing to take part until 1950, although they did play 18 matches against foreign opposition in the 1920s increasing to 28 in the 1930s. Before 1914, the national team had played only 7 fixtures against continental opposition. Scotland played non-British opposition for the first time on a brief European summer tour in 1929 while during the 1920s neither Wales nor Northern Ireland played against foreign opposition at all.

Cricket, although no longer the national sport, continued to flourish in the 1930s and test cricket increased in importance. Between 1928 and 1932, the West Indies, India and New Zealand joined England, Australia and South Africa by playing test cricket for the first time. In the ten years before the Great War and the ten years after the number of Test matches played numbered 52 and 51, respectively. The following ten years saw 96 Test matches played. 1927 was the last summer in England without a test series whereas before 1914 this was a common occurrence. During the 1920s England played 47 Test matches, a number that more than doubled in the 1930s to 102. Indeed, this decade was to witness the most controversial test series in cricket history, the 'Bodyline Tour' to Australia in 1932/33. Controversial it may have been but crowds flocked to the Test match in anticipation of incident and excitement. The arrival of Don Bradman, 'The Don', had something to do with this. Nobody has so outperformed his rivals by such a margin in the history of sport and it could be argued that Bradman remains the greatest superstar in sporting history. Admirers of Usain Bolt and Muhammed Ali might dispute this and it is true that these brilliant competitors outstrip Bradman in terms of personality and impact on their sport in the wider world. But the statistics that confirm Bradman's superiority as the greatest batsman of all time are astounding. A test average of 99.94 runs per innings is 38 ahead of his nearest rival when examining the figures of players who have completed at least 20 innings. It is true that wickets had improved and that the 1930s were a batsman's paradise when compared to the pre-war conditions. Nevertheless, Bradman played like somebody who appeared to have arrived from another planet. Never before, or since, has anybody played with what Neville Cardus called "his singleness of mind and imperturbability." Bradman played with a ruthless efficiency, his secret being, in his own words, the ability to concentrate and to treat every ball as if it was the first ball "whether my score is nought or 200." Bradman's notable arrival on the scene during England's tour to Australia in 1928 was followed by his country's return visit to England in 1930 where 'The Don' proceeded to break records at will. A series total of 974 runs in the five-match series included a score of 334 at Headingley with 309 of them coming during the first day at the rate of 100 runs per session. 'The Don' was no flash in the pan. Years later the great English fast bowler, Harold Larwood, while observing a succession of Australian batsmen sacrifice their wickets playing poor shots, was heard to mutter "how is it when I think back on my career I always seem to be bowling to Bradman." Despite the years lost to the war, Bradman's test career lasted until 1948 when it ended with his famous 'duck' at The Oval.

Internationally sport also continued to grow in popularity. Although some world figures of the 1920s, such as golfer Bobby Jones, began to fade, others took their place. Joe DiMaggio joined Babe Ruth as an American baseball hero while the epic boxing contests involving Joe Louis captured the public imagination. Besides, Jesse Owens was about to appear. Athletics saw the emergence of new international tournaments in South America (1919), Central America (1926) and Europe (1934). Following a Canadian initiative, the British Empire Games were first held in Ontario in 1930. Participation in the Olympics was also increasing considerably. In the 1912 Olympics, the last before the Great War, 28 nations had competed. By 1936 this number had risen to 49. The number of athletes taking part increased at a similar rate — 2,407 in 1912 (48 women) to 3,963 (331 women). These athletes were, from 1924 in Paris, competing in new purpose-built stadiums and, from 1932 in Los Angeles, were housed in an 'Olympic Village' for the duration of the Games. Primitive these may have been by 21st century standards but it was a huge step forward from the rented city locations of previous Games. The Olympics, more than anything else, had also helped to encourage the public to make the link between participation in sport and living a healthy lifestyle. Ironically, the Nazi Party, through the 1936 Olympics in Berlin, set out to encourage this view and the idea spread quickly. As late as 1938 the Bishop of London praised the 'marvellous results' and 'perfectly astounding physical perfection' that the Germans had achieved through their outdoor camps and compulsory exercises. A further significant development during the 1930s was the realisation by politicians that, for the first time, sport could be a useful tool in political debate. The fascist dictators, now in power over great swathes of Europe, saw sport as a vehicle to establish fascism, rather than democracy, as the premier political system. On their part, black African Americans and Jewish athletes saw any success that they achieved as making a big dent in fascist ideas of Aryan supremacy.

Hitler's use of the 1936 Berlin Olympics for propaganda purposes is well-documented but the other fascist dictators also used sport both for propaganda and to produce fit, motivated soldiers. Benito Mussolini had taken time to come to terms with football. He, like his henchmen, had been born too early to have grown up with the game and was irritated that the sport had such a following in England. To him, as to other fascist leaders, football was only good for one thing: breeding soldiers. Mussolini had been given the perfect opportunity to exploit football for his own ends by capitalising on Italy's World Cup victories of 1934 and 1938. Football in Italy was now a major pastime and Mussolini was quick to see its potential. General Franco in Spain also grasped what football could do to enhance his political standing. Josef Stalin in the Soviet Union was not as committed to sport as the others. The USSR took no part in the Olympic Games nor did they play international football matches. Indeed, the communist USSR was seen as something of a pariah state in the world of sport. Yet Stalin did see the possibilities of linking organised sport to economic growth rather than political objectives. Following the Nazi-Soviet Pact of August

1939, Germany and the USSR staged a series of friendly international competitions. Stalin came to see sport as an ideal showcase for the world's first communist state.

Hitler, of course, took this to a new level. He came to see sport as a good way of facilitating the creation of fit young Aryan Germans who were eager to serve him. As early as 1924, when he wrote *Mein Kampf*, Hitler had seen the opportunity that sport presented.

"Give the German nation six million bodies impeccably trained in sport, all glowing with fanatical love of the Fatherland and raised in the highest spirit of attack, and a national state will make an army of them in less than two years, if necessary."

But Hitler didn't totally succeed in manipulating football for his own ends. It was the Olympic Games that provided the perfect propaganda opportunity to encourage this idea. He was keen to establish Berlin as the permanent home to the Games. At first, Hitler had seen the Games as Jewish/Freemason invention, but by 1936 he saw them as the perfect Nazi showcase to help him achieve his political and diplomatic ends. There was little resistance to the Nazification of sport in Germany during these years. Every German who took part in sport did so through an organisation controlled by the Hitler Youth or the KDF. By the time of the 1936 Berlin Olympics, German sport was ready for the challenge. Max Schmeling, World Heavyweight Boxing Champion of the early 1930s, had defeated the up-and-coming American 'Brown Bomber', Joe Louis, by knocking him out in June 1936 while German football had been thriving since the years of the Weimar Republic. In the relatively new sport of Grand Prix racing, Mercedes and Auto Union, both German cars subsidised by the German Government, battled it out for supremacy. In 1934 Bernd Rosemayer, a German driver from Lingen, won the title and quickly became a Nazi puppet and a member of the elite SS. Along with his adventurous, world-renowned aviator wife, Elly Beinhorn, he became a Nazi celebrity until his death when attempting a land speed record in 1938. A glamorous British driver, Dick Seaman, driving for Mercedes, was also used for propaganda purposes until his death in the Belgian Grand Prix of 1939.

Indeed, Seaman, who had given a Nazi salute when winning the German Grand Prix in 1938, was given a Nazi funeral. For Hitler and other leading Nazis motor racing, along with boxing, were the main sports and by now German cars were showcased as being superior.

But the Berlin Olympics didn't quite go to plan. Hitler, anticipating the dominance of his Aryan athletes, made plans to shake the hand of every gold medal winner in Track and Field athletics. Given his views regarding Aryan supremacy, Hitler felt on safe ground until Jesse Owens burst on to the scene and won 4 Gold Medals in 100 and 200 metres, Long Jump and 4x100 metres relay, the very same events as those won by Carl Lewis 48 years later. What is less well known is that 14 other African Americans also won medals that year in Berlin. To cap it all, two years later, in 1938, Joe Louis exacted his revenge on Schmeling, by now a 'Nazi puppet', knocking him out in the first round. Schmeling went on to become an elite paratrooper with the Luftwaffe during the war. Ironically, Schmeling was later credited with saving the lives of two Jewish children in 1938 and after the war become firm friends with Louis, even helping the black American with some of his financial difficulties. Their friendship lasted until the 66-year-old Louis, rated by many as the greatest heavyweight of them all, died in 1981. Schmeling lived until 2005 and died only 8 months short of his 100th birthday, by now a German sporting icon. Louis, on the other hand, was used for recruitment propaganda by the US Army rather than being sent into combat. At the same time he, like countless other black American soldiers, suffered racial abuse and prejudice. Despite this appalling treatment, perhaps Louis did have it better than Jesse Owens. Owens returned from the Berlin Olympics to a life of menial jobs, racing horses in promotional stunts, prosecution for tax evasion and, eventually, bankruptcy. Although his final decade was a good deal happier, Owens died in 1980, like Louis also aged 66, a much loved and respected man but without any of the rewards his talents so richly deserved.

Despite the triumphs of Owens at the Olympics in Berlin and of Louis in the ring, Hitler could be satisfied with how his use of sport was progressing. Although he didn't wait around to hang the medals around Owens' neck, it is easy to exaggerate Hitler's reaction. It was crucial to

Hitler that the Games were a propaganda success so he was unlikely to do anything to alienate international opinion. Rather than use sport to demonstrate 'racial' superiority, Simon Kuper has pointed out that very often the Nazis used sport to make friends. In his book, *Ajax, the Dutch, the War: Football in Europe During World War Two*, Kuper suggests that the Nazis were in desperate need of friends. They were obsessed with how the rest of the world saw them. More importantly, Germany remained weak for much of the 1930s. They needed time to rearm before Hitler's true intentions were become clear. To a great extent he succeeded and few people thought much about the threat posed by Hitler until late in the decade. This was certainly the case in Britain, where sports administers refused to believe that Hitler was aware of any anti-Jewish policies being produced in the Interior Ministry. After all, when the German football team played England at White Hart Lane, the German team and officials behaved impeccably in a ground containing thousands of Jewish supporters. As late as May 1938, the England team gave the Nazi salute at the Olympic Stadium, Berlin, an action ordered in advance by the British Foreign Office as part of Chamberlain's plan to avoid conflict by appeasing Hitler. It is not that some British administrators didn't have some sympathy with Nazi views. Captain Webster, a leading athletics journalist, concurred with the view that black athletes had physical advantages over their white counterparts and therefore should not be allowed to take part.

Now that the Games were over and Germany's standing enhanced, Hitler could further address 'the Jewish problem'. He had begun removing Jews from sport, as in other walks of life, immediately on his election to power. Now he could take things much further but he did remain careful not to make the strength of his views too clear. Helene Mayer was a gold-medal-winning fencer from the 1928 Olympics, who had been stripped of her German citizenship in 1935 as a result of having a Jewish father. She had been allowed to take part in the Games mainly because Hitler saw her participation as an opportunity to deflect criticism from the international community. On winning silver in Berlin, the only athlete of Jewish origin to win a medal at the Games, Mayer saluted the Nazi flag from the podium before returning to the USA where she had been studying. She eventually returned to Germany in 1952 but died a year later from breast cancer. Helene Mayer has been listed by *Sports Illustrated* as one of the top 100 female athletes of the twentieth century but one is left with the feeling that she was used by Hitler in his propaganda campaign. Gretel Bergmann was treated very differently. Despite her Jewish origins, Bergmann had competed successfully for Germany in the High Jump and the German Government appeared keen to also use her abilities for propaganda purposes. However, two weeks before the Games, despite an excellent series of performances resulting in a German record, she was dropped from the team and her records expunged from the record books. Shortly afterwards Bergmann went to the USA where she obtained American citizenship and competed for her new country. Bergmann had quickly realised the direction in which Hitler was taking Germany. In 1934 she had returned to Germany following a spell in Britain. Years later, in 2008, now known by her married name, Margaret Lambert, she recalled the changes that she witnessed in Germany following her brief absence: no Jews allowed in certain restaurants, cinemas or stadiums and training restrictions being placed on athletes such as herself. Bergmann was fortunate to have a long and ultimately happy life. In 2009 her records were restored and she was admitted into both the German and Jewish Hall of Fame. In 2004 a documentary was made based on her life in Germany, *Hitler's Pawn — The Margaret Lambert Story*, followed five years later by the film *Berlin 36*, covering her preparation for, and exclusion from, the 1936 Olympic Games. Bergmann eventually died in New York in 2017 aged 103. Despite the lack of an Olympic medal, Gretel Bergmann had escaped the fate of many other Jewish athletes. Not being used in a Nazi propaganda campaign had proved to be a blessing.

What was the view of the World War 1 Allies to this use of sport as political propaganda? France had always shown a far more casual attitude towards sport in the interwar years but, as war became more and more likely, they tried to match the fascist countries in general fitness and in the health of their youth. Meanwhile, the USA followed an isolationist policy in sport as well as in everything else. The emphasis was very much on domestic, rather than international, sport and racial segregation and discrimination was rife. The 1932 Los

Angeles Olympics was run as a private enterprise with no significant input from the State, a clear contrast to the Italian World Cup and the Berlin Olympics. In Britain, Neville Chamberlain, as Chancellor of the Exchequer, had introduced a National Fitness Campaign which he hoped would produce similar results to the German model. Chamberlain openly praised "the splendid condition of the German youth" and saw no reason why British youngsters should not aspire to these standards.

Britain's policy of appeasing Hitler was also symbolised by a sporting event. By choosing to play a friendly football international against Germany in Berlin in May 1938, Britain was giving an implicit vote of support to the Nazi regime. This was proven later to have been extremely unwise. It wasn't as if the English Football Association would make any money out of this rare excursion into Europe as the German FA were to keep all the gate receipts while the English paid their own expenses. With the spectators numbering 110,000 this was quite a windfall for the German FA. And then there was the matter of the Nazi salute and the England response. Every country playing sport in Germany from 1933 had this diplomatic problem to deal with but, with war looking a strong possibility in the near future, the English FA took the decision that if it took a salute to reduce tension between the countries then it was a price worth paying. The FA secretary, Stanley Rous, also concluded that if a salute put the German crowd in a less hostile mood towards the England players, then there might be some benefit. No doubt when England defeated Germany 6–3, he felt that the decision had been justified. However, this decision later backfired as the salute became a symbol of the British appeasement of Germany. The photograph of the salute appeared in newspapers throughout the world and, according to England's star player, Stanley Matthews in his autobiography years later, the action brought 'eternal shame' on every player and on Britain as a whole. It was easy to be wise after the event and a number of players tried to distance themselves from the decision in later years. But it was too late. English football internationals giving the Nazi salute is an abiding memory of sport in the latter half of the 1930s.

We can, therefore, say with some confidence that on the eve of war sport was central to the lives of vast numbers of people, both in Britain and abroad. Building on the strides made at the turn of the century, participation in, and the supporting of, many teams in a range of sports was a way of life. The use of radio and film backed by greater coverage and analysis in the print media had succeeded in confirming the pre-eminence of sport in many lives. It was the great escape for many when relaxing at the end of a long working day in a coalmine, the docks, factory or steelworks. For others it was the perfect setting to play host, to entertain or just to relax with friends in a desirable social setting such as Wimbledon, Lords or Ascot. From the rugby clubs of the South Wales valleys and the professional football clubs of the industrial north to the more genteel cricket and tennis clubs of 'middle England', the sports club became the hub of the community. Political leaders, both domestic and international, had seen the possibilities offered by sport to enhance their own ideas through the subtle, and not so subtle, use of propaganda. We were now in a world where sport was discussed at government level. In a worldwide sense it was now one important way that people of different nations communicated with one another, a common language for the peoples of the world. It was not going away. In 1914, sport had reacted to the onset of war with a burst of patriotism, heeding the Establishment view that 'this is no time for games'. But in 1939 it was a different world and World War Two a very different war. It remained to be seen exactly how sport would rise to this new, even more threatening challenge.

Bill Edrich

CHAPTER 2
SPORTSMEN AT WAR ONCE AGAIN

From the very beginning, great consideration was given to the role that sport and sportsmen would play in the conflict. The cricket writer HS Altham wrote an essay in the 1940 edition of *Wisden* where he expressed the opinion that the game should be kept going wherever possible. He stated his view quite clearly that the playing and watching of sport would be good for morale and would not have a detrimental effect as the nation had mobilised as never before. Yet it would be wrong to think that the reaction to the start of the war was to encourage the playing of sport. It is just that there seemed to be less dispute as to what should, or shouldn't, be done. Unlike 1914, civilian safety was at the forefront of the authorities' thinking. There was a fear of immediate air attacks to which they felt there was little in the way of defence, articulated by Stanley Baldwin that "the bomber would always get through." In 1914, the Doncaster race meeting began on September 8th when Britain had already been at war for 5 weeks. In 1939, 25 years later, the same meeting was cancelled when the country had been at war for 5 days. This confirms a different attitude, one which led to the steady cancellation of race meetings in the subsequent weeks.

Rugby Union too, acted decisively. The touring Australians arrived on September 2nd, the day before Chamberlain's broadcast. A lunch had been arranged for Monday 4th but this was hurriedly cancelled in the wake of the grave international situation. By the 6th September, the tourists were comfortably settled in Torquay as guests of the RFU but arrangements were already being made for them to make the long trek home. They offered their services to the local authorities and managed to fit in a visit to Twickenham but for these tourists their rugby trip of a lifetime was over before it had properly begun. A journey of 12,000 miles had resulted in one game which had taken between £250 and

£300 at the gate, a small return for a tour that had cost the Australian Rugby Union £5,000. *The Times* reported that matches between Leicester/Bedford and Ebbw Vale/Neath were cancelled as most players were "already engaged on National Service." The WRU issued a statement saying that "this Union, together with its subsidiary organisations and affiliated clubs, suspend their activities during the period of war or until further notice." A week later, on September 12th, the Scottish Rugby Union had cancelled all matches and offered Murrayfield to the authorities for "national purposes" with the recommendation to clubs that they make the same offer. On the 14th September, the RFU followed suit and cancelled all games until further notice. Both Unions did, however, later allow friendly matches to take place as long as there was no interference with national duties or government regulations. Often the Unions had little or no part in organising such games but they did allow them to go ahead. As the war progressed there were even wartime internationals, raising money for charity, although no caps were awarded. More surprisingly, even the very strict rules that prevented rugby union players having any contact with rugby league were relaxed and the players shared the same pitch. Matches were played in good spirit as they were a relief from the horrors and worries of war.

The cricket season was already drawing to a close when war was declared. The West Indies tourists, with their three-match test series already completed, cancelled their remaining six fixtures on 23rd August, already anticipating the events ahead. Sir Derek Birley, an English educationalist and writer of the social history of sport, wrote in his classic *A Social History of English Cricket* that there was "none of the unfortunate disposition to linger over it (the entry into war) as in 1914." Lords was requisitioned by the War Office and taken over by the RAF. There were no more test or county matches until 1946, although the MCC did continue to stage one-day games at Lords throughout the war, raising money for charities such as the Red Cross. There was at least one dramatic event at Lords during this time. During the Blitz of 1940, the ground was hit by a thousand-pound bomb which failed to explode but left a massive crater on the outfield at the Nursery End. In July 1944, a 'doodlebug' threatened to come down very near this crater, although in the end it landed in the vicinity of nearby London Zoo. The Oval, which less than two years earlier had been the scene of Hutton's record-breaking test score of 364, was now commandeered by the War Office and prepared for use as a prisoner-of-war camp for the anticipated German parachutists. Wire cages protected the playing area but no prisoners ever arrived. As the threat of invasion diminished, the ground was used as an anti-aircraft gun site, then as a barrage-balloon and searchlight base and finally as an assault course. The serene nature of an English cricket ground on a summer's day was once again becoming a distant memory. Reminiscing in the manner of those recalling the Edwardian summer of 1914, RC Robertson-Glasgow wrote in the 1940 edition of *Wisden* that reviewing the cricketing summer of 1939 was "like peeping through the wrong end of a telescope at a very small but happy world." Robertson-Glasgow, in the same article, looked forward as well as back. While accepting that the continuation of the County Championship would be wholly inappropriate, he saw nothing wrong with those too old or unfit to fight playing cricket in some shape or form. Some form of regional, one-day cricket was his preferred option. Robertson-Glasgow held firm to the idea that the Counties must be as prepared as possible for the return to normality, whenever that day were to arrive. In the meantime, he was undoubtedly delighted that the RAF, Royal Navy and the Army all had teams which regularly played one another, although the exact makeup of the teams was likely to change right up to the last moment. Teams such as the National Fire Service and branches of Civil Defence were formed while Nottinghamshire, with its strong mining communities, still managed to field a team. Cricket was played in some parts of the Empire, for example New Zealand until 1941, Australia and some parts of the Caribbean. But although cricket in India continued throughout the war, the MCC tour 1939/40 to India was cancelled despite a team having already been selected. In Britain at least, first class and international cricket was over for the next seven years.

Football, as we have already seen, was now the nation's number-one sport. In 1914, football had been the sport that found it most difficult to fully commit to the patriotic demands of the authorities. As professional players who were pretty much owned by their clubs, signing up for 'The Greatest Game' was not always straightforward and the press and politicians did not hold back in attempting to shame players into joining one of the armed forces. Many footballers made significant contributions to the war effort, particularly from 1915 onwards when many lives were lost, but the football authorities had no intention of suffering the criticism of 1914 again. Decisions were made quickly and with little or no hesitation. On the 8th September 1939, the Football Association made the following statement:

"In accordance with the Proclamation by his Majesty's Government under the Rule 27 of the Rules of the Association, all football under the jurisdiction of the Football Association is entirely suspended until official notice is given to the contrary. This does not apply to football arranged by His Majesty's Forces."

Three matches into the campaign, the 1939/40 season was over. Portsmouth remained holders of the FA Cup for the next seven years and Everton remained champions. A law banning the assembling of crowds and a fifty-mile travel limit made the decision inevitable. The lessons of 1914 had been well and truly learned. The result was that footballers didn't waste any time in joining up. In September of 1939, the professionals of Liverpool FC voluntarily joined the Territorial Army and within weeks they were called up for military service. Not that the decision to suspend football met with universal approval. One Bolton supporter took his club to court demanding a refund on his season ticket when football ceased but his efforts failed, although Southend United did refund money to supporters.

Nevertheless, it wasn't long before the authorities relented a little. Not that it was easy to play organised sport as many sporting venues were requisitioned for the war effort: Wimbledon for drilling the Home Guard, Highbury for the HQ of Civil Defence, Twickenham for allotments, White Hart Lane as a mortuary during the Blitz and Epsom for army training as well as the use made of Lords and the Oval already noted. This use of sports grounds in the war effort was not new but it was different. In the Great War, the Talbot Athletic Ground, home of Aberavon RFC, was used for allotments whereas in 1939/40 it was converted into a barrage balloon site. However, there was still a view that the playing and watching of sport was good for morale, so within weeks games resumed subject to the approval of local police and the imposition of strict crowd limits, just so long as it didn't hamper the war effort. The police were fully supportive of this relaxing of the rules. After all, bored young men were more likely to get into trouble if they had nothing to do. It should also be remembered that over half of Britain's army, one and a half million troops, spent most of the war in Britain. These fit young men needed an outlet and some form of entertainment. One of the places where entertainment was to be found was the seaside town of Blackpool. During the war this was the place to be. According to the writer and ex professional footballer, Eamon Dunphy, every pub felt like it was New Year's Eve as soldiers about to go to war thought that they needed to seize the last chance of some fun. Dunphy says that "all the scum, all the prostitutes, all the villains came to Blackpool... There were at least 80,000 airmen and at least as many Yanks."

The War Office agreed to a policy that football should continue but on an ad hoc basis with professionals free to guest for whichever League club was nearest to their Forces base. This did lead to some frustration for the players who found themselves playing for a variety of clubs. One Bradford player reported that he had played for eight different clubs in nine weeks. Notts County used as many as 132 players in one season while the ad hoc makeup of the teams resulted in some bizarre score lines such as Norwich's 18-0 win over Brighton. Regional leagues, ten in total, and cups were set up with a crowd limit of 8,000 (later raised to 15,000) and there was a maximum payment of 30/- a player. In 1940, some survivors of Dunkirk were treated to be present at the first wartime cup final to see West Ham defeat Blackburn 1-0. The positive advantages of playing sport were to be found within the services themselves, as well as in the country at large. As early as September 1939, the Army was given £1,000 by the FA to spend on footballs and football equipment in an effort to ensure that soldiers were involved. And involved they were. England cricketer and Arsenal footballer Denis Compton later wrote that "Cup Finals, League South matches and Army representative games followed on top of one another in a seemingly endless stream." Compton reflected that the war years were the best time of his football (but not cricket) career. Arsenal captain and later Manchester City and England manager Joe Mercer remembered playing 2 to 3 games a week when in the Army. When he asked for a pass to leave camp to play his CO said that he didn't know whether he wanted one to go out or to come in. Mercer, for his part, wasn't sure at times whether he was playing for the Army, England, his unit or his club. Tom Finney too, voiced the opinion that he had never been fitter nor played better than when he was serving in Egypt and playing regularly for the Army. Both Tommy Lawton and that supreme individualist, Len Shackleton, remembered playing two matches on Christmas Day. The sport-loving public appreciated these concessions and interest in sport, although diminished, remained strong. In a poll conducted by Mass Observation, an early social survey organisation, it reported that "people find the war at present completely unsatisfactory as a compensation for sport."

However, it would be wrong to think that, even when involved in active sport, the minds of the participants strayed very far from the dangers of war. Middlesex and England cricketer Bill Edrich, Denis Compton's cricket 'twin', had a very eventful war as a pilot for RAF Bomber Command. As we shall see, Edrich took part in some of the most daring raids of the war, experiences which ensured that he lived every day as if it were his last. Mihir Bose quotes Edrich's description of what it was like to participate in a cricket match between his squadron and a local village team following a raid.

"At times it seemed like a strange dream… Both cricket teams played well and it was a hard and exciting game. Every now and then would come the old, accustomed cry 'HOWZAT' and then one's mind would flicker off to the briefing, and to joking with a pal whose broken body was now washing in the long, cold tides, and one saw again his machine cart-wheeling down, flaming from nose to tail; and then a ball would roll fast along the green English turf and in the distance the village clock would strike and the mellow echoes would ring through the lazy air of that perfect summer afternoon."

The horrors and dangers of war were never far from the minds of those in the frontline of the action.

Despite this, the effect on the public mood was all that the authorities could hope for, although initially the signs were not good. With crowds limited to 8,000, matches often lacked atmosphere and an apprehensive public, fearful of war, had little interest in meaningless games. Chelsea's fixture against Southampton was watched by no more than 2,000 people in a stadium that held 70,000. Simon Kuper, in his book referenced in the last chapter, tells us that only 9% of pre-war fans attended the early wartime friendlies. Supporters found travel difficult due to the blackouts, evacuations and various transport problems. In another poll conducted by Mass Observation, it was found that 49% of people said that the onset of war had lessened their interest in sport, although at the same time, in something of a contradiction, 50% said that they read the sports reports more avidly than news of the war.

However, as the country found itself in a Phoney War, an eight-month period at the start of the war where there was limited action in Europe, interest in football returned. This continued even after the Blitz of 1941. Increases in attendance confirmed this with 323,000 spectators attending the opening matches of the War Cup on Boxing Day 1942. In April 1943, the four quarter finals of this competition drew a total of 100,000 spectators and by January 1945, attendances were up 40% on recent years. The surge in attendances at matches gave an opportunity to recruit potential soldiers. Bolton captain Harry Goslin spoke to the large crowd at one game urging them to join up. His team led the way with the entire Bolton squad joining the 53rd Field Regiment, Royal Artillery while Liverpool players formed a club section of the King's Regiment. The positive effect on sport was confirmed by Mass Observation, one of the first social survey organisations, when it concluded that "sport had a major effect on the morale of the people." Politicians were quick to encourage this enthusiasm, an approval confirmed at the highest level when Winston Churchill himself, along with seven members of his cabinet and 60,000 others, attended the England v Scotland wartime international in 1941. Churchill would also have been well aware of the financial contribution made by wartime football to the war effort. May 1943 saw a good example of this when a match at Chelsea, attended by 55,000 enthusiastic supporters, raised the sum of £8,000 for the Navy Welfare League. Also, in 1943 the Red Cross were able to congratulate themselves on raising the sum of £1,000,000 for the war effort. Football's contribution to this sum was £70,000.

It was not only football where the government pulled back from a total ban on spectator sports. As we have seen, race meetings were quickly affected and there were determined efforts to stop horseracing as it was a drain on resources, a view strongly expressed by government minister Sir Stafford Cripps. But, encouraged by the media who saw racing as good for the morale of the troops and war workers, the public reaction provoked a rethink. Soon races were being run in rural areas such as Thirsk and Ripon where air raids were very unlikely. Indeed, the St Leger was moved from Doncaster to Thirsk for the duration of the war. In return, racing tried to help the war effort by attempting to ensure that, if the owners sold horses, then the money didn't leave the country. Mihir Bose tells us that this proved particularly difficult with the pre-eminent pre-war race owner, the Aga Khan. He was a very important figure in British racing but was known to be an admirer of, and had contacts with, Adolf Hitler. Bose recounts that Aga Khan went to Switzerland in July 1939 and arranged to meet Hitler. However, he developed severe earache and was forced to remain in Switzerland. In the meantime, Hitler invaded Poland so they never met and Aga Khan remained in neutral Switzerland for the duration of the war. Meanwhile, the British war workers' appetite for betting ensured that dog racing and boxing continued to flourish during the war despite government reservations.

The importance of sport to the morale of the public was not confined to Britain. The war was unpopular in Germany from the outset, especially in Berlin, so Hitler was reluctant to deprive the public of sporting contests until absolutely necessary. Some sense of normality was seen as vital to maintaining morale. German football was halted for only the first few weeks of the war and carried on as normal until the spring of 1944. The German Cup Final was watched by 80,000 in 1940 and by 90,000 a year later while the National Championship final was still played a few days after D-Day. There was no ploughing up of football fields in Germany to support the war effort. A total of 35 international matches were played by the end of 1942, although they did stop after El Alamein when the idea became unpopular. Hitler's determination to maintain a form of sporting normality was not confined to Germany. The Nazis hoped that through sport they could secure the loyalty of the population of invaded countries, attempting to convince people in occupied Europe that their lives had not been affected by war. For example, in the Netherlands, Dutch sport carried on as if nothing had happened and sports clubs saw an even higher membership than before the war. In Poland, the Nazis took a different line by recruiting the best Polish player, Ernst Willimouski, for the German national team.

Observing the positive effect that watching top sportsmen was having, British politicians quickly realised that it was important that the public were not constantly being reminded of the horrors of war by reading about the deaths of their sporting heroes. In the Great War some of the household names were protected by the authorities. For example, Jack Hobbs, England's premier cricketer of the day, never quite shook off the claim that he was given an easy ride when part of the newly formed Royal Flying Corps. Frank Woolley too, was seen as having had preferential treatment. Both Wooley and Hobbs spent much of the Great War playing league cricket in the north of England. Nevertheless, many of the big stars of the day served in the most dangerous parts of the Front, as the loss of leading, still active sportsmen such as Ronnie Poulton, Colin Blyth, Tony Wilding and seven members of the table-topping Hearts football team confirms. In 1940, the government was keen to avoid too many high-profile losses, although, as we shall see, some were inevitable. The answer was to recruit the most famous sportsmen as physical training instructors where, as Eamon Dunphy in his book *A Strange Kind of Glory* tells us, "their experience and distinction would help keep the troops fit and in good heart." The list of these instructors is a who's who of British sporting heroes. Len Hutton, Denis Compton, Raich Carter, Stanley Matthews, Joe Mercer and, in Australia, Don Bradman himself all fulfilled this role. Charlie Mitten, possibly the best winger never to win an England cap, was persuaded by Stanley Matthews to give up training to be an air gunner for the much less dangerous role of a physical training instructor. When asked by his senior officer as to his reason for the change, Mitten replied, 'I've decided that I'd like to live a bit longer', a reaction which was greeted with a grunt of approval and the response 'nothing wrong with that Mitten'. As physical training instructors it was much more straightforward to be allowed time to play sport. Sergeant Major Matt Busby cut his teeth as a player manager when taking a team of mainly physical training instructors to entertain the troops behind the lines in Italy. His star-studded team included Joe Mercer, Frank Swift, Tommy Lawton and Cliff Britton, all household names. Busby's assistant manager was Arthur Rowe who after the war managed Tottenham Hotspur to the league title with his famous 'push and run' team. The value of these matches was also becoming recognised. Mihir Bose informs us that in March 1942 a writer in the magazine *Reveille* expressed the view that "Soccer, like cricket, is a shining example of providing entertainment for war workers, except that some of the Service players might be quizzed on how much actual military duty they do in the course of a week."

There can be no doubt that by working as a physical training instructor the chances of surviving the war were much greater. Indeed, footballers came to be called by some 'D-Day dodgers' due to their perceived easy life. In Germany too, following defeat at El Alamein, the German public turned against footballers, seeing them as having a protected experience in sharp contrast to what was happening to their own husbands and sons. Simon Kuper concludes in his book that life as a professional footballer in World War Two was less dangerous than imagined and death rarer. Many British sportsmen died in accidents, not that this made their loss any less tragic, and no professional footballer was killed in the 1944 D-Day landings with the exception of Alan Fowler who was killed by friendly fire. Robinson of Barnsley lost a leg and Bob Thyne of Darlington was blown up but survived to play for Scotland against England nine months later. But none of this should detract from the enormous contribution made by sportsmen during World War Two. Cricket and rugby in particular, as we shall see, suffered some high-profile losses but it is not only with those who made the ultimate sacrifice that we should concern ourselves. The tales of survivors are also very significant and confirm that there were genuine heroes to be found amongst our sportsmen. Moreover, their experiences stayed with them for the remainder of their lives. In 1977, Bob Paisley guided Liverpool FC to their first European Cup Final in Rome. Settling the team in the changing room before kick-off, he urged the team to remain calm before the biggest game of their lives about to take place in one of the most glamorous, historic cities of them all. "I've been to Rome before," he told them. "Thirty-three years ago, when I was in a tank. I helped to capture it." A sense of perspective that surely settled his team before they went out to win the trophy. Paisley, like many others of his generation, never forgot his war experience even though, also like many others, he often passed on the chance to talk about it. It is now time to lift the lid and in the following pages the human stories of our sportsmen will confirm the contribution that sport made and the part that they played in the war against fascism. As we shall see, it was a contribution that, once again, came at a very high cost.

Norman Wodehouse

CHAPTER 3
NORMAN WODEHOUSE: A HERO OF TWO WARS AND OTHER NAVAL HEROES

As Britain prepared for war for the second time in 25 years, memories of the horrors of the Great War were still very fresh in people's minds. In the years between the wars, most people would have gone to great lengths in order to avoid another such conflict. The close on one million deaths suffered by Britain and her colonies by 1918 had inflicted great scars on the country and nobody wanted to see another European conflict as inevitable. Many would accept any compromise as a price worth paying. Nevertheless, by 1939 the Allies were preparing for war in earnest. Hitler had invaded Czechoslovakia in March 1939, concluded the Pact of Steel with Italy in May 1939 and signed the Nazi-Soviet Pact in August. The British people reluctantly had to face the inevitable.

Face the inevitable the country certainly did. Indeed, no country mobilised more effectively. By June 1944, 55% of Britons were in the armed forces or doing civilian war work. Women were used more effectively than in any other country carrying out 'war work' of one kind or another whether it be the civil service, engineering and vehicle building or agriculture. Conscription was enforced from the outset and recruitment of soldiers was done in a much more orderly fashion than in 1914, although there was less moral pressure placed on young men to join up at the earliest possible moment. Daily lives were affected immediately and as early as September 1939, one and a half million women and children had been evacuated from London. The Home Guard was set up around the country through 1940 and the 'Dig for Victory' campaign was launched. Food rationing was introduced early in the war with bacon, butter and sugar rationed by January 8th, 1940. Meat, tea, jam, biscuits, cereal, cheese, eggs, lard, milk and fruit quickly followed. With attacks by German U-boats causing more problems, (833 British vessels were lost in 1943 alone), bread and potatoes dominated the British diet. Both the problems faced by communities and the impressive reaction to the situation were very different to 1914.

The nature of the war itself was also different. World War Two was a war of movement quite unlike the often-static war of 1914–18. Desert warfare took place on a greater scale and jungle warfare presented new challenges, particularly in countries such as Burma. Advances in technology changed the face of war with greater use of aircraft and the greater involvement of tanks. Yet one thing remained the same — the high identification with the national cause. Soldiers not only felt their loyalty to their unit but in particular to their section or close comrades of 5/10 men. The morale of the soldier remained crucial and, just as in the Great War, sportsmen were seen as having all the qualities required for the war effort and the sacrifices that were by now inevitable, namely those of loyalty to one's group, courage and commitment. As in 1914, it would also be recognised that sportsmen were useful agents of propaganda so it was crucial that sport quickly stepped up to the mark.

Just as in 1914, rugby union was quick to commit to the cause and, also like the earlier war, the sport saw some of its best players and most colourful characters make the ultimate sacrifice. Although the numbers of rugby internationals killed was fewer than in the Great War, the figures still make grim reading. Both England and Scotland lost about half the number of internationals when compared to the earlier war, 14 compared to 27 and 15 to 30 respectively, while Wales lost 3 as opposed to 14. The number of Irish internationals was very similar in both wars, 9 in the former compared with 8 in the latter. Australia, with losses of 9 and 10, was the only major rugby nation to suffer more deaths in World War Two than in the First. Fewer certainly but no less significant. A total of 6 players who had taken part in the Calcutta Cup international between England and Scotland in 1939 failed to return from the war, less than the 14 in the corresponding fixture of 1914, but tragic nonetheless. Yet, strangely, the country with the highest losses among former rugby internationals was Germany. When France was ejected from the Five Nations in 1932, following accusations of professionalism in the French leagues, they looked to arrange fixtures against the junior rugby nations such as Italy and Germany. Germany had some success on the rugby field in the 1930s and succeeded in defeating Italy on 5 occasions and even beat France twice before the war ended the playing careers of their emerging team. The Rugby Football Union Museum have uncovered the identity of 16 German international rugby players who lost their lives between 1939 and 1945. But it is to rugby in the British Isles that we look when discovering the identity of the high-profile players killed in the conflict.

Many British citizens, of course, experienced the horrors of both these global conflicts, either as soldiers, civilians or both but some sporting heroes, killed in World War Two, had experienced the beginnings and subsequent horrors of both wars. This certainly applies to rugby union where there are a number of high-profile examples of this. Two of these were the Irish rugby internationals John Minch and John Clune. John Minch was 22 years old when he made his debut playing for Ireland against the 1912 South Africans. The son of the Kildare MP and owner of one of the largest maltsters in Ireland, this Bective Rangers and Army centre played five times for his country but, in a period where Irish rugby was not particularly strong, experienced only one victory in the green jersey, against Scotland in 1914. During the Great War he had served as a lieutenant, and later as a captain, with the Royal Army Medical Core and saw action on the North-West Frontier against the Mohmands and Swatis. Following the war, John Minch took a regular commission and served in India between the wars. By 1938, this keen and popular horseman with a wicked sense of humour had been promoted to Lieutenant Colonel and in 1942 became the commanding officer of Madras Military Hospital. John Minch is buried at Delhi War Cemetery following his death in November 1942 at the age of 52. Unfortunately, the cause of his death is not recorded. John Clune had a similar rugby experience. He also made his debut in the heavy 38–0 defeat to the 1912 Springboks when he was picked as a raw 19-year-old hooker. By 1914, the Blackrock College player had been moved into the second row where he was one of the youngest players to be capped in that position. Two victories against France were the only successes in the six-match international career for this Captain in the Royal Army Veterinary Corps. John Clune died in the Mediterranean on 12th September 1942 when the ship in which he was sailing, the RMS *Laconia*, was torpedoed by a German U-boat. It is unclear as to why he was aboard this particular ship, particularly as it was being used to transfer prisoners of war. Aged 53 at the time of his death, he is commemorated on the Brookwood Memorial in Brookwood Cemetery, Surrey. This cemetery is adjacent to Brookwood Military Cemetery, the largest Commonwealth War Graves cemetery in the United Kingdom, which contains the graves of more than 1,600 servicemen of the British Empire in the Great War and over 3,470 from World War Two.

The highest profile player to serve in the Great War before losing his life in World War Two was not, however, a proud Irishman, he was an Englishman. Norman Atherton Wodehouse was a second row forward whose rugby career culminated in captaining England to her first grand slam in 1913. It was a rugby career that, although somewhat unsung, was almost as distinguished as his naval career, a career during which he rose to the rank of Vice Admiral. He was born in Basford, Nottinghamshire, the son of the Reverend Canon Frederick Wodehouse and his wife Alice, on 18th May 1887 and was destined for a naval career from a very early age. After spending his formative years at the Royal Naval School at Lee on Solent, Norman attended the Britannia Royal Naval College as an officer cadet in 1902. The following year, he was promoted to the post of midshipman and joined the Atlantic Fleet in 1904. His success at Britannia led to Norman being commissioned as an acting Sub Lieutenant, a commission that was confirmed as being permanent in 1907.

It was also in 1907 when Norman began to make his mark on the rugby field as a somewhat uncompromising forward and lineout specialist. He was playing regularly for the United Services and for the Navy, often packing down with future England international Arthur Harrison VC, one of the 27 English rugby internationals killed in the Great War. Norman played in the annual Army v Navy match of 1907 and, despite missing the same fixture the following year, played in a further 6 such games until the outbreak of war in 1914. His reputation began to spread and in 1909 he was chosen to play for the Barbarians in the drawn game with Leicester. By now Norman was seen as one of England's finest lineout forwards and on 3rd March 1910 won the first of his 14 caps when he played in the 11–3 victory over France, a victory that helped England win their first championship since 1892.

Despite this success, Norman did little of note in his early internationals, at least not in the eyes of the press. The first reference to his playing contribution in *The Times* did not come until his 5th cap, when he scored the second of his two England tries, against Scotland in March 1911. Even then it was the English backs, inspired by the mercurial Ronnie Poulton, who got the credit for England's 13-8 victory. His first try, against France earlier that season, hadn't warranted a mention. Nevertheless, by now, despite being something of an unsung hero, he was a permanent fixture in the England side. A dominant display in the lineout helped England to a 15–0 victory over Ireland in February 1912. Following defeat to Scotland a few weeks later, Norman was made captain for the trip to Parc des Princes on 8th April 1912. Leading by example, Norman led England to victory by 18–8 with his team scoring four tries in the process. On the back of this success, Norman would have been confident of retaining the captaincy the following season and, no doubt, had ambitions to lead England to their first Grand Slam.

The 1912/13 international season did not start as planned. In early January, Norman captained England in their clash with the touring South Africans. By the time they faced England, the tourists had already defeated Scotland (16–0), Ireland (38–0) and Wales (3–0), the latter following a Welsh dropped goal that was controversially disallowed and were proving to be formidable opponents. They had lost three matches to Newport, Swansea and London but in the internationals, they had not conceded a single point on the tour thus far. Under Norman's leadership, England gave South Africa a tough test. Ronnie Poulton, in typical fashion, scored one try and nearly went over for two more but South Africa, with two penalty goals and a try proved to be too strong and ran out 9–3 winners. This was to be Norman's last defeat in an England shirt. His ambition to captain England to their first Grand Slam and fourth Triple Crown was fulfilled with victories over

Wales (12–0), France (20–0), Ireland (15–4) and Scotland (3–0). Despite not referring to him at all in the impressive defeat of a strong Welsh team, at last the English press, by way of *The Times*, gave their captain the credit that he deserved.

"Such success as the English teams have had this season could only have been achieved under the best leadership, so let us add to the congratulations showered on Lieutenant Wodehouse, who captained the team throughout the season."

However, it was a sign of different times that the winning of the first Grand Slam took second place to the recovery of the Calcutta Cup.

At least this victory ensured that Norman could retire from international rugby on the highest of notes and he could now direct his time and considerable abilities in pursuing his naval career. With the onset of the Great War in 1914, Norman was quickly in the action. In 1915, he was reported to have dived over the side of a ship in order to save a fellow seaman from drowning. This courageous action earned Norman the Royal Humane Society Silver Medal and he was quickly promoted to the position of Lieutenant Commander. By 1916, Norman was a gunnery officer, primarily serving on the battleship, HMS *Revenge* where he took part in biggest naval battle of the war, The Battle of Jutland, fought off the North Sea coast of Denmark's Jutland Peninsula. This battle, which took place mainly in the 36 hours between the 31st May and 1st June 1916, brought together the two most powerful naval forces of the time, the only full-scale clash of battleships between the two countries in this war. The losses on both sides were significant with the British losing 6,094 killed to the Germans' 2,551. It is estimated that the Royal Navy lost 113,300 tons made up of a total of 14 ships compared to the German Navy's loss of 62,300 tons and 11 ships. However, despite losing more men and ships than the German Navy, the Royal Navy could not be more pleased with the outcome as the German Navy was too diminished to put to sea again while the war lasted. The long-term aim of denying Germany access to the United Kingdom and the Atlantic did succeed and the Germans avoided fleet-to-fleet contact for the remainder of the war. Norman had certainly made his contribution to the British war effort.

Norman's successful naval career continued after the war. In 1919, following the Armistice and the subsequent Paris Peace Settlement, he was promoted to the position of Full Commander and was posted to China as a fleet gunnery officer. On this tour of duty Norman was awarded the Chinese Order of the Striped Tiger, an award for military or naval service awarded by the Republic of China. In 1923, he returned to Britain and, in October, married Mrs Theodosia Swire, the widow of Captain Douglas Swire who had died earlier in the year. She was the daughter of Commander Edward Boyle and his wife, Theodosia Ogilvie. They had two sons. By 1926, Norman was promoted to the position of captain and attended the Imperial Defence College in order to undertake a senior officer's war course. Following a period commanding the cruisers HMS *Ceres* and HMS *Calypso*, in 1931 Norman took command of the Royal Navy College at Dartmouth, a position that he held until 1934. This varied and distinguished career continued with a tour as Flag Captain, a term used to signify the captain of an admiral's flagship, in the Mediterranean on HMS *Barham* before being appointed as head of the British Military Mission in Portugal in 1938. While in this post, Norman was given credit for ensuring that Portugal did not fall under the influence of Spanish fascists currently involved in the Spanish Civil War. Finally, before the outbreak of war, Norman was appointed as aide-de-camp to King George VI, a fellow veteran of the Battle of Jutland, and awarded the Companion of the Order of the Bath. This former England rugby captain had come a long way since the triumphs of 1913 and England's first Grand Slam but, with war looking ever more likely, Norman was determined not to miss out on the action.

Three months before the outbreak of war, Norman was recalled to active service and became a Rear Admiral given the task of taking charge of the Naval Docklands in Gibraltar, a highly significant strategic position for the British Navy. On May 8th, 1940, he was made a Vice Admiral but quickly accepted a demotion to the position of Commodore (2nd Class) Royal Naval Rescue. This drop in rank was common for returning officers and allowed Norman to use his considerable experience and talents in the best way possible to help the war effort. Men such as Norman were needed urgently. The Royal Navy were to be crucial in providing cover during evacuations and operations, to guard the sea lanes thereby allowing British Armed Forces to fight in remote parts of the world such as North Africa and the Far East, to escort convoys across the Atlantic and Arctic Oceans as well as protect them from air, surface and submarine attack. Naval warfare had changed since the Great War and the technology available to both the British and German navies had advanced a good deal. By 1940, the outcome of a battle was often determined by the quality of radar or communications equipment, the intensity and accuracy of antiaircraft fire and the ability to use established systems to limit the impact of fire, explosion and other battle damage. Naval organisation was more flexible than land and aerial forces, so fighting fleets were put together as the situation demanded and that the availability of units allowed. On the other hand, this multiplicity of roles and the frequent unavailability of purpose-built types often exposed warships to challenges that they had not been designed to meet. At the same time, the Germans had made huge efforts with a surface commerce raiding campaign, which involved operations in every ocean, action which caused disruption and tied down British warships needed in other theatres. This led to a trade crisis in the South Atlantic, Indian Ocean and the coastal waters of Australia as well as in those waters nearer home. Naval warfare in World War Two was as important and dangerous as it had ever been. In carrying out their vital tasks, the Royal Navy suffered 50,758 deaths and the Merchant Navy a further 30,248.

In the summer of 1941, Norman got the chance to put his experience to the test when he was given command of convoy OB337 aboard the merchant vessel *Robert L Holt*, which was attached to HMS *Eaglet*. Norman's new duties of taking responsibility for the safety of convoys of merchant vessels was not without its problems. Norman's leadership skills were badly needed as Masters of Merchant Fleet vessels were used to a high degree of autonomy on their own ships. However, morale in the British Navy must have been lifted by the success, on 27th May, in sinking the first modern German battleship,

The Bismarck, after it was relentlessly hunted down and destroyed. The destruction of this formidable threat was significant but did nothing to reduce the dangers faced by the convoy vessels.

The plan when Norman set sail on June 20th 1941 was to head for a variety of ports in southern Africa, the *Robert L Holt* itself bound for Warri in Nigeria. The intention was for the convoy to disperse 750 miles from Land's End and for the vessels to go their own way but this left them very exposed, especially along the coast of Africa. Shortly after dispersal, the Robert L Holt, with Norman aboard, came into contact with a German U-69. There was no real contest and on July 4th the *Robert L Holt* was subjected to intense gunfire and, somewhat inevitably, was sunk. There were no survivors and Vice Admiral Norman Wodehouse, 54 years old, hero of two world wars and captain of the England Grand Slam winning team 1913, was one of those who perished. Norman was remembered as one of the most successful of England's rugby captains, a name to place alongside fellow leaders of the stature of second row forwards and captains Bill Beaumont and Martin Johnson. Norman is remembered with a memorial tablet placed in St Lawrence's Church, Gotham, Nottinghamshire, and on the Liverpool Naval Memorial, one of the approximately 800,000 military and merchant marine casualties of the war.

The year 1941 had already seen two notable England rugby internationals lose their lives while serving in the Royal Navy. The first of these was William George Ernest Luddington, a highly respected, mobile prop forward in England's Grand Slam winning teams of 1923 and 1924 under the captaincy of WJA Davies and Wavell Wakefield, respectively. The son of a veteran of Rorke's Drift where his father had assisted the surgeon James Reynolds VC in treating the injured, William was born in Aldershot on 8th February 1894 and grew up in Devonport keen to follow his father into the services. However, it was to the Royal Navy, rather than the Army, that William looked and it was here that his rugby career developed. He was a regular for both Devonport Services and the Royal Navy and he won his first England cap at the age of 29 in 1923. William's international career lasted only three years but during that time, he experienced great success. In his 13 internationals he was only on the losing side once, winning 10 and drawing 2 of the other games, and making his mark in this glorious period for English rugby. On winning his first cap, against Wales, it was reported that "he did not spare himself or anybody else in the mauls" and at the end of that season he won the Calcutta Cup for his country with a last-minute touchline conversion, reminiscent of John Taylor's historic kick at Murrayfield in 1971. Like Taylor, as a forward, William was not considered an obvious choice to be given this responsibility but, also like Taylor, he had the ability to rise to the occasion. Later that year he converted the winning try in a combined England/Wales XV that beat Scotland/Ireland in a thrilling match celebrating the centenary of rugby. In 1925, in front of 70,000 eager spectators, William scored the first points in the new Murrayfield stadium, although this was the game in which he suffered his first, and only, defeat in an England shirt. By the time his rugby career ended in 1930 William had become the first non-commissioned officer to captain the Royal Navy and become the most capped player from that particular service, a record that he held until 1979. Dai Gent, a highly respected former England scrum half and journalist, remembered his important place in English rugby history.

"England had short bulldog types in the front row, powerfully shouldered, of boundless energy, and capable with their feet and in open play generally. The names of the best of them will occur to all followers of the game: WGE Luddington and GS Conway."

As a regular in the Royal Navy, William inevitably saw action in World War Two and in 1939, he was a Master at Arms on the aircraft carrier, HMS *Illustrious*. By this time, aircraft carriers had become a very important part of the war effort. This particular carrier joined the fleet in August 1940 and carried 36 aircraft to the Mediterranean after which the ship saw action at Maritza on August 31st and a further mission against Benghazi on September 16th. HMS *Illustrious* became the first aircraft carrier to strike against an enemy fleet when, on November 11th, one Italian battleship was sunk and two others damaged. Following this action, HMS *Illustrious*, still with William on board, returned to protecting convoys, as we have seen, a dangerous activity. On January 10th, 1941, HMS *Illustrious* was attacked by enemy aircraft east of Sicily. The ship was hit by a 500-pound bomb and six other bombs also found their mark. William, who bravely remained at his post to the end, was killed in this attack, aged 46. William is remembered on the Plymouth Naval Memorial and at Twickenham where his daughter has allowed his rugby memorabilia to be placed on display.

Another England rugby international to lose his life in 1941 while serving in the Royal Navy has a particularly heroic story. Christopher Champain Tanner, better known as Kit, was born in Cheltenham on 24th June 1908. Kit was educated at Cheltenham College, where he first developed his love of rugby, and then at Pembroke College, Cambridge. Although initially missing out on a 'Blue', Kit's rugby ability as a strong and pacey winger did come to the attention of the England selectors. He is remembered as being a wonderful sight in full flow, aggressive in his running and a real crowd pleaser, popular with the supporters of all the teams that he played for. Playing for the Barbarians against the East Midlands in the Mobbs Memorial match, Kit scored three tries in front of the England selectors. *The Times* noted that "the strong and determined running of Tanner had been one of the features of play" and two weeks later, in March 1930, Kit was picked to play for England against Scotland at Twickenham. Despite the match ending in a 0–0 draw, Kit provided the highlight with a strong run, only to be recalled for an alleged knock-on. *The Times* acknowledged his contribution when reporting that he "did his best… and, in fact showed such power of stride he looked every inch a scorer." Although Kit gained a blue in December 1930 in a 3–3 draw, he lost his place in the national team despite playing well for the Barbarians and, occasionally, for Gloucester. By January 1932, Kit was back in favour and picked to play against the 1931/32 South African tourists. Defeats to the Springboks followed by another loss in Wales did not affect his place in the side. Victory over Ireland (11–8) in Dublin and then Scotland (16–3) surprisingly, following their poor start, gave England a share of the championship. In this deciding match Kit scored his first and only England try when "he went at full tilt for the corner turning in a bit to hand off Macpherson just before he crossed the line." Nevertheless, despite playing several more times for the prestigious Barbarians and in subsequent England trials, Kit never played for England again.

Rugby, however, was only part of the popular Kit's life. In 1935 he was ordained and became a Curate at Farnham Royal in Surrey. He remained here until 1937 when he moved to St Mary de Lode, Gloucester for the next two years, once again as Curate, before becoming Rector at Haslemere in August 1939. Kit's time here was brief as, with the outbreak of war, he was elected to serve as a Chaplain with the Royal Naval Volunteer Reserve. Kit was posted to HMS *Fiji* and quickly took to navy life, being a popular and highly respected Military Chaplain. HMS *Fiji* was commissioned in May 1940 and, in April 1941, was despatched, along with the destroyers HMS *Kandahar* and HMS *Kingston*, to support the operations to relieve the besieged island of Malta before being redirected for tactical reasons to prevent a landing on the island of Crete. In the attempt to achieve this, HMS *Fiji* came under heavy aerial attack from the German Luftwaffe and, with only one anti-aircraft gun and little ammunition it was inevitable that the captain would order the men to abandon ship. As Chaplain, Kit had no direct role in combat but he was expected to support the men in the best way he could. Kit's interpretation of this was particularly brave. After overseeing the removal of 60 wounded men from the sickbay, Kit, along with 500 other survivors, was forced into the water. He helped some men onto the small rafts and lifeboats that were available and, in the most dreadful of conditions, attempted to raise morale of those, like him, who were still in the water by leading them in song. It has been reported that the songs were more reminiscent of the rugby club rather than church but it helped maintain the spirits of me who were facing the direst of situations. When, after about four hours in the water, help arrived, Kit helped the men to safety before returning to the sea to give further help to those too weak to help themselves. It is estimated that at least 30 men owed their life to Kit's efforts during the night of 22nd/23rd May.

Alas, it proved too big a task for even as strong a character as Kit. Exhausted from his Herculean efforts, Kit died a few minutes after he was pulled to safety. For his bravery Kit was posthumously awarded the Albert Medal, an award given for lifesaving and the equivalent of the George Cross, one of the very few to be won in World War Two and the only one to be awarded to an English rugby international. Kit was 32 years old and left a wife, Eleanor, who he had married in 1937. Their daughter was born later in 1941, a matter of months after his death. The bravery and sacrifice of Kit Tanner is recognised both by a Rood cross at St Christopher, Haslemere and on the Commonwealth War Graves, Plymouth Naval Memorial. Kit is remembered as one of the bravest of men and, along with Norman Wodehouse and William Luddington, one of the three England rugby internationals to be killed at sea in 1941.

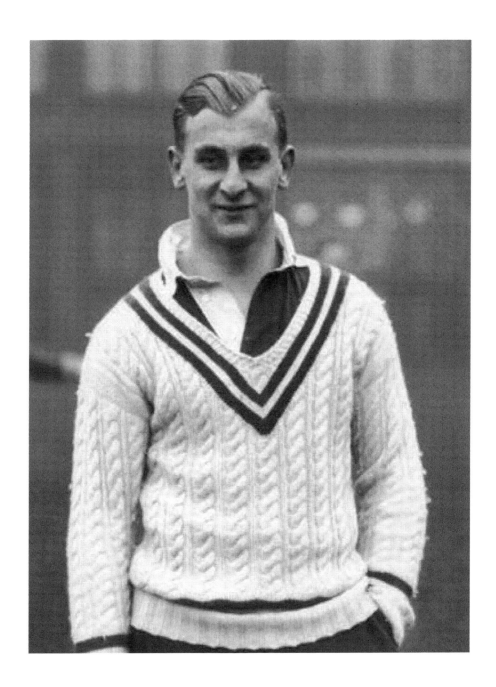

Prince Alexander S. Obolensky

CHAPTER 4
ALEXANDER OBOLENSKY: THE FLYING PRINCE

There is no doubt that Norman Wodehouse was one of the great England rugby captains and that he had a very distinguished naval career. However, despite this, Norman Wodehouse has disappeared under the radar when discussing England's rugby history. The same is also true of William Luddington and Kit Tanner. However, this cannot be said of our next subject, one of the most high-profile losses, and certainly one of the most glamorous, Prince Alexander Obolensky. Alexander was born in St Petersburg, then known as Petrograd, on 17th February 1916, the son of Prince Serge Obolensky, an officer in the Tsar's Imperial Horse Guards, and Princess Luba. As a descendant of Rurik — who had established a dynasty in 862 which later dissolved into the independent principalities and went on to form medieval Russian States — Alexander came from very distinguished stock. Following the 1917 Revolution, Serge and his family, including baby Alexander, fled to England where they settled in Muswell Hill in north London. Alexander received an education befitting an English gentleman, attendance at Ashe Boys Preparatory School in Etwall, Derbyshire followed by Trent College, Long Eaton. From here he progressed to Brasenose College, Oxford University where he studied PPE, although he made a much greater impression on the rugby field than in his academic studies.

Alexander's prowess on the rugby field as an exceptionally quick and elusive wing three-quarter first became obvious at Trent College. Here he was the 16-year-old star player of a team that went unbeaten throughout the season, scoring 539 points against a mere 22 conceded. In 1935, he won his first blue in a scoreless, forgettable encounter with Cambridge. Yet the match, in which he made a try saving tackle on the Cambridge wing JR Rawlence, not a facet of the game for which he would become renowned, was the game which first brought him to the attention of the England selectors. Welsh rugby writer, JBG Thomas, called this "the tackle of a lifetime" and it certainly offered him the chance of a lifetime, one that he was keen to take. He came into the final England trial, scored 3 tries and, in the words of *The Times*, "was in the side to stay." Not yet a British citizen, the 19-year-old was known to drink Champagne and eat a dozen oysters before Oxford matches. But the selectors had seen enough to not let this rather unorthodox preparation affect their decision to select this unique character. In the manner of 1970s England hero David Duckham, Alexander was a supremely balanced athlete who maximised the use of his great pace while retaining the ability to swerve and sidestep, in his newly designed light boots, through the bewildered opposition. *The Times* saw his speed as his greatest asset but in the trial match they reported that his defence, too, was as good as anybody's.

Although clearly the most glamorous England three-quarter since Ronnie Poulton led England to the 1914 Grand Slam before his death in Flanders, the selection of Alexander for the national side was certainly a gamble, all the more given the opposition. The third New Zealand All Blacks had arrived, and despite a narrow defeat to Wales and an early loss to Swansea, they were looking as powerful as their illustrious predecessors. There couldn't really be a bigger test for the young winger. The selectors, however, had every confidence in him, knowing that he could cause Jack Manchester's 3rd All Black team problems and so asked the established, crisp passing centre Peter Cranmer to play left centre rather than right so that "he could get the ball to Obolensky." The preparation for the match however was rather chaotic and gave Alexander and Cranmer little time to cement their partnership. The team wasn't finalised until Friday afternoon and so only one full training session was possible before the team settled down to their evening meal at the Metropole Hotel, Northumberland Avenue, where they were staying, which ironically was the hotel where their opponents were also based.

The final match of the 3rd All Blacks tour of the British Isles took place on 4th January 1936 and has gone down in history as one of the great English victories. The afternoon began with the teams being introduced to the Prince of Wales, just 16 days away from becoming the ill-fated King Edward VIII. On being introduced to the Russian Prince, the future king, well aware of Alexander's lack of British citizenship, asked "By what right do you play for England?" Alexander, no doubt of the opinion that the Prince of Wales was his only social equal in the 73,000 crowd, answered "I attend Oxford University, Sir." He carried this confidence into the game where he ensured a staggering 13–0 England victory with two superb individual tries. For the first, receiving a pass from Ronnie Gerrard, he cut between two opponents before swerving outside another and racing over for the opening try. In the second half he produced an even more individual effort, an arching run from the right to score on the opposite side of the pitch, beating numerous would-be tacklers in the process. A try by the other debutant wing, Hal Sever, and a dropped goal by Cranmer completed the convincing victory, the biggest international defeat suffered by the New Zealanders on British soil before or since. Alexander had made rugby history, helped no doubt, by the unorthodox nature of both tries, what New Zealand's premier rugby writer, Terry Maclean called "a stupendous exhibition of the hypotenuse in rugby", and the happy chance of his efforts being caught on film for Pathé News and subsequently viewed in British cinemas.

Following this performance, Alexander had a whole new set of admirers. *The Times* described the match as "remarkable" and the result "still more remarkable" while the England captain, Bernard Gadney, thought that Alexander's first try disillusioned the All Blacks while at the same time giving his side more confidence, helped no doubt by the violent roar that greeted both tries, worth according to Gadney, five extra points to his team. EHD Sewell, the rugby journalist, wrote that Alexander "glides with the easy sinuosity of an antelope at full speed" and there were plenty of others who now saw him as much more than a sprinter. Cranmer agreed saying later that Alexander "just went straight though the gap and his feet did the rest for him." *The Morning Post* went further:

"Runners we have seen before but never such a runner with such an innate idea of where to go and how to get there. His double swerve to gain his first try was remarkable enough, but the extraordinary turn-in and diagonal right-to-left run which won him his second and which drew forth that great Twickenham rarity, a double roar of applause, will never be forgotten by anybody who saw it."

The match itself was never forgotten by those who witnessed or played in it. Hal Sever was another debutant who had a game to remember by scoring England's third try. Although Sever went on to gain 10 caps, a sizeable number in the days of the Four Nations and infrequent touring teams, this was his most memorable moment, with the memory of his co-winger firmly at its centre.

"My most thrilling game? I played in many but I must place my first international against the All Blacks in 1936 as the most exciting of all for me. Not that we had a grandstand finish: we didn't. We won more easily than anyone imagined. But I shall never forget the deafening roar from the capacity crowd at Twickenham when Obolensky scored his two tries. No game could ever quite match that one."

It was reported that Alexander mused after the game that "it is difficult for me to believe that I am anything but an Englishman, and as one, I simply did my best at Twickenham." It was no surprise when two months later, in March 1936, Prince Alexander Obolensky was made a full British citizen.

Following this sensational start, a long career of international rugby looked sure to follow. England's next game, a few weeks later, was against Wales at St Helen's, Swansea and Alexander was expected to cause the hosts serious problems. With a veiled reference to his privileged upbringing, *The Times* saw him as a wing who would not expect the ball "on a proverbial silver salver" but would go looking for work and who would support breakaways. In the event, in front of a big crowd of 50,000 in excellent conditions, the attacking players cancelled each other out and the match finished in a 0–0 draw, a result that satisfied nobody. Closely marked, Alexander had a few chances to shine but the Welsh defence held firm. Three weeks later England were defeated 6–3 in Lansdowne Road, Dublin and the press were quick to conclude that, although he made great effort to run around the opposition, Alexander's exceptional pace was wasted. Following the victory over Scotland at Twickenham on 21st March, *The Times* concluded that "he has been a wasted force ever since the match with the All Blacks." They didn't blame Alexander personally as he "tried in vain to remind his centres that he could run pretty fast."

Despite the failure to build on his sensational introduction to international rugby there was much to look forward to including the forthcoming British Lions tour to Argentina. This has come to be thought of as 'the forgotten tour' as in playing terms it did not place the demands on players as tours to New Zealand and South Africa. It was also an understrength Lions team which, although captained by England skipper Bernard Gadney, included a small number of 'capped' players. But the glamour of the team's destinations ensured that it would never be forgotten by the players. Sailing on *The Andalucía Star*, a ship that was to be sunk by a German submarine off the coast of Africa in 1942, the players stopped off at exotic locations such as Lisbon, Madeira, Tenerife, Montevideo and Rio de Janeiro before docking in Buenos Aires. The facilities on board for the 20-day voyage were first class and the players even managed to keep themselves reasonably fit by completing some light training on the deck during the journey. There was an element of fun evident throughout the tour, not least when the team adopted Madeira hats as part of the official tour uniform. A warm-up game was played against Brazil at Santos in which it is reputed that Alexander scored 17 tries, still a world record. Although the details of Alexander's exploits are a little vague, the Lions did win this game 81–0 and went unbeaten throughout the tour with 10 further victories. *The Times* referred to Alexander's "fine try" against the Combined Argentina XV and his two "dashing" tries when playing the Argentine Pacific Athletic team. However, it was the other English wing on the tour, the as yet uncapped Jim Unwin, who grabbed the headlines in Argentina. He scored 17 tries in the Argentine leg of the tour, including one in the 23–0 win in the only Test match. No caps were awarded in this game, despite it being played in front of an enthusiastic 15,000 crowd, and there are no details of Alexander's contribution. Indeed, remarkably, with the exception of seven games for the Barbarians and a couple of wartime internationals, Alexander's representative career was over.

On his return to England, Alexander did continue to play rugby. He missed the varsity match through injury in December 1936 and played less rugby in the 1936/37 season which resulted in Alexander losing his place in the England team but by December 1937 and the varsity match he was back. Although there were still, possibly unfair, question marks about his defence, it was thought by many that Alexander's searing pace could win the match for Oxford. By a score that seems strange to the modern supporter, Oxford did indeed win, and win comfortably, by 17–4 or by 5 tries and one conversion to one dropped goal. Ironically, Alexander made his greatest contribution through valuable work in defence and had few opportunities to shine. It was left to others, including future Scottish international Willie Renwick, to score the tries. Renwick, like fellow three-quarter Herbert Freakes and opposition Scottish international centre John Forrest, became a casualty of the war a few years later. Alexander also played 7 games for the Barbarians during these years, a much greater honour in those days than is currently the case. Two of these appearances were in the Mobbs Memorial match, the annual fixture between the Barbarians and the East Midlands in memory of England rugby captain Edgar Mobbs who had been killed at the Battle of Passchendaele in 1917. But it was late in 1938 before Alexander was back in the England reckoning following a series of appearances for Rosslyn Park. He played in all three England trial matches, playing on the left rather than his preferred right wing, but he barely received a pass in any of the games. His frustration was complete when he received a dog bite which led to a brief stay in hospital. *The Times* talked of Alexander's "rare speed" and "occasional revelations of real football ability" but thought that the "thoroughly competent, small but polished" RH Guest of Liverpool University and Waterloo deserved his place. It would seem that Guest's sound defence was to be preferred to Alexander's speed. The possibility of playing both was discussed but was seen as too much of a risk. Alexander's chance of a recall to national colours had gone.

Out of the England set up he may have been but for Alexander, life went on. His glamour was still very apparent and he had no shortage of female company, often as a result of him regularly attending debutante balls. Add to this his enthusiastic theatrical reviews in the Oxford University's *Isis* and frequent dining engagements with Russian émigré society, it is no surprise that academic study took a back seat. This was confirmed when Alexander received his 4th class honours degree.

As early as 1938, Alexander had joined the Royal Air Force Auxiliary and while at Oxford he had shown his willingness to serve his adopted country. In Oxford University debates Alexander had voted to 'fight for King and Country', determined to prevent Britain falling in the manner of Russia in 1917 and suffering the consequences that resulted from such a defeat. With war imminent, Alexander was, on August 12th, 1939, commissioned as an Acting Pilot Officer with 615 Squadron, Auxiliary Air Force stationed at RAF Kenley. Shortly after, with war declared, he joined RAF 504 Squadron, equipped with Hawker Hurricane fighters. It is important to remember the crucial role which the RAF played in the war effort. Although they did not win the war on their own, praise of 'the few' is well-deserved. Whether it be in tactical bombing, the bombing of cities, supporting land forces or protecting and defending ships at sea, this work was crucial in gaining a successful outcome. At the outbreak of war Bomber Command possessed just 352 aircraft, fewer than in 1918, but by 1945 the average daily strength was 1,420 with most now possessing four engines. The number of RAF personnel also increased hugely, from 175,692 in September 1939 to 1,185,833 by July 1944. The training that these new, inexperienced pilots completed was much more dangerous than is sometimes realised. Realising that thorough preparation of pilots shaped the efficiency of a unit, the training was improved as the war progressed. However, the threat to Britain was so serious that the emphasis was on quantity rather than quality of pilots, with a high count of accidents being an inevitable result. According to an article published in the *Daily Telegraph* in February 2014, a total of 7,847 officers and aircrew were killed in training accidents in World War Two. All were volunteers. Bomber Command lost more than 3,000 on its own, deaths barely noticed save by their families.

One of the most bizarre of fatal accidents involved two promising sportsmen of note. Claude Ashton, son of Hubert Ashton, president of

Essex County Cricket Club, was a fine footballer and cricketer. He was a wing half with the Corinthians who represented the England Amateur XI on 12 occasions and captained England in his only full international. He was also a successful cricketer, an all-rounder for Cambridge University who, like his two brothers before him, he captained before joining Essex. Claude also won two hockey blues while at Cambridge, a truly exceptional sportsman whose work as a chartered accountant in the city prevented him from gaining further success. On the outbreak of war Claude trained as a pilot and quickly became a flight lieutenant. He was killed on 31st October 1942 when flying as a navigator/observer in a British Beaufighter X7845 when it collided in mid-air with a Vickers Wellington in a training session over Caernarfon. The pilot of the Wellington was Squadron Leader Roger Winlaw, a fellow Old Wykehamist, who had played 52 first-class matches for Cambridge University and Surrey as well as spending 7 years of Minor Counties cricket with Bedfordshire. In case one is lulled into thinking that this was uniquely a British problem, it is worth remembering that the USA lost approximately 15,000 airmen in training accidents.

During the period of 'The Phoney War', pilots had little to do other than this very important training and flying defensive patrols while waiting for the inevitable conflict to begin. It did, however, mean that Alexander could return to playing some rugby. In December 1939 he played for a joint England/Wales XV that defeated Scotland/Ireland XV 17–3 at Richmond and in March 1940 he played for an England XV against Wales where he scored a typical solo try in a 18–9 victory. The money made from both matches went to the Red Cross to support their work. Tragically those matches were the last that Alexander ever played. By now he had been posted to Digby, where Martlesham Heath, Suffolk was being used as a forward base and it was here that he completed his training. Here he confided to fellow Oxford Blue and Wales full back Vivian Jenkins that, although his pilot training was going well, he still experienced some difficulties when landing the aircraft. Nevertheless, on March 26th, 1940, he was promoted to become a full Pilot Officer and two days later learned of his selection for the England team to play Wales in another Red Cross fund-raiser on April 13th. The following day, March 29th, 1940, Alexander was killed when he overshot the runway while landing his Hawker Hurricane Mark 1 at Martlesham Heath. It appears that his aircraft dropped into a ravine where Alexander broke his neck. There has been some suggestion that he was performing acrobatics but this has never been confirmed and is unlikely given Alexander's concerns over his ability to bring the aircraft to a safe landing. The official cause of death remains 'an accident resulting from overshooting the runway'. He was 24 years old.

There was great sadness at Alexander's death, the first high-profile sportsman to be lost in World War Two. His death was even recorded in the *New York Times* where the headline read, "Prince Obolensky, 24, Killed in Air Crash" followed by the subheading "British Flier Was Also an Outstanding Rugby Back." His England captain, Bernard Gadney, himself a rugby hero of the 1930s, thought Alexander to be "a nice young chap" and visited his grave in Ipswich New Cemetery each year on the anniversary of his death. This glamorous Russian prince left an impressive legacy in his adopted country. Twickenham has a suite named after him as well as including him as one of the 100 players in their 'Walk of Legends' while an annual lecture is also given in his honour. Rosslyn Park RFC have an annual award in his name and a building has been named after him in Trent College, Long Eaton where he had studied in his youth. In 2009, a memorial was unveiled in his honour by his niece Princess Alexandra in Ipswich, some money for which was given by Roman Abramovich, the Russian owner of Chelsea Football Club and billionaire businessman and investor. His time as a household name may have been short but there is no doubt that Prince Alexander Obolensky will be forever remembered as the most glamorous of England rugby players and a tragic loss to British sport.

Ronald Gerrard

CHAPTER 5
RONNIE GERRARD: "A MAN OF A STOUT COUNTENANCE"

The Flying Prince was certainly the most glamorous member of the England rugby team that defeated the 1936 All Blacks and, quite rightly following his two tries, his is the name that has been remembered in the history books. But there were other heroes. England were captained by scrum half Bernard Gadney, a six-foot two-inch scrum half who had captained England to the Triple Crown in 1934 and was to lead his country in eight of his fourteen internationals. Against the All Blacks, Gadney as usual led from the front, his aggressive, confrontational style giving Jack Manchester's team plenty of problems. Hal Sever was a dangerous winger who raced 35 yards to score England's third and final try in this famous victory. The pacey winger continued to have a good England career winning the Triple Crown in 1938 and finishing with ten caps. Both Bernard Gadney and Hal Sever saw wartime service but survived the conflict to live to the ripe old age of 91 and 95, respectively. Centre Peter Cranmer was the other scorer with a dropped goal. He later captained England and later became a distinguished rugby and cricket broadcaster with the BBC.

One of the other heroes of that January day in 1936 was not fortunate enough to have the long life enjoyed by Bernard Gadney and Hal Sever. Ronald Anderson Gerrard was born in Hong Kong on 26th January 1912 and developed into an outstanding all-round sportsman. While studying at Taunton School, the tall and strongly built Ronnie won the Public Schools shot-putting at Stamford Bridge in both 1929 and 1930. He opened the batting in the school cricket XI and headed the averages for three years impressing everybody with his forceful, attacking style. Ronnie had a highest score of 130 in schoolboy cricket but this was not his only area of sporting excellence. Lawn tennis, table tennis and Fives (a form of hand-tennis) champion, Ronnie was also a member of the school water polo team and a first-class rifle shot. His cricketing ability brought him to the attention of the Somerset County Cricket coaching staff and in 1935 he played three first-class games for the county. Unfortunately, he achieved little of note in these matches scoring only 36 runs from his five innings. Not that this mattered too much as by now Ronnie was making his mark in his true sporting love as a highly dependable, steady centre in the England rugby XV.

Ronnie's senior rugby career had begun early, alongside his other sporting successes. By the age of 18 he had made his senior debut for Bath and it wasn't long before he made his mark. A good all-round rugby player who could make a clean break and kick goals, it was in defence that Ronnie excelled. He was a ferocious tackler who thought nothing of his own wellbeing, always being prepared to put his body 'on the line'. Although early reports say that he had all the skills with a good swerve and hand-off, it is his defensive qualities that shine through. The reports of his early games in the Bath Chronicle indicate that Ronnie was set for a great career. They were right. By 1931 Ronnie was playing in the England trial and, although *The Times* reported that despite making "many fine breaks… he still needed to learn when to pass the ball", he did not have to wait long to step on to the international stage. On January 2nd, 1932, three weeks short of his 20th birthday, Ronnie faced the mighty South Africans in front of a 70,000 crowd at Twickenham. Expectations were high and *The Times* expected "at least a great defensive effort" from Ronnie. They were not disappointed as Ronnie acquitted himself well regularly making breaks on the few occasions that he received the ball. An inexperienced England team, however, with seven other debutants, did disappoint and were beaten 7-0.

Ronnie, by now often known as 'Gerry', kept his place for the opening match of the 1932 home championship but England suffered another seven-point defeat (12–5) to a strong Welsh XV. The remainder of the championship brought a change in fortune with victories against Ireland (11–8) and Scotland (16–3) which gave England a share of the championship with Wales and Ireland in a topsy-turvy international season. Following these two victories, Ronnie was beginning to look like an England regular, no mean achievement for a twenty-year-old. Despite a perceived lack of pace, Ronnie was seen as a dependable centre who was capable of making a break but who could be relied upon to be steady in defence with his decisive tackling and solid kicking game. It appeared that Ronnie was in the England side to stay.

Ronnie was soon joined by another player destined to be victim of the war. Making his return to the England team to win the ninth of his ten caps in the decisive victory over Scotland was try scoring hero and pick of the pack, Brian Black. A second row or No 8, Brian Henry Black was that rare creature, a goal kicking forward who scored 30 points for England as well as four more in his five test appearances for the British Lions over his distinguished career. He was also rare among international rugby players in being a South African Rhodes Scholar, born in Grahamstown, Eastern Cape, who studied at Oxford University. Although sometimes inconsistent with the boot, Brian Black was a prodigious kicker who in 1931 kicked a penalty from the halfway line with the last kick of the game to deny Wales their first win at Twickenham. Two years later, when Wales finally achieved their long awaited first success at rugby's HQ, Brian Black played his last game for England. Not that his sporting successes had come to an end. In 1937 he was part of a gold-medal-winning two-man bobsleigh team in the World Championships held in Cortina d'Amprezzo, Italy. Later he won the four-man event in St Moritz, Switzerland. On the outbreak of war Brian Black became a Pilot Officer in the Auxiliary Air Force but the thirty-three-year-old was killed in a flying training exercise over Wiltshire on 29th July 1940, as we have already seen, not the first or last international sportsman to die in this tragic way.

As Brian Black's international career was drawing to a distinguished close, Ronnie Gerrard was going from strength to strength. Newspaper reports show clearly how many of Bath's tries he had a direct hand in and there is no doubt as to his contribution to Bath's success during these years. In January 1933, he was selected to face a strong Wales team still searching for their first win at Twickenham. Here he would directly face an equally strong tackling, robust centre Claude Davey. The Swansea and Sale centre is still remembered as one of Wales's best centres, a player who won twenty-three caps and led his country in eight of those games. Ten minutes into the second half, Ronnie was led from the field with blood pouring from his eye following a tackle from Davey. According to Huw Richard's in his book *The Red and the White*, a history of England-Wales rugby internationals, Ronnie "fell to the ground like a stone." Wales leading 4–3 at the time went on to win by 7–3 with star wing three-quarter Ronnie Boon scoring all of Wales's points. Some England supporters claimed that the injury to Ronnie was deliberate but this seems unlikely. It was probably more a case of a clash of two crash-tackling centres coming up against each other. Something had to give.

Despite this injury, three weeks later Ronnie was back to face the Irish at Twickenham. Despite giving two scoring passes in the 17–6 victory *The Times* felt that his pace was suspect and that "his constructive play had been disastrous this season." This does seem a rather harsh assessment when one considers that England scored five tries in an impressive victory. In England's final international of the season, against Scotland at Murrayfield, Ronnie was once again injured, this time suffering the effects of cramp. *The Times* cut him no slack and were once again critical of his lack of pace taking little account of him being reduced to being a passenger before the end of the game. Scotland won 3–0 and went on to clinch the Triple Crown in Dublin two weeks later.

The following season 1933/34 saw Ronnie gain a more favourable press coverage. Playing for Bath against Swansea in September 1933 the local press reported how he saved his side with a run where "he beat half a dozen opponents before relieving the pressure", thereby enabling his team to hang on for a 5–3 victory. Later that month, newspapers talked of "Gerrard again in the picture with a lightening cut through" and in the fixture against Harlequins at the end of the month it was reported that Ronnie "capped a perfect display of running by diving over wide out."

The international season was about to be even more successful for Ronnie and for England. It began with the eagerly awaited clash in Cardiff with Wales and another battle with Claude Davey. The England selectors had addressed Ronnie's perceived lack of pace by selecting the quicker Peter Cranmer as his co-centre. This proved to be an ideal combination and one which would serve England well in the next few seasons. A brilliant all-round sportsman, Cranmer played in 16 rugby internationals between 1934 and 1938, when he was made captain, as well as captaining Warwickshire County Cricket Club between 1938 and 1947. During the war Major Cranmer served in Burma, Egypt and India. Ronnie nursed Cranmer through his first game as well as having another titanic struggle with Davey. England scored three tries, one set up by Ronnie, in a 9–0 victory. The brilliant, mercurial new Welsh outside half, Cliff Jones, was tackled out of the game and England won convincingly. It proved to be the launch of a Triple Crown season as Ireland were beaten 13–3 and Scotland 6–3, after which *The Times* dubbed him "The Prince of all tacklers." High praise indeed from his former critics.

Also, part of this unbeaten England team of 1934 was the Exeter-born front row forward Henry Rew, whose international career came to a close following the victory over Scotland. A sturdy prop who could also play at hooker, Henry made his international debut against Scotland in March 1929 when his country suffered a 12–6 defeat. Nevertheless, Henry kept his place for the next two seasons, missing only the game against Wales in 1930 through injury. At the end of the 1930 season, he was part of the British Isles team to tour New Zealand and was selected for all four tests in a 3–1 series defeat. On his return Henry kept his place in the England team during a poor season during which England failed to win a single game. This resulted in a three-year absence from the international scene. However, Henry returned for the England trial in January 1934, following an injury to Douglas Kendrew, "alive and full of vigour" according to *The Times*. His subsequent return to the England team for the whole of the 1934 championship was something of a swansong for a player who the press reported had "relapsed into honourable rugby old age." The Welsh media were quite happy to see Henry's selection, voicing their opinion that he had "lost his spring", a comment which resulted in the England team presenting Henry with his own three-foot-long spring. Kendrew returned to the England team during the season but was picked as a No.8 due to Henry's impressive form.

The onset of war had very different outcomes for the rival forwards and teammates. Henry became a Major in the Royal Tank Regiment and led A squadron of the 7th RTR in Operation Compass in December 1940. Despite being successful in taking more than 2,000 prisoners, Henry was one of 56 British soldiers killed or injured in the operation, tragically dying of his wounds at Nibeiwa Fort, Egypt on 11th December 1940, aged 34. His death was reported in the *Sydney Herald* where he was remembered as a member of the 1930 British Isles team and "one of the best footballers Devon has produced." Henry is buried at El Alamein War Cemetery. Major General Douglas Kendrew DSO with three bars, became one of the most highly decorated soldiers of World War Two.

The season, 1934/35 began well for Ronnie. Following a 14–6 victory against Camborne in September 1934, the Bath Chronicle reported that "Gerrard's genius was noticeable in all he did" while earlier that month, despite a 14–3 defeat to Llanelli it was reported that "Gerrard was magnificent. He did a couple of men's work, collected a black eye, and was proud of it." A week later, following a victory over Bedford, Ronnie was chaired from the field. His versatility was also coming to the fore. For a later match against Camborne, in December 1934, the England selectors requested that he play at full back. Reports described "his gathering as superb, his kicking thorough and, if you want a stopper, Gerrard is your man." Ronnie was also known to turn out as outside half if the occasion required. Nevertheless, by January 1935, Ronnie was back playing at centre where the press talked of his "thrust fullness."

Ronnie was to miss the 1935 international championship but the climax of Ronnie's career was fast approaching. He was picked to partner Peter Cranmer in the centre in the historic clash with the 1935/36 All Blacks, at 23 years of age, the old man of the midfield backs, with outside half Peter Candler 20 years old inside him, and Cranmer at 21 outside him. They were expected to feed 19-year-old winger Alexander Obolensky which, as we know they did to spectacular effect. Ronnie's part in the 13–0 victory was significant. After being given the job of kicking off, Ronnie and his young partner Cranmer were "supremely sound" in their roles and both contributed to the try scoring exploits of Obolensky and Sever. It must have seemed to Ronnie that his future was bright. This victory, however, was the high point. Although Ronnie was only 24 years old during the 1936 championship, it was to be his last in the England shirt. He was criticised during the season for not releasing Obolensky more often. Both men paid the price and neither played for England again. Ronnie and Alexander Obolensky both played their final match against Scotland on 21st March but, at least ended on a high with a narrow 9–8 victory. Although the *Bath Chronicle*, partisan to the last, described Ronnie as "fighting fit", injuries began to take their toll the following season when Ronnie only played in 16 matches. This was followed by 13 and, finally, 7 in the two years before the outbreak of war. Given Ronnie's all-round abilities, it is surprising that he never scored for his country in any of his 14 appearances but, although a distinguished career had ended in something of an anti-climax, Ronnie could look back with pride in his achievements on the rugby field as one of the best defensive centres of the decade.

World War Two was to confirm Ronnie as something more, among the bravest of men, an assessment that would have come as no surprise to those who had played rugby alongside him. After joining the Royal Engineers, Ronnie rose to the rank of major where one of his jobs was to clear mines and booby traps. While engaged on this task while under heavy fire at the Second Battle of El Alamein, Ronnie was awarded the Distinguished Service Order (DSO) in the autumn of 1942. The conditions faced by Ronnie and his colleagues were dreadful, made more difficult by frequent sandstorms, some of which exposed the minefields. The injuries sustained by some of the soldiers were also horrendous. The Reverend Douglas Thompson, a Chaplain with the Essex Regiment, tells us that severe burns were among the worst problems. Injured soldiers would be likely to lose a great deal of skin when their clothes were removed. Corporal Vernon Scannell of the Argyll and Sutherland Highlanders confirms the suffering of his colleagues.

"One of the most memorable and still chilling and nightmarish things is hearing the voices of those who had been badly wounded, their voices raised in terror and pain… one badly wounded sergeant was sobbing and calling for his mother which seemed to be so demeaning and humiliating and dreadful. I felt a kind of shock that I can't fully understand even now because he'd been reduced to a baby."

The living conditions were also dreadful, all too reminiscent of the Great War. Bodies were sometimes not recovered until a week or more after death and so had deteriorated dreadfully. Their discovery was extremely traumatic for those who had survived. Soldiers told of the flies, the shortage of water and "the monotony of the deadly diet of bully beef and hard biscuits." In other respects, it was very different environment from 1914–18 Western Front as soldiers experienced a bleak landscape with little vegetation, hot days followed by cold nights and only scattered settlements and towns. Lawrence of Arabia would certainly have recognised these conditions, while the toilet facilities were very similar to those described so vividly by soldiers who experienced Gallipoli.

Ronnie fortunately survived this battle and was able to learn of his DSO. The victory was to prove to a major turning point of the war. Churchill himself said that "before El Alamein we didn't win a battle but after El Alamein we never lost one." Not strictly true of course but it makes the point of the importance of this victory. For Ronnie there was no time to reflect on this success. Three months later, on 22nd January 1943, he was killed in action near Tobruk. Ronnie was buried at Tripoli War Cemetery, aged just 31 years old. In 2016 D Crichton-Smith wrote a biography of Ronnie entitled *Men of a Stout Countenance — The Life of Major RA Gerrard DSO, RF*. One year earlier, in 2015, Ronnie Gerrard had been one of the six Bath players inducted into the club's new Hall of Fame along with a legendary centre of a later era, Jeremy Guscott. Fitting memorials to a brave soldier and distinguished English rugby player.

Bob Alexander

CHAPTER 6
FIVE NATIONS RUGBY HEROES

It is clear that rugby union paid a high price for their involvement in World War Two and, like England, the Celtic nations of the United Kingdom once again, lost a significant number of high-profile internationals. We have already seen that a total of 14 Scottish internationals were lost along with 8 Irish and 3 Welshmen who had represented their country. The cause of their deaths varied with some being lost whilst performing heroic deeds while others perished in accidents, inevitable perhaps as the warring nations tried to come to terms with the rapid advancement in military hardware and equipment.

One of the Irish internationals who met a particularly heroic death was Charles Hallaran, a lock forward who played 15 times for his country during a five-year period, February 1921 to February 1926. The splendidly named Charles Francis George Thomas Hallaran was born on the 10th June 1897 in Ceylon, the son of Colonel William Hallaran who was then serving in the Royal Army Medical Corps. William Hallaran himself was an international rugby player having represented Ireland in their match against Wales in 1884, only the second encounter between the two countries and the first to be held in Cardiff. Not that many would have known. William played under an alias, R.O.N. Hall, (although later the records were amended to give the correct name), an action taken to avoid the wrath of his clergyman father who clearly did not see the playing in such a game as a good use of his son's time. William, who was still serving in the Royal Army Medical Corps during the Great War, was killed on January 23rd, 1917. Although father and son were to suffer the same fate in two different World Wars, Charles' rugby career was a good deal more successful than his father's had been.

Educated at Eastman's College, Royal Naval College Dartmouth, United Services Portsmouth, Charles played his rugby for the Royal Navy and Surrey where he established his reputation as a consistent and highly respected lock who was soon to make his mark on the international scene. Despite finishing on the losing side in 7 of his first 8 matches Charles kept his place for most of the subsequent games. His last 7 games resulted in 5 victories as the Irish began to establish themselves as a force in the game once again following the Great War. Indeed, Charles last international season (1926) saw Ireland claim a share of the championship, their first success since 1912. During these years Charles also played for the Barbarians.

Away from the rugby field, Charles' personal life also had its share of ups and downs. In February 1924, at the height of his rugby career, Charles married Anita Sinclair but the marriage was not to last and they divorced, a rare occurrence in the 1930s. In 1934, both Charles and Anita remarried, Charles to Elizabeth Joyce Philpot. This marriage too, was ill-fated but for very different reasons. On the night of the 21st March 1941, a motor boat came alongside Commander Hallaran's ship and, as a result of the swelling sea, the motor boat rolled and a stoker was thrown overboard. Seeing that the man was likely to be crushed between the two boats, Charles dived in to rescue him. He succeeded in dragging the man to safety but tragically Charles was thrown against the boat in the rough seas where he suffered a fractured skull. Before he could be rescued, Charles drowned. He was posthumously awarded the Albert Medal, just as Kit Tanner was to be for his bravery just two months later. Charles' body was recovered and he was buried in Belfast City Cemetery. He was 43 years of age.

It is sometimes difficult to gain a clear picture of the character of such a man nearly 80 years after his death but the tribute paid by a fellow officer in *The Times* on 4th September 1941 gives as clear a picture as one could hope to see. "I had only known him a few months... but in that time I, and all of us, had come to rest upon him as the pillar of his ship's existence. He had a sure sense of affairs and was an utterly loyal senior — a priceless man. In duty inflexible, in pleasure he was warm and the widespread company of those who mourn him will testify to the gaiety and sunshine of his spirit. His tantrums were great — as tremendous as himself. He had a mighty joy in a row, whether he was right or wrong. What did it matter! All was soon blown over, and once more that slow and attractive smile would take the sting from any words of his. We his messmates miss him. We are leaderless. No greater tribute can we give than to say how hollowly we feel an absence where once so latterly dwelt, such a massive presence."

Irish rugby heroes were not only to be found in the Royal Navy. Possibly the most notable Irish rugby player to lose his life in World War Two was Bob Alexander, a captain in the Royal Inniskilling Fusiliers. Born in Belfast on 24th September 1910, Bob was a renowned Irish sportsman who, besides representing Ireland on the rugby field in 11 internationals between 1936 and 1939, also played cricket for his country. A right-arm fast-medium bowler, his appearance for Ireland in their victory over Scotland in 1932, where he scored 7 and 22 but failed to take a wicket, was his only contribution to Ireland's cricket history. Rugby, however, was a different story. A student at Queen's University, Belfast, Bob represented his university and various police teams as a quick, aggressive flank forward and in 1935/36 he was selected, as an uncapped player, for the Barbarians. His appearance on the international stage quickly followed. In February 1936, Bob was chosen for the game against England to be played at Dublin's Lansdowne Road, where, in front of 36,000 spectators, he made an instant impression. *The Times* was fulsome in their praise of Bob's contribution in a 6–3 victory.

"Most of their aggression had to come from the new man R Alexander, whose quickness on the man and ball was phenomenal and, what is equally to the point, generally legitimate."

Victory over Scotland followed and, although the Triple Crown was lost as a result of a 3–0 defeat to champions Wales, Bob was now in the Irish team to stay. In this period, during which France was excluded from the championship following claims of professionalism and a time when no touring teams visited Britain, he went on to play in 11 of the 12 Ireland international matches before World War Two.

The following season, 1937, saw two more victories, this time over Scotland and Wales but it was England who won the Triple Crown and championship. Bob did score his one and only try for his country in the

11-4 win over Scotland at Lansdowne Road but it was England's year. The following season saw Scotland win the Triple Crown and Ireland lose all three games. *The Times* praised Bob's performance in the heavy defeat to England (36–14) but he was left out of the clash with Wales. *The Times* blamed his non-selection on Bob having played too much rugby. Having joined the Royal Ulster Constabulary in 1937, Bob was now playing for the Police on a regular basis and this was seen, probably with some cause, as having taken its toll.

Being rather stale did not, however, prevent Bob from being selected to tour South Africa with the 1938 British Isles, a tour that in many ways was the highlight of Bob's rugby career. Not yet known as the 'British Lions', a term first used to describe the 1950 touring side, selection for the British Isles team did not necessarily mean that you were the best in your position. Selection still depended to some extent on availability. For example, neither Wales' Cliff Jones, probably the best outside half in Britain at that time, nor the other contender for that title, Wilson Shaw of Scotland or the powerful Welsh centre/wing Wilf Wooller were available but there is no doubt that Bob was worth his place in the touring party. The media reported that, despite his heavy workload, he was still Ireland's key player in the loose and there were high hopes that he would do well.

Bob did not disappoint his admirers. In the second match of the tour, he scored a try in the 22–9 win over Griqualand West and followed this with another in the 16–9 defeat to Transvaal. Despite picking up an injury to his instep, Bob returned with two more tries in the impressive 45–11 victory over Rhodesia. Although the tourists suffered clear defeats in the first two Test matches, Bob continued to play well being particularly prominent in the loose rather than in scrums and lineouts. This was confirmed in the narrow win over Eastern Province and when he scored another try in the victory over a Border XV. The third and final test saw what was probably Bob's finest moment. The big, deceptively quick flanker showed an impressive burst of speed which brought the crowd to its feet when scoring the try which helped to give the British Isles a 21–16 victory. It was Bob's 6th try of the tour, a record at the time for a forward.

Following this tour Bob played all three of Ireland's games in the 1939 championship but his great rugby days were behind him. Following two victories his international career ended in Ravenhill, Belfast when a Willie Davies inspired Wales defeated Ireland 7–0. Playing in the backrow, alongside Bob, in this game, as in many others, was another flanker of distinction playing in his final international. Mike Sayers, the son of Sir Frederick and Lady Sayers of Waterford had been educated at Stoneyhurst College and Sandhurst and was a regular in the British Army. He was also a key member of a fine Irish side who were expected to defeat Wales and win the Triple Crown. Mike had already tasted success when part of Ireland's championship winning team of 1935 and he went on to win a total of ten caps for his country. The high point of Mike's career was scoring a drop goal from a mark which secured the win against Scotland in 1939, a score carried out when executing a fierce hand off. Mike, by now a Major in the Royal Artillery, was tragically killed in an air crash on 6th December 1943. He is buried at Aylesbury Cemetery.

With the onset of war, Bob Alexander joined the Royal Inniskilling Fusiliers and was commissioned as an officer in 1940. By the following year he was a highly respected captain. As a fit 31-year-old, Bob still took the opportunity to play the sport he loved and when home on leave in 1942, he captained Ireland in a friendly match against the British Army. This was to be a short distraction. Bob soon returned to action and in July 1943, he was instructed to lead his troops in an attack across the Simento River in Sicily. This was, he realised, an extremely dangerous and even hopeless mission. Fellow officer Sir David Cole wrote later that Bob knew the dangers. On being wished good luck by Cole he replied with a smile, "it's suicide." Unfortunately, Bob was proved to be right. He was killed on 19th July 1943 and buried with his comrades in Catania War Cemetery, Sicily. His Commanding Officer wrote to the family following the death of this much respected officer and Irish rugby international, "I cannot put on paper what a loss he has been to the Regiment as the finest type of officer and leader, and to us personally as a friend."

Like Mike Sayers, Bob was just 32 years old.

Possibly the most flamboyant Irish rugby international to lose his life in World War Two was Ted Hunt, an exciting centre or full back who played the game in a way that thrilled and excited his many admirers. The first hint as to his future flamboyance comes in his name, Edward William Francis De Vere Hunt, and his playing career certainly lived up to this image. Born on 12th December 1908 in Dorset, the son of John Theodore and Ada Mary De Vere Hunt, Ted was educated at the Dragon School, Oxford and then at Rugby School before he joined the Army in order to follow what would become a very successful career. Ted's rugby career developed when he played for the Army and then for Roslyn Park and it was not long before he was making his mark. Andrew Wemyss, a Scottish international, tells of his first appearances for the Barbarians on their traditional Easter tour of Wales in 1929. In the match against Newport, he dropped a goal from about 50 yards in the last minute to win the game 4–3, a remarkable feat in the days of the heavy leather ball used at the time. Ted's rugby career was up and running.

The following season, 1930, Ted was selected at full back for Ireland in the game against France. Played at Ravenhill, Belfast, it was not a very successful beginning to his international career as Ireland lost 5-0. For the next two years Ted was in the international wilderness until his recall in 1932, this time at centre for the match against England where he faced Army colleague and fellow centre Ronnie Gerrard. Despite narrowly losing 11–8 to England in Dublin, Ted kept his place for the remainder of the season. Indeed, *The Times* acknowledged his performance in this game reporting that "Hunt was the keen and tireless player that the English members of the crowd of 30,000 already knew him to be." In the following game, against Scotland at Murrayfield, Ted scored his first international try in a convincing 20–8 victory, an effort which was described as "daring and clever" in one match report. Two weeks later, he played a role in preventing Wales from winning their first Triple Crown since 1911 when Ireland held on for a famous 12–10 victory at Cardiff Arms Park. As if to ensure that the Welsh crowds appreciated his skill, at Easter he returned to Wales with The Barbarians and set up a sensational try against Cardiff. Collecting the ball almost on his own line and facing a pack of marauding Cardiff forwards, Ted set off on a mazy run which brought the crowd to its feet before sending Ben Tod over for a magnificent try. According to Andrew Wemyss, the crowd, in a state of "laughing immobility", did not know whether to laugh or cheer. In the end many did both.

It is Andrew Wemyss who gives us the fullest picture of Ted on the rugby field, referring to him as "a unique Irishman." In the book *Barbarian Football Club 1890–1955*, the Gala, Edinburgh Wanderers Scottish international talks of the "tall athletic figure with the fresh complexion of an unshaven boy, his flaxen hair parted in the middle and wearing Roslyn Park stockings." Wemyss describes how Ted had the remarkable ability, very evident in the victory over Wales, of getting out of seemingly crunching tackles. Ted kept his place in the centre for Ireland's first fixture in the 1933 championship and once again faced Ronnie Gerrard, this time at Twickenham. Despite scoring a try in the 17–6 defeat, Ted's international rugby career came to a sudden and surprising end.

Away from the rugby field, however, life went on in the same positive manner as Ted had played his rugby. On 5th June 1934, he married Nancy Rudkin, the daughter of Major Hugh Rudkin OBE, at Compton near Guildford, a marriage that appeared most suitable for this career soldier. In 1933, Ted had progressed from the rank of 2nd Lieutenant in the Royal Artillery to the position of full Lieutenant. In 1935, he joined the Royal Horse Artillery and served as a captain in Egypt and Palestine. On Christmas Day 1938, Ted was posted to Hong Kong and Singapore where he served as a Major. Tragically Ted's war was relatively short-lived. On 20th December 1941, he was killed at Wong Nai Chung Gap during a Japanese attack on the island. However, it proved difficult to confirm exactly what had happened to him and his death remained unconfirmed. On 14th March 1942, Nancy advertised for information of his whereabouts in *The Times* newspaper but to no avail. Ted's death was finally confirmed in June 1944, two and a half years after the battle that claimed the life of this 33-year-old Irish rugby hero. His name appears on the Sai Wan Memorial in Hong Kong.

One of Ted Hunt's close rivals on the rugby field was another Irish war hero, Paddy Coote. As a regular in the Royal Air Force Paddy, also a centre three-quarter, had faced Ted directly in Inter Service matches and when Paddy was playing for Leicester. Indeed, their clashes were much discussed in rugby circles. Born at Eton on 7th January 1910, the son of Commander BT Coote OBE RN, Patrick Bernard Coote was a pupil at Woking Grammar School where he soon distinguished himself as an excellent all-round sportsman. On leaving school in 1925, Paddy enlisted in the RAF as an aircraft apprentice stationed at RAF Halton and by 1928, he had been awarded the Sir Charles Wakefield Scholarship of £75 to complete an apprenticeship/cadetship at RAF Cranwell College. Here his sporting prowess was quickly apparent when he represented the college in athletics and hockey. He was the RAF squash champion in 1931 and runner-up the following year despite carrying a rugby injury. Paddy represented the Britain in the Gold Cup International Bobsleigh Championship held at St Moritz and played tennis for the RAF where his doubles partner was up-and-coming rugby player and future war hero Douglas Bader. Despite Paddy's love of competitive sport, his career continued to go from strength to strength and in 1930 he was awarded the Sword of Honour, given to the most outstanding student, and beating the equally competitive Douglas Bader into second place. Paddy was also awarded the Air Ministry Prize for aeronautical engineering after gaining the highest marks in the examinations.

Yet of all the sports that captured his attention, it was rugby union which gave Paddy his greatest thrill. In January 1928, he played his first game for the RAF against Cambridge University but this was just the beginning. Over the next few years, Paddy established himself in the RAF team, played for Leicester when he wasn't required by his Service team and represented the East Midlands in the County Championship. In October 1931, Paddy played his most demanding fixture yet when he represented London in their match against the touring South Africans. A heavy 30–3 defeat didn't put off the Irish selectors, who were by now showing an interest. In January 1932, he had a trial for his country. It did take Paddy another year to find favour with the Irish selectors but on the 1st April 1933, he took the field to make his international debut in the centre against Scotland at Lansdowne Road. Although Ireland lost 8–6, they can be counted as having been extremely unlucky. In scoring two tries to Scotland's two drop goals, this result would have been reversed under later scoring systems. Moreover, Paddy nearly dropped a goal from 50 yards to win the game as well as having a hand in one of Ireland's tries. A long international career seemed assured but it was not to be. In December of that year, just 8 months after his Irish debut, Paddy was seriously injured when playing for Leicester against Swansea. He suffered a serious neck injury and severe concussion and spent a few months in hospital before being advised that his rugby career was over.

His rugby career might have come to a sudden close but life for Paddy still looked full of promise. On 1st June 1935, he married Muriel Elsmie at St Peter's Church in Ealing and the newlyweds settled down in Chobham where they had two daughters. By the time of the war, Paddy's career was one of unblemished success and by 1941, he was a Wing Commander. In February 1941, he was serving with 211 Squadron during the Greek campaign and leading in an 80 Squadron Gladiator. He took part in an air battle over the Tepelenë coast, Albania where he was credited with shooting down an Italian Fiat CR42a Falco. Following this success, in April 1941, Paddy went as an observer to assess the progress of the German advance in a group of 6 Blenheims. Just 40 miles short of their target area, on what is now the border between Greece, Macedonia and Albania, all 6, without a fighter escort, were shot down on 13th April by 3 Messerschmitt planes based in Libya. They came down near the village of Trigono where the two survivors from the six crews buried their dead comrades before making their way by foot and mule to Larissa, 150 miles away. Paddy Coote, at 31 years of age and in the prime of life, was later buried with his colleagues at the Phalron War Cemetery, Kalamaki, near Athens.

An equally distinguished RAF officer and fellow Irish international centre met a similarly tragic death. Reginald Vere Massey Odbert was born on 9th February 1904 and was educated at Blackrock College, Dublin, a breeding ground for numerous Irish rugby internationals. On his arrival at Dublin University, 'Oddy', as he was usually known, was soon in the university 1st XV. On completion of his studies Oddy joined the RAF and was able to continue his rugby career with some success. In both 1928 and 1932, he captained the RAF team playing alongside

Paddy Coote and succeeded in beating his younger, talented colleague onto the international stage when he was selected for his country in January 1928. In front of a crowd of 20,000 at Ravenhill, Belfast, Ireland defeated a plucky French team 12–8 and Oddy played his part. However, despite continuing to play for a number of years, this was his only international appearance.

Oddy's RAF career, however, went from strength to strength. In 1930/31, he served in the Middle East and in 1934, he was appointed to be an experimental pilot in the Armament Testing Squadron. In June 1936, Oddy was made a squadron leader and in March 1939, months before the outbreak of war, he was appointed as a Wing Commander. In September 1941 Oddy became Group Captain Reginald Vere Massey Odbert, an officer who won huge respect when dealing with the difficult problems that he faced in this role.

Unfortunately, his time in this job was relatively brief. On the 18th July 1943 Oddy, along with 6 others, was on board a Wellington 111 BK235 to take part in a gunnery demonstration where he could see what the training involved. Soon after taking off from RAF Fulbeck, Lincolnshire, they were involved in a corkscrew fighter affiliation exercise with a Martinet HN 877. Witnesses on the Martinet saw the starboard wing of the Wellington break off resulting in it crashing just south of Appleby, also in Lincolnshire. All 6 crew members and passengers were killed. The obituaries were fulsome in their praise. *The Times* described Oddy as a man with "honesty of purpose and tenacity" who gave his utmost and that his "simplicity of living was exemplary." They added that "he closely approached the ideal officer" and that his "only luxury was his generosity." Oddy was buried in Newark-upon-Trent cemetery.

Losses of brave young men were not confined to Ireland when considering the Celtic rugby heroes of World War Two. Scottish rugby too was hit by the untimely deaths of some of their best players during these war years. When reading about sportsmen who died in the Great War, we are often reminded that 14 of the 30 players taking part in the Calcutta Cup match of 1914 were killed in that horrific war. What is rarely told is that 6 Scottish rugby internationals who represented their country in 1939 were killed in World War Two. The 6 players: Tom Dorwood, William Penman, George Gallie, Donald Mackenzie, William Renwick and George Roberts, all failed to return and joined another veteran of the 1914 Calcutta Cup, Archie Symington, on the Scottish Rugby Roll of Honour held at Murrayfield Stadium. The home of Scottish rugby also houses a memorial outside the ground to the 'Scottish Rugby Men' lost in two World Wars.

One of the best known of the Scottish rugby internationals owed his fame, at least in part to his success in another sport, namely rugby league. He also carries a name which continues to be well known even today but in a very different walk of life. Roy Kinnear is the father of the well-known character actor of the same name who entertained audiences right up to his untimely death in 1988. The actor Rory Kinnear is the grandson of the rugby playing Roy and the son of actor Roy, a face that is very familiar with modern audiences. Roy senior was born in Scotland on 3rd February 1904 and first made an impression playing in the centre for the famous club, Heriot's Former Pupils. Such was his impact that Roy was selected to play for the British Isles team that toured South Africa in 1924. Although many of the 'big names' were unavailable to tour, it was an achievement for Roy to be selected and then to play in all four Test matches. Only 9 of the 21 matches were won with the 4-Test series ending in a convincing 3–0 defeat, with the third test drawn but Roy had taken his chance. Two years later he was in the Scottish team winning caps in the victories against France and Wales as well as in the defeat to Ireland.

The following year young Roy, still only 23 years old, succumbed to the lure of the professional game and he joined Wigan. During the next six years, Roy played 182 games for Wigan and scored 81 tries, his most famous against Dewsbury in the Challenge Cup Final at Wembley in 1929, a match his team won 13–2. The result confounded the critics as Wigan had lost their previous five matches but they prepared well for the final. This was the first occasion that Wembley had been used to stage the final, it more usually being held in the north at Headingley, Wigan or Manchester. The press, particularly in the north of England, were quick to sing the praises of this Wigan team describing the southern rugby union teams as "weak and watery" when compared to northern professionals. Wigan had played a particularly expansive game which gained the upper hand over Dewsbury's tighter, forward-based style and it paid off. *The Manchester Guardian* concluded that both Wigan and Dewsbury had "speed that amazed southerners" and Roy was described as "far too speedy for those who wished to stop him" despite having gained "fortunate procession." A total of 41,500 fans witnessed this success, more than twice the number attending previous finals, and a further 20,000 lined the streets of Wigan to welcome the team home. The decision to move the final south had paid off handsomely as those supporters enjoying a weekend in London would testify.

That season, 1929, also saw Wigan win the Lancashire County Cup when they beat Widnes 5–4 in the final. Roy benefitted personally from this success when he represented the Great Britain team which faced Australia in 1929 and was also picked for the 'Other Nationalities' team, mainly made up of Scottish and Welsh players, to play England on three occasions in the 1929/30 season. In these games, Roy scored a total of three tries. However, his career soon began to wind down and Roy played his last game for Wigan in 1933. On joining the RAF, 38-year-old Roy played rugby once again and tragically in 1942 he suffered a fatal heart attack during one of these friendly games. He is buried in Uxbridge. Gone maybe, and not in a heroic battle, but this rugby hero was not forgotten. Even today the Scotland Rugby League Student Player of the Year Award is named after him.

One of Scotland's most successful seasons thus far occurred in 1938 when Wilson Shaw led his country to the Triple Crown. One of the stars of this team was John Gordon Scott Forrest, a three-quarter equally at home at wing or centre. Born in Rhodesia on 28th April 1917, John was educated in Strathallan School, Perthshire and then at St Catherine's College, Cambridge where he studied medicine. John had been an outstanding sportsman at school where he captained both the rugby and cricket teams but his rugby career really blossomed at Cambridge and he gained his blue as a fresher. In 1936 he played in the narrow 6–5 win over Oxford where the Oxford try was scored by Willie Renwick, a future Scottish three-quarter destined to be killed in Bolsena, Italy in 1944. A year later, playing in the centre, John made an impression with his stout defence despite losing the game 17–4. The following year, John was captain and made the try that won the fixture 8–6 for Cambridge, a result that confounded the predictions of most newspapers and exacted revenge for the sound defeat of 1937.

By this time, John had made his mark on the international stage. In 1938, he was selected to play on the wing for all three matches in Scotland's 8th Triple Crown triumph. He made his debut in the 8–6 victory over Wales at Murrayfield, scored two tries in a convincing 23–14 victory over Ireland, also at Murrayfield, before the climax of the England encounter at Twickenham. This, the first rugby match ever to be shown live on BBC television, is remembered as 'Shaw's match' as the Scottish outside half and captain scored two of his sides five tries against their greatest rivals. Although the score was 21–16 to Scotland, a try count of 5–1 confirms Scottish dominance, particularly in attack and John was an important cog in this exciting backline.

Surprisingly, this was to prove John's only season of international rugby. Injury, followed by the outbreak of war, prevented any further triumphs and at only 21 years of age his days of representing his country on the rugby field were over. Not, however, in other respects. John became a lieutenant in the Air Branch of the Royal Naval Volunteer Reserve based at HMS Blackcap in Cheshire. On 14th September 1942, during formation practice, two Spitfires (AB873 and BL487) collided with one another at a height of 7,000 feet. Spitfire AB873 crashed at Pownall Green Farm, Tabley, near Northwich, and 25-year-old John was tragically killed. The obituaries were fulsome in their praise. *The Scotsman* newspaper thought that he "never gave a bad or poor game in my seeing" and that every time, whether as a wing or centre, "he pulled more than his weight." DR Gent, writing in *The Sunday Times*, thought that John was "a magnificent player, whether on the wing or in the centre. I preferred him in the centre, where his running and swerving and side-stepping and kicking and passing gave me no end of pleasure." Gent concluded with feeling that "in this modest and charming young Scotsman we have lost a great rugby footballer in the making."

The Scotsman, in its tribute to John Forrest, made reference to the equally tragic loss of one of his rivals. Facing John in each of the three varsity matches 1936–38 was the England full back Hubert Dainton Freakes. Although not a Celtic hero, Hubert's career is one to note. He was born in Durban, Natal on 2nd February 1914 and attended Maritzburg College where he excelled at all sports but especially rugby, cricket and athletics. By the time Hubert was eighteen years old, he was opening the batting in Currie Cup matches and succeeded in scoring three centuries in his ten first-class matches. Academically Hubert was equally successful. By the age of sixteen, he had gained acceptance to study at Rhodes University, Grahamstown, where he gained a distinction in his MA and was accepted to further his studies as a Rhodes Scholar at Magdalen College, Oxford. But his rugby career was now taking off. Six weeks after arriving in Oxford, he was a member of the University 1st XV. It was quickly apparent to all that Hubert was a talented full back, cool under pressure and safe under the high ball with a strong relieving kick. All of these skills came to the fore in his first varsity match where he played well despite the 6–5 defeat to their Cambridge rivals. Before the game *The Times* felt that his presence gave Oxford an advantage and following his side's defeat, this newspaper talked of his "outstanding ability." Some did blame him for missing a tackle, which allowed Cambridge to score a decisive try but it was clear that Hubert had a great rugby future.

The following year, 1937, Hubert was surprisingly selected at centre where he directly opposed John Forrest. *The Times* called this "a stroke of genius" and, despite the valiant efforts of John Forrest, Hubert came out on top with an excellent display in the 17–4 victory. He was now in demand and later that month, December 1937, Hubert was selected for the Barbarians in their 34–0 victory over Leicester. A place in the England team was now assured for this 24-year-old South African, and his adopted country had high hopes for a successful run in the side. These hopes, however, were dashed when, in gale force winds, Wales defeated England 14–8. *The Times* concluded that Hubert had been "subject to the fiercest of tests" but, although he had kicked a conversion, he was dropped for the remainder of the season.

By the next time that England faced Wales, this time at Twickenham, Hubert was back. Despite losing the varsity match 8–6, Hubert, this time as captain, had played well in his more recognised position of full back. Although some pundits thought that he should have played in the centre, Hubert had done enough to impress the England selectors. England beat Wales 3–0 and *The Times* was full of praise concluding that "HD Freakes at full back was a splendidly sound defender and ready enough to turn defence into attack." He kept his place for the game against Ireland, once again at Twickenham but this did not end so well. Ireland, the better balanced team, harried and pressured England to a 5–0 defeat and Hubert took some criticism for his part in the loss. The England centres lacked pace, and this sometimes left Hubert exposed, as on one occasion when he was caught near his own line resulting in Ireland's winning try. That mistake signalled the end of Hubert's England career.

With the outbreak of war, Hubert became a Pilot Officer in the RAF and by February 12th, 1941, he was a Flying Officer. He was attached to the RAF Ferry Command to deliver aircraft from Canada and the USA to British air bases. During the war, Ferry Command transported around 9,000 aircraft to squadrons but it was a dangerous activity attempted by only 100 aircraft. Only around half of these successfully completed the journey and, sadly, Hubert's Hudson bomber was not one of them. On 10th March 1942, it spun out of control and crashed into the ground at Honeybourne Airfield, Worcestershire, killing Hubert and his crew. Hubert, one of the most talented sportsmen of his generation, was 28 years old.

Wales losses, when considering international rugby players, were far less in World War Two than they had been in the First but none the less significant. Maurice Turnbull was one of the greatest talents of his age and played international sport in two different disciplines and, as we shall see, demands a very close examination of his sporting and military career. John Raymond Evans less so, at least in the sporting context, but his career is of interest nonetheless. He was born in Newport, the son of William and Alice Evans on 12th September 1911. A versatile forward, capable of playing anywhere in the pack, John played much of his rugby as a hooker where he was instrumental in moulding the Newport pack into a unit to be respected. He made his debut for his home club in 1930 as a raw 19-year-old but soon he was an established member of the team. Nevertheless, it was a major shock when, in January 1934, John was made captain of 'The Probables' team due to face 'The Possibles' in the Final Wales Trial. Welsh rugby had only recently experienced one of its major high points with the first ever win at Twickenham the previous year. However, this team had broken up and the selectors were intent on creating a new team.

They didn't make this change gradually. For the England match at Cardiff two weeks after the trial, there were twelve new caps in the Wales XV, a number that increased by one when Viv Jenkins, a highly respected full back, pulled out on the morning of the game. Only Claude Davey and Dai Thomas had international experience. John was to captain the side on his debut — a feat repeated 50 years later when Mike 'Spike' Watkins, another Newport hooker, captained Wales during the 1984 season. Most of the pack were made up of locks or wing forwards and the press were united in seeing this selection as both strange and controversial. *The Times* remarked that it was unheard of for an international side to have a captain who had never played representative rugby before. Although they saw it as a "mystery pack", *The Times* thought that despite this "JR Evans is a good man and is the hooker in the Newport pack that at last has been showing signs of the old Newport teamwork and finish." For them it highlighted the decline in Welsh rugby, inconsistent since the war and badly hit by defections to the professional code. The backs had looked weak for some time, the paper argued, and now the pack was made up of a unit in which no two players had played with each other before. Indeed, seven of the team played outside Wales.

These concerns were justified when England won by 9–0, scoring three tries in the process. John came nearest to scoring when he failed with a long penalty kick. He was dropped for the next game when a further five new caps were introduced. Wales won both their remaining games against Scotland (13–6) and Ireland (13–0) so there was no way back for John or for the four other 'one cap wonders'. The basis of the 1935/6 team that would beat the All Blacks was taking shape and John was out of the picture, although he did captain his club in their 17–5 defeat to New Zealand. More tragically, John was to make the ultimate sacrifice in a war that saw so many such sacrifices. A lieutenant in the

Parachute Regiment AAC 3rd Battalion, John was killed in action on 8th March 1943 and is buried in Tabarka Ras Rajel War Cemetery, Tunisia. He was 31 years old.

Maurice Turnbull

CHAPTER 7
MAURICE TURNBULL: A HERO OF TWO SPORTS
AND A WAR

It is clear that rugby union lost some very high-profile international players as a result of World War Two. Cricket was to suffer as many, if not more, tragic losses, many of them household names. One man, however, could claim to be a top-class sportsman in both rugby and cricket. Maurice Turnbull played rugby with distinction for both Cardiff and Wales and played test match cricket for England as well as keeping his county, Glamorgan, afloat financially in very difficult circumstances during the interwar years. As the only Welshman to play international-level cricket and rugby, as well as representing Wales in both squash and hockey, Maurice can lay claim to possibly being the greatest all-round Welsh sportsman of the twentieth century.

Maurice Joseph Lawson Turnbull was born in Cardiff on 16th March 1906, the son of a Yorkshire-born ship owner, Philip and his wife Marie who raised a family consisting of eight children. Maurice's grandfather, Lewis Turnbull, had created a shipping line at the then thriving Cardiff Docks and this became the family's passage to very comfortable middle-class lifestyle. Following the Depression of the 1930s, the family disposed of their vessels and they went into business as ship brokers. A strongly religious family, the Turnbulls were considered to be one of the most prominent Catholic families in South Wales and were fervent supporters of St Peter's R.C. Church, Cardiff. But it was to be the family's excellence in the sporting arena that was to bring them to the attention of the wider world. Sport played a major part in family life from the beginning as Maurice's Uncle Bertrand played hockey for Wales on 19 occasions and represented Great Britain at the 1908 Olympics. Bertrand also played Minor County cricket for Glamorgan, served on the committee from 1922 and was chairman between 1928 and 1939 during the period when his nephew was the county's star performer. Maurice's father Philip was a fervent supporter of Yorkshire cricket while elder brother, Bernard, played rugby for his country and captained them in the 1927 game against England. Described as a "dour, unimaginative centre", Bernard had a difficult international career. Despite scoring a try on his debut against Ireland, he finished on the losing side in each of his six games for Wales between 1925–1930.

Like his brothers, Maurice was educated away from home in Downside School — the famous Roman Catholic boarding school — near Bath where his sporting talent quickly became apparent. It was as a cricketer that he made his greatest impact during his time there, but he also excelled in rugby, hockey, tennis and boxing. His determination to participate in all sports never left him as his later achievement in becoming the South Wales Squash Racquets champion confirms. On leaving school, Maurice progressed to Trinity College, Cambridge where he read History. He had been offered a place to start in October 1924 following an impressive set of examination results but, to ease the financial burden on his parents, Maurice decided to stay on at school a little longer in order to sit the scholarship examination. This he did successfully and therefore took his place at Trinity College in October 1925. Arriving with the reputation of being an immensely talented sportsman, Maurice quickly secured his blue in cricket, missing a rugby blue in 1925 and 1926 due to the presence of future England international Wilf Sobey and in both 1927 and 1928 through an injury to the cartilage in his right knee. This injury also prevented him from gaining a hockey blue, although he did make amends when selected by Wales for the Home Internationals in the 1928/29 season. Maurice, probably to nobody's surprise, scored the winning goal on his debut against Scotland. He achieved his cricket blue in 1926, the same season that he scored his maiden first-class century for Glamorgan CCC at Cardiff. By 1929, he was captain of the university side and scored over 1,000 runs for them during the season. Maurice's cricket career was well and truly up and running.

But what of his rugby career? Cricket was the sport where Maurice left a lasting legacy but, before examining that in detail, it is important to consider his success on the rugby field. On leaving university, Maurice played his rugby for St Peter's, a junior club in his home city of Cardiff but it was clear that he could perform at a higher level. As he was a strong scrum half with a long, swift dive pass, it was clear that Cardiff, where brother, Bernard, was still playing, would be interested in his progress. During season 1931/2 Maurice played his first games for Cardiff, including an appearance alongside Bernard against the 1931 South Africans in a plucky performance after which Bernard was described by the *Western Mail* rugby writer, 'Old Stager', as "the best centre on the field." Bernard must have relished this report as he was not always given such praise but it was Maurice who by now was attracting the attention of the national selectors. By late 1932, Maurice was representing Glamorgan. This swift rise to prominence continued when he was selected to represent the Possibles against the Probables in the Welsh trial of January 1933, just weeks before the trip to Twickenham, a ground where Wales was yet to record a victory. The Possibles recorded a shock win which threw the selectors into turmoil, so much so that they requested a match be hurriedly arranged between Glamorgan and Monmouthshire to act as a further Wales trial. The selectors requested that certain players be picked to play in this game.

The result of this rather 'hit or miss' selection process was a Wales team containing seven new caps, including the scrum half, Maurice Turnbull. When the Wales team arrived at Twickenham, hopes were not high. It was true that in recent years there had been some very close games, for example when Bernard was captain in 1927 and Wales lost 11–9 despite playing most of the game with 14 men. On Wales' last visit in 1931, a strong Wales team had forced a 11–11 draw but they had lost on their previous eight visits and, in selecting seven new caps, the press did not give Wales much of a chance. *The Times* reasoned that England had an advantage at half-back and that this would decide the outcome. They acknowledged that Maurice was an improving, developing player but, while possessing a good pass, did not have "a box of tricks." Half-back partner Harry Bowcott was similarly underestimated. The unexpected result was an historic first Twickenham victory for the inexperienced Wales team. A try and dropped goal by fellow Glamorgan cricketer Ronnie Boon ensured a 7–

3 victory in which Maurice played a crucial part. Throughout the game Maurice harried his opposite number, Alan Key, not letting him settle while also providing a swift, consistent service to Harry Bowcott allowing the outside half to turn the English defence with a series of deft kicks. *The Times* gave qualified approval but couldn't help making the point that Maurice was "a little slow" although he succeeded in "getting his passes away." Nevertheless, Bernard's defeat and twenty-three years of hurt had been avenged.

Wales must now have expected to kick on and secure their first Triple Crown since 1911 but it was not to be. Injuries led to several players, including Maurice, withdrawing from the Wales team for the next game and the result was an 11-3 defeat to Scotland at Cardiff. Fitness restored, Maurice was back for the trip to Belfast but from the beginning this was an ill-fated adventure. Poor player behaviour was reported on the boat to Belfast while, on landing, the captain, Watkyn Thomas, made several positional changes to the team against the wishes of the WRU. Wales gave a poor performance and lost 10–5. *The Times* said that Maurice "hardly ever gave Harry Bowcott a decent pass all day." The following season saw a clear-out of 11 players. Maurice was one of them and he never played for Wales again. Although his rugby career continued, his time in the rugby limelight was over. Even as late as 1935, *The Times* reported that Maurice, following a Cardiff victory over Swansea, was "still incomparable so far as sending out a long swift pass is concerned." But, despite that defeat, the future belonged to the Gowerton schoolboy half-backs, the cousins Hayden Tanner and Willie Davies and the mercurial Cambridge University outside half, Cliff Jones. Maurice could concentrate on his cricket.

Maurice had always excelled in cricket. When at Downside School, he once hit a score of 184 in under three hours when playing against King's Bruton, another independent school in Somerset. During this season, 1924, Maurice made three centuries and had a batting average of 84.7, an outstanding performance in the context of schoolboy cricket, which was duly noted by his home county, Glamorgan. During the holidays that summer Maurice was invited to represent Glamorgan against a Lancashire side at Swansea containing big names such as Ted McDonald, Cecil Parkin and Richard Tyldesley.

Maurice was not overawed and he made a contribution of 40 and 16 in a match where the highest total in a completed innings was 153. Glamorgan won the match, the most significant win by a county that had only gained first-class status three years before.

This debut performance set the template for the rest of Maurice's career. He was a gifted right-hand batter who often made runs when, as in his debut match, they were most needed. Indeed, he was a lot better than his still impressive figures might suggest. He had all the conventional strokes as well as a few of his own and was always looking to attack the bowler. He had little interest in figures himself but looked to play the innings that was in the best interests of his team. Add to this his ability as a fine short-leg fielder and his later excellent leadership skills and you have a complete cricketer. Maurice might not have been particularly interested in figures but it didn't prevent him making nearly 18,000 runs and taking over 300 catches in his first-class cricket career. On his debut, the *Western Mail* described Maurice as "batting with the assurance, coolness and judgement of a veteran" and this was a judgement that proved to be very accurate over the next fifteen years.

By the end of 1924, Maurice, along with Cyril Walters, was seen as one of 'the bright young things' of Glamorgan cricket. Cyril Walters retired from Glamorgan in 1928 before joining Worcestershire as their captain and permanent secretary. He also had a Test career which saw him play 11 times for England, including once as captain, and averaged over 50. Maurice, on the other hand became the face of Glamorgan cricket. His first century for the county was made in 1926 at the Arms Park against Worcestershire and great things were expected of the local Cardiff boy. Unfortunately, Maurice had a setback in 1927 when he spent much of the summer injured following a rugby injury, a particular risk when playing two sports at such a level, and it took most of the following year to recover. Without 'the bright young things', Turnbull and Walters, Glamorgan struggled. By 1929 they had been bottom of the County Championship on three occasions, since their admission into the County Championship in 1921 and were seen as something of a 'shambolic outfit'. It was time for somebody to emerge and grasp the mettle.

Maurice soon proved to be that man. In 1929, he scored over 1,000 runs for Cambridge University, his final year there. Glamorgan, meanwhile, had used seven different captains during that year alone. Johnnie Clay, one of their best players and a great friend to Maurice, described them as "a flock without a shepherd" so, in somewhat desperate circumstances, Maurice was offered the job, initially on trial at the end of 1929 before being ratified as the full-time leader for 1930. The club's historian, Andrew Hignell, described Maurice's captaincy in the following way:

"...he was an inspirational leader, always getting the best out of both the professionals and amateurs at his disposal and putting great faith in the young Welsh players... he led with a cool and debonair authority and always insisted that the professionals made an appointment if they wanted to see him, whilst he ensured that the amateurs always travelled in first class accommodation."

Players in the team described Maurice as a "fantastic and passionate leader of men who led without fuss, without ever shouting but who made men feel valued, wanted and important." Glamorgan had found their man.

The England selectors were also taking more than a passing interest in Maurice's progress and the winter of 1929/30 provided the ideal opportunity to take a closer look at him. The MCC had arranged for an England team to tour New Zealand to play a four-match Test series, the first to be played by that country. Under the leadership of Harold Gilligan, a late replacement for his brother Arthur, the tour also included a fixture in Ceylon, five first-class matches in Australia and eight in New Zealand, four provincial games and four Test matches. The tour party was an inexperienced one, especially so as at the same time Freddie Calthorpe was leading another England tour party to play in the West Indies where the hosts would play their first Test series. With experienced players like Frank Woolley, KS Duleepsinhji, Les Ames, Patsy Hendren, Wilfred Rhodes and Andy Sandham split between the parties, there was a chance to blood new players. This was true of the New Zealand leg of the tour while the team that went to the West Indies was the oldest tour party of all time averaging 38 years.

On 10th January 1930, one day before England were due to take the field against the West Indies at Bridgetown, Barbados, Maurice was making his debut in Christchurch, the first Glamorgan-born Test cricketer. England won the game by eight wickets, the only result of a series where all the other games were drawn. Maurice was dismissed for 7 and, disappointingly, played no further part in the series. He admitted later that he had found it difficult to adapt to the hard wickets, the glare of the sun and the pace of the ball. A century against New South Wales, before the team travelled to New Zealand for the Test series, was the only high spot of the tour for Maurice. He was not forgotten however and the following winter, Maurice was selected for the MCC tour to South Africa. A Bradman inspired Australia had defeated England 2–1 in the summer of 1930, a series in which Maurice played no part. In South Africa, however, Maurice played in all five Tests, this despite the MCC selecting a very strong batting line-up which included Walter Hammond, Maurice Leyland, Patsy Hendren and Bob Wyatt under the captaincy of the flamboyant Kent batter, Percy Chapman. Despite an innings of 61 from Maurice, the first Test was lost and, with all the other Tests ending in a draw, so was the series. The conditions in South Africa — two Tests affected by rain and three played on matting — didn't appear to suit Maurice and he performed well below his best. He was left out of both the home series against New Zealand (1931) and the notorious 'Bodyline Tour' to Australia in 1932/3. Although he was recalled for the first Test, and then the third, against the West Indies in 1933 and the first Test against India at Lord's in 1936, Maurice did little of note in these games. England won all three comfortably so Maurice had no opportunity to bat when runs were needed, the match situation at which he excelled. Despite batting well against India in the second innings and being at the wicket when the winning runs were scored, his rather 'stop start' Test career was over. Four wins, four draws and one defeat in his nine Tests were not enough to save him.

It might have been a different story but for Maurice's decision to turn down the opportunity to tour India with England in 1933/4 when he preferred to concentrate his energies on rescuing Glamorgan from financial ruin. Possibly of even greater significance was his falling-out with the England selectors over the issue of illegal declarations. Maurice has been seen by some as possibly the best cricket captain of his generation never to captain England but he must have come near to it, particularly when leading The Rest in a Test Trial in 1934. His cause was probably not helped when he fell out with the England selectors and the MCC over his policy regarding declarations. Maurice, much like Percy Fender of Surrey, believed in declaring the first innings as quickly as possible in a rain-affected game, thereby effectively turning the contest into a one innings match. This, of course, made a result far more likely. Maurice saw it as a boost for 'entertaining cricket', a view which he wholeheartedly shared with the maverick Fender. This policy was followed twice in 1931, against Northamptonshire and against Surrey. Glamorgan won both games. The authorities took a dim view and thought the decision 'illegal'. Maurice received a reprimand and his chances of ever captaining England were probably adversely affected.

Not so his career with Glamorgan and it is in his commitment to his home county that Maurice shows his true greatness. His captaincy was of huge importance to the county during this time, not that his success in this area would have been a surprise to his teammates. Maurice had given warning of how he thought intelligently about the game from the outset of his cricket career. With Surrey fast bowler Maurice Allom, he had written books on both the tour to New Zealand and the trip to South Africa. Allom, an ex-Cambridge University teammate and friend was also a member of both tour parties and they produced interesting analysis of both tours, appropriately titled 'The Two Maurices' and 'The Two Maurices Again'. Allom played in five Tests for England, four in New Zealand and one in South Africa. He later became both Surrey president and president of the MCC. Maurice had always used his astute cricket brain to good effect and was especially encouraging of youngsters making their way into the side. As Andrew Hignell has said, Maurice was the "architect of Glamorgan as a first-class county." The responsibility of captaincy didn't affect his batting. Indeed, in 1932 at Cardiff Arms Park when Nottinghamshire's bowlers Harold Larwood and Bill Voce experimented with 'Bodyline' ahead of the winter tour to Australia, Maurice scored 205, possibly his finest innings against the bowlers who six months later were subduing the great Bradman. It was not enough to take him to Australia that winter so instead he spent his time sorting out Glamorgan's perilous financial situation.

By the end of 1932, Glamorgan had a debt of £5,000 so each village and town was encouraged to raise money in support, often through organised dances or other similar functions. In his new role as Glamorgan Secretary, Maurice set out to solve the problems partially caused by the high rents imposed by Cardiff Athletic Club as well as Swansea Cricket and Football Club for the use of the Arms Park and St Helen's. As Bradman danced away from Larwood's near 100mph deliveries, Maurice was doing something similar around the dancehalls of South Wales. Johnnie Clay, with him most evenings, recalled that Maurice danced as many miles as some players made runs that year. One of the Glamorgan team, Dai Davies, a future Test umpire, tells of Maurice taking the whole team to a dance, after a full day fielding, in order to raise money for the player's wages. "Dance our feet off we would", recalled Davies, "and there would be the skipper at the door by midnight handing out the pay packets." As we have already seen, the following winter, 1933/34, Maurice turned down the chance to tour India with England in order to continue his financial rescue of his club. It worked. The club avoided bankruptcy and by 1939 Glamorgan reported a surplus of £1,000. Regardless of this improvement, Maurice continued to put his own money into the club, a sum of £200 in the winter of 1937/38.

Managing the finances was not Maurice's only achievement in his joint role of captain and Honorary Secretary. By amalgamating Glamorgan and Monmouthshire for cricketing purposes, the catchment area greatly increased and the club began to acquire a sharper Welsh dimension which was not there in the early years when players were often 'cast offs' from other counties. Monmouthshire had been a Minor County but Glamorgan replaced them with a 2nd XI that could now play in Minor County cricket, a great breeding ground for future stars. Local talent was encouraged and interest widened as players such as Emrys Davies, Alan Watkins, Dai Davies and Haydn Davies came to the fore.

There is no doubt that, after the war, Maurice was destined to be one of the great cricket administrators.

Glamorgan were not the only 'unfashionable' county to struggle during these interwar years and Maurice was not the only county captain to see the need to lead both on and off the field. The same could have been said of the captain of Northamptonshire, Robert Nelson. Born in 1912, Robert Nelson was a free scoring left-hand batsman and occasional left-arm spin bowler who had shown great promise as a schoolboy cricketer while attending St George's School, Harpenden. From here, after brief spells with Hertfordshire and Middlesex, Robert progressed to Cambridge University where he gained his blue in 1936. His stylish innings of 91, in partnership with future England captain Norman Yardley, helped Cambridge to an eight-wicket victory. On leaving Cambridge Robert joined Northamptonshire where he was quickly made captain. The team he inherited was seen by the Honourable Secretary, WC Brown, as "a disorganised rabble" who had finished bottom of the championship for five consecutive seasons. Brown later wrote that Robert moulded them into a team that was almost impossible to recognise from the team that he took over. Like Maurice at Glamorgan, Robert managed his limited resources most effectively, getting the best out of his teammates with his patience and encouraging manner. Leading by example both on and off the field, Robert, through his popular, buoyant personality, lifted Northamptonshire from the bottom of the table. At the same time, he, like Maurice, was able to raise large sums of money, in this case for the Red Cross. There is no doubt that, if he had survived the war, Robert would have become 'Mr Northants' and had the same impact as Maurice at Glamorgan. Tragically it was not to be. By now a Second Lieutenant in the Royal Marines, 28-year-old Robert was killed in action on 29th October 1940. He is buried in Deal Cemetery where his headstone reminds us that he was "a lover of cricket who maintained in his life the spirit of the game."

Although much of his time was taken with administrative matters, Maurice still had time to contribute on the field. In 1939, in his very last first-class match, he made 156 against Leicestershire while the previous year, he had taken on the role of England selector as the home side attempted to regain the Ashes from Australia. The following year, he was one of four selectors, including the captain, who selected the touring party to tour India. This sixteen-man team was not a full-strength England touring party but they were scheduled to play three Test matches. The tour, of course, never took place due to the war and only four of the party played for England after hostilities ended. In the absence of a tour, one of those selected, the Oxford Blue and Worcestershire all-rounder Roger Human, joined the Oxford and Buckinghamshire Light Infantry. Tragically, on 21st November 1942, Roger, by now a respected master at Bromsgrove School, was killed in action, ironically in India, and was buried in Madras War Cemetery. Aged 33, he left a wife and two young children.

Meanwhile Maurice did not confine his interests to cricketing matters. Before the war, on discovering an absence of decent squash courts in Cardiff, he was instrumental in the formation of Cardiff Squash Club in 1936. Squash had by now replaced rugby as his main winter sport and Maurice soon confirmed his ability. In 1938 he won the Welsh Squash championship and was rewarded with selection for the Wales national team.

Despite this seemingly never-ending catalogue of sporting success, Maurice did develop other interests. Andrew Hignell, in his biography of Maurice, refers to his business interests in the insurance world and the likelihood that he would have followed a career in the Stock Exchange but for his success on the sports field. Maurice was also something of a gourmet and wine buff who enjoyed good food and a fine claret. Following his studies at Cambridge, Maurice expanded his interest in poetry and literature by taking a course on 'The English novel', an experience that helped his writing when he dabbled in journalism and wrote his two books during the 1930s. Maurice even found the time to marry Elizabeth Brookes in 1939. They had first met in Cardiff Squash Club when the sporty, squash-loving Elizabeth had come to Cardiff from Scunthorpe to stay with her brother. Despite an unpromising start to their courtship when Elizabeth found Maurice to be 'the most conceited person she had ever met', he soon won Elizabeth around. The couple married on 7th September 1939, just after war had been declared. They had three children, Sara, Simon and Georgina. The future for Maurice and his young family could not have looked brighter. The war was soon to change all that.

The leadership skills that Maurice had shown in abundance on both the cricket and rugby fields were soon apparent when he went to war. Maurice enlisted as a Second Lieutenant with the Welsh Guards on 18th November 1939, just ten weeks into his marriage. By the end of 1939, he was a Welsh Guard completing the necessary training for inexperienced, new recruits in Colchester. He still found time for some cricket and met up with Bill Edrich, an old adversary who, as we shall see, was due to have an eventful war as a fighter pilot followed by a successful test career and notoriety as Denis Compton's 'Middlesex twin'. During the early part of the war, Maurice was part of the Eastern Coast Defence Scheme, a job that continued through the Battle of Britain and the Blitz. In July 1942, Maurice was promoted to acting captain which resulted in him attending courses at both R.A.C. Sandhurst and R.M.C. Camberley before he was struck down with appendicitis. In May 1943, Maurice moved to King's Lynn, Norfolk to begin training for Operation Overlord and the planned liberation of Europe. By the time of the Normandy landings, Maurice had reached the rank of Major in the First Battalion, an officer loved and respected by his men in the same way as cricketers had responded to him on the cricket field. These leadership skills were about to be put to the most severe test in the coming days.

The D-Day landings were clearly a major event, a defining moment of the war. By June 1944, the stage was set for the Allies to launch the invasion of Europe in order to liberate France. The troops had trained and prepared; the planners had completed the invasion scheme and the resistance cells in France had prepared a programme of sabotage to support the landings. But nothing would be straightforward. Planning was the key but there had already been one tragedy before the first man had landed. At Slapton Sands near Dartmouth, a training exercise was spotted by 9 German motor torpedo boats on a routine patrol. Three USA tank landing ships were torpedoed killing 749 American soldiers and sailors. Following a weather induced 24-hour postponement many men went to church, even agnostic or atheist soldiers finding some comfort in prayer as the magnitude of what was before them became clear. Men have told how Montgomery inspired his troops the night before the landings while in a cinema in Portsmouth. One soldier, Brigadier Arthur Walter, recorded how Montgomery was a true "leader and I would have followed him to hell."

A kind of hell was where Maurice was heading. The success of the operation often disguises to us, living nearly eighty years later, the horrific nature of the fighting and the sheer terror that men must have felt as they advanced up the beaches. Recent work carried out by oral historians such as Max Arthur, have brought this to light. Able Seaman Ken Oakley a Royal Naval Commando, was told by his senior officer on the eve of the landings "not to worry if all the first wave of you are killed, we shall simply pass over your bodies with more and more men." He was right. On the 6th June at dawn 18,000 paratroopers landed, according to Captain Jim Sim, in a "tremendous exciting light hearted atmosphere", with the aim of capturing essential bridges and to disrupt German lines of communication. The first USA troops landed with their tanks at Utah Beach at six thirty a.m. followed by the British at Gold and Sword Beaches. The Canadians landed at Juno Beach while the remaining Americans were tied down at Omaha Beach. By midnight 155,000 Allied troops were ashore but at a great cost. Sergeant William Spearman was told that he had two choices, either stay on the beach and die or get off and live. He said later that "there were bodies — dead bodies, living bodies… All the blood in the water made it look as though men were drowning in their own blood. That's how it looked." Francis O'Neill, a photographer in the Army Film and Photographic Unit, was horrified at what he found as he came off the beach.

"…bodies — British bodies! I remember the first one I saw was an infantryman, and what fascinated me was that he had no head. He was just lying there, with no head. There was no sign of his head…"

O'Neill's experience was more common than might be supposed. Max Arthur records how some soldiers were so badly injured that they were given a lethal shot of morphine while Sergeant Major William Brown of the Durham Light Infantry saw a 40-year-old soldier self-inflicting wounds, his nerves shot to pieces. Nevertheless, there was also relief that the invasion had finally taken place. Max Arthur records how a soldier expressed his relief,

"I found myself banging the bridge with my clenched fist… By God, we are ashore in France, we've done it, we're back in France again."

What of Maurice at this point? Maurice had left Brighton for Normandy on 18th June, 12 days after the first soldiers had fought their way ashore. Following the landings, Maurice and his men headed south through Normandy, crossing the Orne River and onto the Caen Plain as the Germans retreated. Maurice helped to lead attacks on the towns during this retreat and by early August they had reached Pont d'Eloy, two miles outside Montchamp. It was in this hamlet, under constant shelling, mortar attacks and sniper fire, that Maurice wrote his last diary entry, reaffirming his Catholic faith, and his last letters to Elizabeth in which he writes affectionately about photographs that he had received of his three much loved children.

It was also here that the Germans counter attacked in an attempt to halt the progress of the Allied tanks. The version published in Wisden, tells us that Maurice was killed instantly by a German sniper as he voluntarily led a recce in an attempt to re-establish contact with other units. Sergeant Fred Llewellyn, who with Rex Fowles recovered Maurice's body, remembers the incident in far more detail. He says that, as German tanks and foot soldiers launched a counter-attack along a sunken road towards Maurice's unit just outside Montchamp, he told his men to hide alongside the hedge lining an orchard. He tried to immobilise the lead tank so as to halt the advance but the Germans opened fire with machine guns. Maurice was killed instantly as the leading tank's gun turret swung through the hedge. Llewellyn and Fowles came across the body and carried it back to safety thus ensuring that their highly respected officer could receive the dignified burial that he deserved. Llewellyn came across personal belongings including a photograph of Maurice's wife with a young baby in her arms and two young children by her side, which he returned to the padre so that they could be returned to the family. Over fifty years later, an emotional Fred Llewellyn met with Maurice's children and gave them details of the dreadful day and their father's heroic actions. The family remained forever extremely grateful to Fred Llewellyn for this information. Maurice was buried in Bayeaux War Cemetery, one of over 100 casualties sustained by the Welsh Guards as they fought in and around the village of Montchamp. A devastated Elizabeth did eventually remarry and had another son while each of Maurice's children went on to have successful lives and careers. Yet there can be no doubt that Maurice's death left a huge void in the lives of all the family.

The loss of such an iconic figure was bound to be keenly felt in sporting circles. Maurice's great friend Johnnie Clay, in the *Wisden* obituary which he composed, quotes a letter from an admiring soldier who served with Maurice in France.

"Maurice was such a grand person. So often have I seen him go into action and never have I seen him rattled. He was always the same: quiet, confident, thinking always of his men and disregarding all danger to himself. A really great person."

Clay goes on to describe his value to Glamorgan where "he played his own game until the end." As a player and captain, Clay had no doubt as to his importance.

"Mere facts and figures do him scant justice. A great player he may have been, but an astute brain made him an even greater captain — the best of his generation who never captained England — and there is little doubt that he would have become one of the game's foremost administrators."

Glamorgan, of course, had already benefitted from these administrative skills.

"He was indeed a most efficient Secretary; always on the job and his suggestions were based on practical knowledge and experience. He went all out successfully for an increased membership and paid great attention to the comfort of the spectators. In short, by 1939, he converted a shambling, shamefaced, bankrupt club, into a worthy and respected member of society."

The legacy of this fine cricketer and brilliant captain was Glamorgan's first County Championship under the leadership of Wilf Wooller in 1948, a team that contained many of Maurice's protégées. Wooller, with Maurice, a surprise selection for the Welsh rugby XV which defeated England at Twickenham in 1933 and a Glamorgan teammate, won eighteen caps for Wales in the 1930s and played a key role in Wales 13–12 victory over the 1935/36 All Blacks. Like Maurice, Wooller was a superb all-round sportsman who once scored a hat-trick for Cardiff City and also represented Wales at squash. While studying at Cambridge, Wooller won his blue in both rugby and cricket but the demands made by his business interests cost him the chance to play Test cricket both in 1948/49 and 1951/52, although he did later become a Test selector. Remarkably Wooller had survived incarceration by the Japanese in Singapore following his capture at Java in 1942. Indeed, at one point he had been reported as missing but survived imprisonment at Changi jail due to his determination. As he said himself, "If I was to get anywhere, I'd have to achieve it myself by sheer drive and force." After successfully bartering for a strip of land, he succeeded in growing bananas, eating the skins for extra fibre. Wooller returned to confirm himself as another great all-round Welsh sportsman and cricket administrator.

Tragically, we can only speculate what Maurice might have achieved as a leading cricket administrator following the end of the war. But there can be no doubt that he, along with Wilf Wooller, would have played a vital role in the future of Glamorgan and England cricket. In Maurice, Wales had lost one of its greatest sporting figures and Glamorgan its greatest servant.

Hedley Verity

CHAPTER 8
HEDLEY VERITY: "MIND AND BODY HARMONISED AND CONTROLLED"

Maurice Turnbull was a fine cricketer, rugby player and a brilliant all-round sportsman but there can be no doubt as to the finest cricketer to be killed in World War Two. Captain Hedley Verity of the Green Howards (Yorkshire Regiment) and Yorkshire and England bowler was one of the finest spin bowlers to ever play the game. It is a sad irony that the most distinguished cricketer to die in each of the twentieth century's two world wars was a slow left-arm bowler: Colin Blyth of Kent and England and Hedley Verity. As the Commonwealth War Graves Commission information leaflet, 'Playing the Game — Cricket of the Two World Wars' tells us, "Both were 38 years old and were conspicuously decent, modest men who attracted universal respect and popularity." Colin Blyth was killed at Passchendaele in November 1917 while Hedley Verity succumbed on the last day of July 1943 in the Italian campaign at Caserta, Campania.

Hedley Verity was born on the 18th May 1905 in Headingley, Leeds, the perfect setting for a future Yorkshire and England left-arm bowler to follow in the giant footsteps of fellow Yorkshire and England spinners Wilfred Rhodes and Bobby Peel. Hedley was named after his father who supported his wife, Edith, a Sunday school teacher, son and two daughters by working in a coal company. Hedley, encouraged by resourceful and dedicated parents, attended Yeadon and Guiseley Secondary School where he quickly acquired a taste for cricket. He started by bowling medium pace in swingers and out swingers after discovering that he did not possess the required pace to become an out and out fast bowler. On leaving school and joining his father in the coal business, Hedley began to gain a good reputation in local cricket as a very promising bowler and an improving batsman. In 1921, he was playing for Rawdon before moving to Horsforth Hall Park where his reputation continued to grow. He was soon spotted by Bobby Peel, a left-arm spin bowler who had played in 20 Test matches for England, a sizeable number for the time, and a Yorkshire legend keen to acquire young Yorkshire talent for the county. This led to Hedley receiving coaching from the great Yorkshire and England all-rounder and now coach, George Hirst. Hirst, concluding that Hedley needed experience in the highly competitive and professional Lancashire League, recommended him to Accrington Cricket Club. In September 1926 Hedley made the move.

Unfortunately, the move to Accrington was disappointing. Hedley received little help or guidance with his bowling while his batting went backwards. There was a further problem as Accrington refused to release him to play for Yorkshire, not that at this time he was anywhere near good enough to be picked for the First XI. It had been the intention of both Hirst and Hedley that further coaching and playing would take place back in Leeds, eventually resulting in a county career with Yorkshire. A year later, a frustrated Hedley joined Middleton in the Central Lancashire League, signing on for less money but with the promise of playing time back in Yorkshire. This was the turning point. While working in the nets with Hirst, that other legendary Yorkshire all-rounder, Wilfred Rhodes, saw Hedley's potential. Rhodes was moving slowly towards the end of one of cricket's most remarkable careers with well over 4,000 first-class wickets and 40,000 first-class runs. During his test career, which stretched from 1899 to 1930 and consisted of 58 tests, Rhodes proved to be a truly great slow left-arm bowler and a batsman who progressed from being the last man in the batting order to opening the batting with the great Jack Hobbs. Nobody knew the game as well as Wilfred Rhodes so when he suggested, supported by his great friend George Hirst, that Hedley turn to left-arm spin bowling there was no resistance. With typical understated praise of "he'll do", Rhodes acknowledged his successor.

There was still work to do, but in the summer of 1929, his first summer of bowling spin, Hedley took over 100 wickets for Middleton and in a game for Yorkshire Colts he had the most impressive figures of 5/7. By now he was, as cricket historian Derek Hodgson has pointed out, "arriving in Yorkshire as a hardened and experienced performer." Hedley made his debut in May 1930 in the friendly against Sussex, a match which also saw Syd Buller, later to become a renowned umpire, make his one and only appearance for his home county. By Hedley's fourth match, against Glamorgan, he was really making his mark by taking 9 wickets in the second innings and 12 in the match. Playing alongside Rhodes, it was quickly apparent that, although he didn't spin the ball sharply, Hedley was deadly accurate and almost impossible to play on wicket that had given him some help, especially one affected by rain. In 12 games he took 64 wickets and topped the national bowling averages. Rhodes, his job done, departed the scene, although the debt that Hedley owed his mentor was never forgotten. Bill Bowes, Hedley's colleague for Yorkshire and England, later expressed the debt both owed to Rhodes and his fellow senior professional, the equally tough Emmott Robinson, when he wrote "to Wilfred Rhodes and Emmott Robinson... I owe most for what I learned of first-class cricket — and Hedley Verity shared my debt." Robinson was just as difficult to please as Rhodes. When Hedley took 9/60 against Glamorgan, Robinson told him that it should have been 9/20.

It wasn't just Hedley's cricket career that was now falling into place. On 7th March 1929, he married Kathleen Alice Metcalfe, a bookbinder and the daughter of a sales agent. The couple had first met in their home area of Headingley, Leeds, when children but reconnected while attending a Rawdon Youth Club social event. The marriage was to prove a happy one, producing two sons. Cricket was never far away and Hedley even named his sons Wilfred and George Douglas after his cricket mentors Rhodes and Hirst, the 'Douglas' being a reference to Douglas Jardine who was to captain Hedley in the victorious Ashes winning team of 1932/33 in Australia, the famous 'Bodyline Tour'.

Hedley's first full season with Yorkshire, the summer of 1931, was an outstanding success. Not only did he, on his 26th birthday, take all ten wickets against Warwickshire at the cost of 36 runs, only the second bowler ever to do this, he repeated the feat against Nottinghamshire the following year at the cost of only 10 runs. This was followed closely by taking 5/8 against Essex at Leyton. This bowling performance followed

Holmes and Sutcliffe's record opening partnership of 555 as Yorkshire set the highest of standards. As the country lurched towards an economic and political crisis, which by August had seen the fall of the second Labour Government and the formation of a National Government, Yorkshire were unsurprisingly wrapping up the County Championship title and Hedley was being named one of Wisden's Five Cricketers of the Year. Indeed, by the onset of World War Two, Hedley had won a further six county championship titles, a remarkable decade of success for both Hedley personally and Yorkshire cricket. Nevertheless, *The Cricketer* saw the need for him to further improve his technique and *Wisden* suggested varying both pace and flight in his bowling, this despite his having taken 188 wickets during the summer. Some also saw him as a negative bowler, unable to dismiss batsmen on perfect wickets. This criticism proved unfair as Hedley learned to vary his length on such wickets and was able to 'think' the batsman out. There was, however, some evidence of a need to tighten up his bowling in these early years especially on good wickets. Frank Woolley hit him for four sixes in an innings in 1931 and a year later Eddie Paynter went one better. Arthur Wood, another county and test colleague, once shouted to Hedley, "You've got him in two minds... He doesn't know whether to hit you for four or six." Even the best spin bowlers get hit from time to time. But Hedley was quick to learn the lessons and he soon learned to vary his pace and to bowl more economically on good wickets.

Not surprisingly, England recognition came quickly. Hedley made his debut against New Zealand, newly recognised as having 'Test match status', on 29th July 1931 at the Oval and began well taking 4/75. He kept his place for the rain-affected third test at Old Trafford. The following summer saw disappointment as Hedley was not selected for the tests against India despite taking 162 wickets and finishing second in the averages. It appeared very unlikely that he would be selected for the forthcoming Ashes tour of 1932/3, particularly as nobody expected an English left-arm spin bowler to have much help from Australian wickets. As it turned out, England captain, Douglas Jardine had decided to curb Bradman's phenomenal scoring by using a three- or four-man pace attack, unheard of at the time. He also needed a slow bowler who could exercise some control so, despite the efforts of Woolley and Paynter, Hedley was seen as that man, although it must be said that expectations were not that high and he was not expected to play a major role in what turned out to be an historic tour and England victory. During the tour, Hedley learned the art of bowling defensively, giving Larwood and Voce in particular, time to rest between spells. Hedley had his own successes against Bradman. In their respective careers, Hedley dismissed Bradman 8 times in seventeen tests, more than any other bowler, at an average score of about 50, delivering 932 balls at the cost of 401 runs. This is an excellent record against a batsman with a career average of over 94 and test average of a fraction under 100. Such was his success in the 'Bodyline' series that he finished second to Larwood in the averages, with 11 wickets at the cost per wicket of 24 runs and played in all 4 England victories, missing only the second test which England lost. At the end of the tour Jardine, showing man management skills not always appreciated at Lords or Sydney, wrote to Hedley's father,

"Hedley has come through his first tour triumphantly, no mean feat to start with the stiffest tour, but particularly for a slow left hander. On and off the field, Hedley has been a real friend and a grand help to me."

Given that Jardine, as a qualified and practising solicitor, was most definitely an amateur and Hedley a professional, this mutual respect should not be taken for granted. The difference in social standing was still most relevant in 1933 and there were difficulties even in this team. Gubby Allen, the amateur, Australian-born, England fast bowler who refused to bowl 'Bodyline' on the tour, referred in a letter home to "swollen-headed, gutless, uneducated miners." Both Larwood and Voce, of course, were Nottinghamshire miners. Quite possibly Allen had similar views regarding Hedley with his modest background and lack of an Oxbridge education. If so, Allen was very wrong. When chosen for the Ashes series in Australia under Allen's captaincy in 1936/37, Hedley spent the month-long voyage reading T. E. Lawrence's *Seven Pillars of Wisdom*, the pastime of a self-educated, rather than an uneducated, man.

Whatever Allen thought of Hedley's social status, the Yorkshire spinner was now a master craftsman of his trade. Although he was not known as a big spinner of the ball, certainly not when compared to Australian wrist spinners like Bill O'Reilly and Clarrie Grimmett, Hedley had learned the art of control. Bowling at pretty much medium pace, rather quick for a spinner, he bowled accurately and straight from a slightly long, yet graceful, run-up. He had learned to vary his pace which more than compensated for any perceived lack of spin, and on a rain-affected pitch, he was almost impossible to play. To find the nearest modern equivalent you have to look back to Derek Underwood in the late 1960s and 1970s, another bowler who thrived on damp wickets yet could be relied upon to cause problems when the conditions favoured batsmen. When comparing Hedley with Underwood it should be said that the Yorkshireman was the better batsman. By modelling himself on Yorkshire and England colleague Herbert Sutcliffe, Hedley opened himself to the criticism of being the 'poor man's version' of the great opening batsman, "Sutcliffe gone stale", as Robertson-Glasgow once described him. However, he was a useful lower-order batsman who was good enough to score three half centuries for his country and average around 20. On the field, Hedley showed a keen sense of humour, which he sometimes used to lighten a tense atmosphere, and was slow to anger, often not minded to show his feelings if a catch was dropped off his bowling. Yet he could demonstrate his strength of feeling as he did against Surrey in 1933 when he bowled underarm as a protest against his opponent's unwillingness to declare. His delivery was called a 'no ball' but the point had been forcibly made. The most powerful man in Yorkshire cricket, AB Sellers, while not prone to extravagant praise, thought highly of Hedley from the beginning. His first impressions were "of a very quiet type of man who did not say very much but had a great sense of humour." Even more important to Sellers was that Hedley made "no fuss and got on with the game" yet who would "not be driven into something that he didn't want to do."

Following the 'Bodyline Tour', Hedley's place in the England team, as England's leading spinner, was reasonably secure. In 1933, he played in two of the three tests against the West Indies while the following winter he was selected for the first ever tour of India, once again under the captaincy of Douglas Jardine. By now Jardine rated Hedley as the best slow left-arm bowler in the world, possibly ever, and backed this assessment by picking him in all three tests in a 2–0 series victory. Hedley returned his captain's confidence by taking 23 wickets in the series. Earlier in 1933, Hedley had achieved something more remarkable when he matched World War One victim, Colin Blyth's, record of seventeen wickets in a match. Hedley managed this feat in one day against Essex. When studying the newspaper reports of these years, the most common word to describe Hedley's bowling is 'irresistible', certainly the most appropriate word term to describe his performance at Lords on 23rd June 1934 in the second Ashes test of that year. On the third day of this test Hedley took 14 Australian wickets at the cost of 80 runs, with six of these dismissals coming in the last hour. Neville Cardus was full of praise for his bowling, observing that Hedley "bowled not more than six loose balls all day; and he bowled for hours, lovely to see, grace concealing his deadliness. He kept an alluring length, and his break pitched on the middle stump and whipped across." Hedley finished with match figures of 15/104, the best return by an England bowler against the old enemy at that point and still second only to Jim Laker's 19/90 in 1956. England squared the series, winning by an innings and 38 runs, the only test victory against Australia at Lords in the twentieth century. Indeed, no England spinner took 5 wickets in an innings against Australia at Lords until Graeme Swann achieved the feat in 2013. Don Bradman mused that "With Hedley I am never sure. You see, there's no breaking point with him", a comment that was born out when Hedley dismissed 'The Don' in both innings. Bradman later conceded that Hedley, in his view, was the greatest left-arm spinner of all time.

Despite Hedley's efforts, the series was finally lost 2–1 when two draws were followed by defeat at the Oval. After missing the winter tour to the West Indies, the following season Hedley returned to the Test match arena for the series against South Africa. After, by his standards, an undistinguished series, Hedley was dropped from the final test, replaced by Glamorgan's Johnnie Clay. The series was lost 1–0, South Africa's first series win on English soil. One steady performer in his first series for South Africa, with 15 wickets and an average of 30 with the bat, was Chud Langton from Natal, Transvaal. He was a six foot three inches attacking, forceful batsman and effective medium-paced bowler who varied his pace and manage to achieve both lift and swerve in his accurate deliveries. Chud was a regular for his country in the second half of the 1930s and played in 15 Test matches, his final appearance being in the 'timeless test' in Durban. Details of the war service record of this lieutenant in the South African Air Force are sketchy but he was reported killed in action on 27th November 1942 and buried at Maiduguri Cemetery, Nigeria. Chud was 30 years of age.

It was at this period in his career that the story began to take hold that Hedley couldn't threaten on good wickets. Nearer the truth was, as cricket historians Alan Hill and RC Robertson-Glasgow both testified, that he needed to be appreciated, even told that everything depended on him. In Yorkshire they clearly understood this. In 1935, he took 211 wickets as Yorkshire claimed another title, and the following year he achieved his highest ever total of 216, when he topped the national bowling averages despite Yorkshire losing out to first-time winners Derbyshire in the County Championship. That year he also played in all 3 tests against India, topping the bowling averages and making an important 66* in the drawn test at Old Trafford.

The tour that winter was, of course, the visit to Australia, the first since the infamous 'Bodyline Tour' four years earlier. The tour party was led by Australian-born, anti-Bodyline, fast bowler Gubby Allen, who, as we have already seen, had refused to use this tactic in 1932/3. Larwood and Voce were left behind as the MCC tried to repair relations so badly damaged four years before. Hedley began the tour bowling well and maintained this form, without much reward, for the first two tests. No matter as England took a 2–0 lead into the third test at Melbourne but this was the turning point in the series. A magnificent 270 from Bradman resulted in as convincing a win for his team as England had achieved in the first two tests. The pendulum had now swung dramatically. Two more decisive Australian victories followed and the series was lost, despite Hedley's steady bowling and commendable efforts when asked to open the batting in the fourth test at Adelaide. The wickets hadn't really suited him and on returning home, he found himself out of favour, playing in only one of the three tests against New Zealand in 1937. One of Hedley's two victims in this test was the New Zealand debutant Sonny Moloney, a steady bespectacled right-hand batsman, one of the first cricketers to play while wearing spectacles, who was also a useful medium-pace change bowler and reliable fielder. Sonny played in all three tests but did little of note and never played test cricket again. During the war, he was a lieutenant in the 20th Battalion, New Zealand Armoured Regiment who was wounded and taken prisoner at the First Battle of El Alamein. He died, a prisoner of war, on 15th July 1942, aged 31. Originally buried by the Germans, he was later reinterred in El Alamein Cemetery.

Hedley was back for the 1938 Ashes series but Hammond, by now an amateur and therefore an acceptable cricketer to captain England, appeared to trust his pacemen, Farnes and Bowes, rather than the spinners. England drew this series, in the main thanks to a remarkable innings from Yorkshire colleague, Len Hutton. His record-breaking 364 in the final test at the Oval enabled England to reach a huge first innings total of 903/7 and a victory by an innings and 579 runs. Hedley played his part in this momentous occasion, perhaps more off the field of play rather than on it. On the rest day, Hedley took his young county colleague, Hutton, 160* overnight, to the seaside in an effort to release the tension of the occasion. Later, Alan Hill tells us that Hutton said,

"I owe Verity the kind of debt that one can never fully repay… His quiet natural dignity was an immense source of strength to me during those long hours."

During the following winter, Hedley toured South Africa with the MCC and took 19 wickets in a high-scoring series which England won 1–0. He returned to England to play in what was, unknown to anybody, to become his final season. His England career came to a disappointing end, although rather appropriately it ended at Lords, the scene of his greatest Test match triumph. Playing in the first test, he contributed to an eight-wicket victory, the only result of the three-match series, but was then dropped in favour of Tom Goddard. Hedley's last wicket in Test match cricket was that of Learie, later Sir Learie Constantine, one of the truly great men of West Indian cricket. In county cricket, Hedley had a far more dramatic final season as Yorkshire won their third consecutive championship and Hedley's seventh title in all. In that final summer, before Hitler invaded Poland, Hedley took 191 wickets and finished second in the national averages. As we have already seen, the title was clinched at Hove in a strange atmosphere, combining the festive, rather hyper, end-of-season mood with apprehension at the imminence of war. Hedley took 7/9 on a rain-affected pitch and, despite the strained, tense atmosphere, it was a fitting end to a glorious career.

Hedley, a man who had a keen interest in current affairs and the world around him, had fully expected another world conflict so was not surprised as the events of September 1939 unfolded. He had begun his own preparation in 1937 by reading military literature but prior to the declaration of war, he had other concerns. Kathleen had begun to suffer ill health and it was decided that by accompanying Hedley on a trip to South Africa, where he had been offered a coaching job, her worrying condition would improve. The war scuppered those plans. Instead, along with Bill Bowes, Hedley enlisted, serving briefly in Air Raid Precautions in Guiseley and then as a sapper in the Royal Engineers. In January 1940, Hedley was commissioned as a Second Lieutenant, and later Captain, in the Green Howards. Following a spell in the Infantry Training Centre he was posted to the 1st Battalion where he met up with Yorkshire and England colleague, Norman Yardley. They were not the only Yorkshire and England cricketers serving in the Green Howards. Herbert Sutcliffe, Maurice Leyland, Len Hutton and Arthur Woods could all be found in their ranks.

Hedley's first posting was to the regimental depot at Richmond, Yorkshire where he was responsible for the training of recruits. In the spring of 1941, he was posted to Omagh in Northern Ireland where he completed further training. Here he was joined by Kathleen before his first posting overseas. This followed in early 1942 when the Green Howards were transferred to Ranchi in India. Here, Hedley found that the climate affected his health and he suffered a bout of dysentery, the first of a number of health problems that were to cause him difficulties. From here Hedley was posted to Persia and, in March 1943, to Kibrit Air Base in Egypt and then Qatana in Syria, all moves made in preparation for the invasion of Sicily.

The invasion of Sicily, codenamed Operation Husky, was to prove to be one of the most significant actions of the war, leading as it did, to the overthrow of the Italian dictator Benito Mussolini. Led by Commander-in-Chief General Dwight Eisenhower, it began with a large amphibious and airborne operation, followed by a six-week land campaign. Max Arthur, in his oral history, *Forgotten Voices of World War Two*, tells us how Lieutenant-Commander Roger Lewis, supported by, amongst others, the Hollywood actor Douglas Fairbanks Junior, set up a hoax landing on a beach that the Americans had no intention of using. They set up PT boats with towered balloons made to look like a large assault convoy. The Italian and German troops fell for the hoax and hundreds of their soldiers were moved to the beach. When dawn broke, they discovered the 4 PT boats and 4 balloons and realised that they had been tricked. Indeed, this action initiated the Italian Campaign which would continue until the Allies liberated Rome on 4th June 1944, two days before the Normandy landings.

Meanwhile, Hedley's health difficulties had not gone unnoticed and it was agreed that, once the Sicily campaign was over, he would be transferred to work in a staff position at Headquarters. First of all, before Hedley could take advantage of this opportunity, there was a campaign to fight, and a particularly difficult one it proved to be. Although initially the campaign was successful, when they reached the plains outside Catania, conditions became very difficult. A full description of Hedley's involvement has been described by RC Robertson-Glasgow.

"He received his wounds in the Eighth Army's first attack on the German positions at Catania in Sicily... The objective was a ridge with strong points and pill boxes. Behind a creeping barrage Verity led his company forward 700 yards. When the creeping barrage ceased, they went on another 300 yards and neared the ridge in darkness. As the men advanced, through corn two feet high, tracer-bullets swept into them. Then they wriggled through the corn, Verity encouraging them... The moon was at their back, and the enemy used mortar-fire and fire-bombs, setting the corn alight."

Robertson-Glasgow went on to describe in detail how Hedley, bravely leading his men, came to suffer his soon to be fatal injuries.

"The strongest point appeared to be a farmhouse to the left of the ridge; so Verity sent one platoon round to take the farmhouse while the other gave covering fire. The enemy fire increased and, as they crept forward, Verity was hit in the chest. 'Keep going', he said, 'and get them out of that farmhouse'. When it was decided to withdraw, they last saw Verity lying on the ground, in front of the burning corn, his head supported by his batman, Pte Thomas Reynoldson of Bridlington."

In the same attack, Hedley's second in command, Laurie Hesmondhalgh, was killed while Hedley had been hit by shrapnel. With chaos all around, the Company retreated and, in desperation, were forced to leave without him. The following day Tom Reynoldson, returned to where his captain had fallen accompanied by "a nice young German officer who spoke English." Here he was captured and removed to a field hospital, a very badly injured prisoner of war. An immediate operation was essential if Hedley was to live but before the operation was able to take place it was necessary to remove a grenade from his shirt pocket. This very dangerous task fell to Tom Reynoldson, who needed to remove the detonator so that the grenade could be made safe and Hedley could be taken to the makeshift operating theatre.

On his return from the operation Hedley was able to share a tin of soup with Reynoldson. However, their reunion was short-lived. Tom Reynoldson was sent to a prisoner-of-war camp in Austria while Hedley was forced to make the torturous route to Naples. They never met one another again. Corporal Henty from Leeds was present as these events took place and he is quoted by Alan Hill as saying that, once the operation was over, Hedley was determined to show fellow prisoners photos of his wife and family. Ever the family man, they were uppermost in his thoughts, despite the pain and suffering that he was experiencing. One can only begin to imagine his thoughts as he travelled by boat across the Strait of Messina to the Italian mainland and to the hospital in Reggio Calabria. From here it was decided that he should undertake a two-day rail journey to Naples where he was taken to the Italian hospital at Caserta. By this time, Hedley was extremely ill and needed another operation in order to relieve pressure from the rib on the lung. Tragically, he went downhill quickly and, three days later, on the 31st July 1943, Hedley Verity, one of England's greatest cricketers, died. As Robertson-Glasgow later wrote, "So, in the last grim game, Verity showed, as he was so sure to do, that rare courage which both calculates and inspires."

The news that Hedley was a prisoner of war, and possibly dead, was greeted with the utmost concern back in England. His old captain, Douglas Jardine, wrote to the family before the death was confirmed hoping that "you will soon have better news of the cricketer and man I most admire." Confirmation of Hedley's death came on September 1st, four years to the day since his last match for Yorkshire at Hove where he clinched the Championship title with his remarkable bowling figures of 7/9. He was buried with full military honours, his body finally laid to rest in the Caserta town military cemetery. At the end of the war, Yorkshire promptly organised a two-day Hedley Verity Memorial Match which raised an impressive sum of £3000 for his grieving family.

But how great a loss as a cricketer was Hedley Verity? Given his age it is unlikely that Hedley would have played much cricket after the war but his career figures over a ten-year period, 1956 wickets at a cost of 14.87 during a period when wickets tended to favour batsmen, place him in the front rank of bowlers. Not that, as Robertson-Glasgow said, he would have pressed these claims as "he never dwelt on decimals." And there is no doubt that he would have remained a huge influence in Yorkshire cricket. Despite appearing to some supporters to be 'a little stiff and aloof', Hedley was a humble and kindly man who would have been an enormous help to the young Yorkshire cricketers, Brian Close, Fred Truman and, most of all as a fellow spin bowler, Raymond Illingworth. Following in the tradition of Peel and Rhodes, it can be debated as to whether or not he reached their greatness but between the Wars he stands alone among English spinners. Les Ames certainly thought so naming him as the best left-arm bowler he faced while even Bradman admitted that "he never completely fathomed Hedley's strategy."

Bradman also spoke of Hedley's sportsmanship during a career in which "he exemplified all that was best about cricket" and somebody "who I grew to respect as a gentleman and a player." Robertson-Glasgow, clearly a huge admirer of both the player and the man, called him the "ever-learning professor, justly proud yet utterly humble." This legacy would last well past the end of a war in which so much talent was lost. More than ten years after Hedley's death, his former Yorkshire and England colleague, Len Hutton, led England on the Ashes tour down under. Stopping off en route to Australia, England's first professional captain led members of his team and a group of journalists to visit Hedley's grave where they laid a wreath, a single white rose and a Yorkshire scarf in his memory. As if to further highlight the terrible losses suffered through war to sportsmen of the first half of the twentieth century, they were accompanied by former Yorkshire and England cricketer, Abe Waddington. It was Waddington who, on the first day of The Battle of the Somme, had held in his arms the mortally wounded Yorkshire and England all-rounder Major Booth. With the loss of Hedley Verity, Yorkshire and English cricket had suffered another irreparable blow. Perhaps the last word should rest with the incomparable Don Bradman who concluded that, "more than his cricketing skill was his sportsmanship and manly bearing under all circumstances... I never once heard him complain or offer a criticism... and I deem it an honour and privilege to have been on the stage with him in those golden days of the 1930s."

Ken Farnes (left)

CHAPTER 9
KEN FARNES: "ESSENTIALLY A NATURAL CRICKETER"

When one thinks of English fast bowlers of the 1930s, it is inevitable that thoughts turn to the exploits of the Nottinghamshire pair, Harold Larwood and Bill Voce. The name of Larwood, in particular, evokes memories of the 'Bodyline Tour', Cabinet meetings and crisis in the Empire. Such was the impact of the tour culminating in England's 4–1 series victory, that when Larwood hobbled from the field of play following Bradman's dismissal in the final test at Sydney in 1933, he could not have imagined that he had played in his last Test match. Refusal to apologise to the MCC authorities for his 'unfair' bowling meant that England's fastest bowler never played for his country again. The search was now on to find a replacement. That search took the England selectors to Essex. Here they found Kenneth Farnes, a bowler of whom Dudley Carew wrote was "one of the nicest, gentlest and most modest of men... the one bowler England had who could conceivably make up for the loss of Larwood."

Ken Farnes was born on the 8th July 1911 in Leytonstone, Essex, the son of Sydney Heath Farnes and Florence Susanna Georgiana Farnes and the younger of two boys. Given the middle names of the parents, it is perhaps surprising that Ken was christened with such a straightforward name. Sydney was company secretary and accountant to Truman's Brewery in London's East End, one of the largest brewers in the world at the time of Ken's birth. During the second half of the twentieth century Truman's declined and the brewery closed in 1989, although it did revive in 2010 and since 2013, Truman's brand has been brewed once again in the East End of London. Ken was educated at the Royal Liberty School in Gidea Park, near Romford, where the Farnes family had lived since Ken was five years old. Although the area was very metropolitan, Ken was able to find 'The Green', an area of parkland, which Ken and his friends used for cricket. Ken was later to write fondly of 'The Green' in his book *Tours and Tests*', stressing the care with which the boys looked after their cricket pitch. It was while attending the Royal Liberty School that, encouraged by his headmaster, Mr SB Hartley, Ken gave notice of his cricketing ability. This ability did not come as a surprise to his family given that Sydney himself was a prominent club cricketer and Ken himself was soon playing club cricket at Gidea Park. Here he was spotted by Percy Perrin, an Essex batsman with over 30 years' experience of playing county cricket. Ken's career was underway.

Ken continued his education at Pembroke College, Cambridge, a decision which allowed him to further his cricketing experience by playing for the university in term time and Essex in the holidays. Indeed, by the age of 19 he was already playing in the county side as a very promising fast-medium, right-arm bowler. The decision to become a fast bowler had been made early on, inspired by seeing Arthur Gilligan knocking a stump out of the ground at Lords. Ken later referred to it as a "wonderful, unforgettable, inspiring sight." As he later wrote, Ken was determined to experience the thrill for himself.

"The sight of a stump seen hurtling out of the ground has always struck me as one of the finest in cricket. It sends shock through the spectators and from the middle you can hear a gasp all round."

Ken was destined to be a fast bowler. He certainly had the physic for it. Perfectly proportioned at six feet five inches tall and weighing nearly fifteen and a half stone, Ken was the ideal build for the job. Sending down his deliveries from a height of over eight foot, he was able to generate good pace from a relatively short run of eleven strides and, with a last second downward flick of the wrist, he was able to add a little extra nip when required. In the 1932 varsity match, Jim Swanton, at the beginning of his splendid journalistic career, told Ken's future biographer, David Thurlow, how impressed he was with young fast bowler and that "I can still hear the ball thudding around Peter van der Bijl's ribs and Peter giving great groans which you could hear in the

Tavern." Carew writes of his inconsistency but confirms Swanton's impression and saw him "like some engine of fabulous gear which only on rare occasions could wind itself up to its full might... in these moments of inspiration he was a devastating force."

Ken's introduction to county cricket, however, did not start well. Despite taking 5/36 against Kent in only his second championship game, the two matches against Yorkshire in 1932 stand out. In the first, Yorkshire won by an innings and 313 runs, the exact number of runs scored by Herbert Sutcliffe as he and Percy Holmes (224*) put on a world record 555 for the first wicket. In the return match at Scarborough, Sutcliffe and Maurice Leyland hit Ken for 75 runs in 4 overs, a pasting that reduced the young Essex bowler to tears. The onslaught continued with 239 runs being added in the two hours between lunch and tea with Sutcliffe scoring 94 in only 40 minutes. After the game Ken confided to Bill Bowes that he would never make a fast bowler. The wise Bowes, destined to be Ken's partner opening the England attack in future years, gave the youngster sound advice. He stressed that, although you could bowl short-pitched bouncers against many batsmen, you could not bowl in this way to renowned hookers such as Sutcliffe and Leyland. "Know your man", advised Bowes. Bowes knew what he was talking about. In Essex first innings, he had taken 9/121 in 44 overs in a wonderful display of controlled fast bowling.

There were also problems with Ken's run-up, not an unusual problem for young up-and-coming pacemen. In one match Ken was no balled 21 times. The issue was eventually addressed when Ken reverted to a short, easy run-up of 11 paces. Part of the difficulty was that Ken didn't cut the image of an aggressive fast bowler. Most of the successful bowlers of the first 40 years of the twentieth century were professional players. Rival fast bowlers like Larwood, Voce and Bowes tended to emerge from the heavy industrial areas of Nottinghamshire and Yorkshire. The same could be said of spin bowlers like Rhodes and Verity. Successful amateurs were much more likely to be free-flowing batsmen, playing without the pressures of having to earn a living. Ken, unfairly, was seen as lacking the aggression needed to be a highly successful fast bowler. Time would prove this to be unfounded but the feeling that Ken was hard to arouse persisted for some time.

The following year, 1933, confirmed that Ken was right to persevere with his dream of being an international fast bowler. In the varsity match this summer he went a long way towards showing the necessary aggression. Bowling to a field of 4 short legs Ken bowled short, fast leg theory in the manner of Larwood and Voce. An Oxford opener was hit in the neck, the last man on the jaw, while between these victims, others took blows to the ribs, chest and arm. The summer continued to bring success. Against Surrey at Southend in August, Essex recorded victory over their near neighbours for the first time since 1914. And a convincing win it was with Essex crushing Surrey by 345 runs. Ken's contribution, were match figures of 11/114 including 7/21 in the second innings. By the end of the summer Ken had taken 113 wickets at a cost of just over 18 runs per wicket. The 22-year-old Ken Farnes had truly arrived.

Ken's surge in form was well timed as, of course, English cricket was in a post-Bodyline world so Larwood was out of the picture. Ken had shown enough promise to earn a call-up to the England team to play Australia in the first test at Trent Bridge and he wasted no time in making his presence felt. With figures of 5/102 and 5/77, Ken became one of only six Englishmen to take ten wickets on his test debut. Not that this magnificent effort paid dividends for England, who were comprehensively beaten by 238 runs, but it did announce the arrival of a genuine fast bowler who would be crucial to his country given the absence of Larwood and Voce. The second test, played at Lord's, saw a complete reversal in form with a convincing innings victory for England but no wickets for Ken. This match, Verity's test, was, as we have seen, the only victory England gained over Australia on this ground in the twentieth century. It also saw England open the bowling with two genuine fast bowlers, Ken and Bill Bowes, a decision that was far from inevitable before this series.

An injury prevented Ken playing any further part in this Ashes series which Australia won 2–1, helped by Bradman scoring his second consecutive triple hundred at Headingley followed by a double hundred at the Oval. He was selected to tour the West Indies that winter under the leadership of Bob Wyatt. Ken wrote that he "was delighted to be leaving England's grey December for sun-drenched coral beaches fringed by palms" but the team was, as Wisden described it, "sufficient for the occasion." They were wrong as the series was lost 2–1. Moreover, the amateurs in the party were out of pocket—the MCC saw it as an honour to play for England so only paid amateur players £25 in expenses. Ken had sacrificed his £100 a term pay, as a schoolteacher to make the trip. Another series defeat was notable for Ken and Jim Smith becoming two of the very few players to open both batting and bowling in the same test. In the second innings of the first test, Wyatt decided to reverse the batting order calculating that the wicket would play a little easier the longer the innings continued so that it made sense to place his best batsmen lower down the order. The gamble paid off and Hammond, batting at number six, guided England to her only win of the series. Ken played in one further test on the tour before picking up a knee injury which was serious enough to keep him out for the whole of the 1935 season.

The road back was not an easy one. Despite bowling very quickly for the Gentlemen against the Players in 1936 and taking 11/131 in a famous victory over Yorkshire at Southend, the first victory over the champions since 1911 and a win which could be viewed as revenge following the humiliations of 1932, Ken was not selected for any of the three tests against India that summer. Perhaps the new England captain, Gubby Allen, had seen enough and the fellow fast bowler was happy to take Ken on the 1936/7 tour to Australia in a bid both to re-establish friendly relations with the Australian cricket authorities and public and, of course, to regain the Ashes. Ken appeared well-suited to helping England achieve success in both these objectives. Although Sutcliffe held the opinion that Ken's action was easy to spot and Hutton felt that the lack of histrionics signified a lack of ambition, these critical Yorkshiremen were in a minority. With his magnificent physique, toned by following a 'Mr Universe' course, and his great height, Ken looked a superb athlete, ideal for the arduous tour ahead. Bill Frindall describes Ken as "one of the fastest bowlers of all time and the leading amateur opening bowler of the 1930s." Robertson-Glasgow elaborates on this when he described Ken as a "magnificent sight" whose bowling was "always good and, when need called, often great." Yet the image of a man lacking that 'nasty streak' that often accompanied the very best fast bowlers provided some contradictions. Bill Edrich remembered the occasion when, having been hit by a ball from Ken bowling at his fastest, he recovered to hear his opponent consoling him with the words "have some water, there's no hurry." A love of poets such as James Elroy Fletcher, novelists including the Irish writer George Moore and the philosopher JW Dunne added to the belief, held by some, that Ken was something of a soft touch. Yet Robertson-Glasgow was adamant that "when you were hit by Ken Farnes, you stayed hit." Perhaps the combination of a genuine fast bowler who was also the most agreeable of men would be the ideal man to lead the England attack following the controversies of 'Bodyline'.

It didn't quite go to plan. England won the first two tests most convincingly and appeared on course to regain the Ashes. But as ever, when Bradman got going, Australia was always on top. Double centuries at both Melbourne and Adelaide capped by another century in the deciding test, once again in Melbourne, resulted in Bradman inspiring his country to a 3–2 victory. Ken only played in the final two tests, Bowes and Allen being seen as a strong enough pace attack. Perhaps the presence of three pacemen would have revived the atmosphere of 1932/33, although when Ken did play it was as a third pace bowler. Nevertheless, at the end of the tour Wisden described him as England's most consistent bowler.

Facing the recalled Ken in the fourth test at Adelaide was a young Australian for whom a bright future seemed assured. Gerald Ross Gregory, known by his middle name, was a gifted right-hand batsman who, at twenty years of age, was already a regular in the Victoria team that was about to win the Sheffield Shield. First representing his state whilst still at school, Ross had already taken a century off Gubby Allen's tourists. Although below medium height, Ross had strong forearms which enabled him to play very effective shots in front of the wicket. Like Bradman, Archie Jackson and Stan McCabe, Ross made his test debut before he came of age and was quick to make his mark, making 50 in Australia's second innings, an effort which helped to square the series. In the deciding test Ross made 80 as the Australian batsmen ensued an innings victory and it must have seemed that he would go on and make many more runs in test cricket. Nobody could have thought that, despite missing the 1938 tour to England, Ross had played his last Test match. Ironically, his dismissal in this test occurred on his 21st birthday when he was caught by Hedley Verity off the bowling of Ken Farnes. Tragically within six years all three were dead, victims of this truly worldwide war. Ross, by now a qualified accountant, had joined the Royal Australian Air Force as a Sergeant-Observer and Pilot Officer. He was killed on active service near Ghafargaon, Assam on 10th June 1942 aged 26 and is commemorated on the Singapore Memorial to the Missing.

Despite missing the 1937 series against New Zealand and the first test against Australia the following summer, Ken was coming into his prime. In 1938, after being omitted from the test team, Ken bowled extremely quickly at Lord's for the Gentlemen against the Players. Bill Edrich, batting for the Players, said that Ken was now as quick as anybody that he had ever faced. "His first ball jumped off the completely dead pitch and flew outside my off stump, head high, from only just short of a length. The next ball pitched at the same length on the leg stump, jumped like a lightning bolt straight at my eyes."

Ken finished with figures of 8/43, giving him 11 wickets in the match, and it was said to be the best bowling in these series of matches since Arthur Fielder took all ten Gentlemen wickets in 1906. When he followed this with his best ever figures of 11/113 against Glamorgan at Clacton, it could be safely said that Ken was in his prime. He played in the three remaining tests that summer, (the third test at Old Trafford having been washed out without a ball being bowled), taking 17 wickets in the series at the cost of 34 runs per wicket. By the end of this drawn series, Ken was a firm fixture in the England team so it was no surprise when he was invited to tour South Africa in the winter of 1938/9.

As the senior fast bowler on the tour, it is no surprise to discover that Ken played in all five tests. He opened the bowling with Bill Edrich in three tests and Walter Hammond in one, neither of whom, although more than useful, could be considered a frontline fast bowler. Ken, along with Hedley Verity, carried the England bowling attack on his very considerable shoulders. The series was won 1–0, which might have been 2–0 if the 'timeless' fifth test had not been abandoned with England 42 runs short of victory with five wickets left. Rain in the tea interval on the tenth day prevented further play and the England team had a boat to catch. Ken had more than done his bit as 16 wickets at the cost of 32 runs each testify.

Nobody could have thought that the 'timeless test' would be Ken's last. He played no part in the series win over the West Indies in the summer of 1939 and, with war looming on the horizon, test cricket would cease for nearly seven years. Ken would, however, leave test cricket on a high when he was named as a Wisden Cricketer of the Year in 1939. His autobiography, *Tours and Tests*, was published the following year and was well-received. In this book, Ken confirmed that he was a man with a social conscience and his sensitive, questioning mind shone through. He wrote passionately of the hardships that he had witnessed in the East End and reflected on the sights seen on his recent tour of South Africa. The direction in which the world was heading and the lack of education offered to many in particular caused him concern. When war was declared there was no doubt that Ken would play his part in the war against fascism.

Given Ken's background it should be no surprise that he would offer to place himself at the heart of the conflict. Sergeant Farnes joined the Royal Air Force Volunteer Reserve and was quickly sent to Canada for training. On his return, Ken was commissioned as a pilot officer in September 1941 when he was expected to play his part as a night-flying pilot. Four weeks later, on 20th October 1941, Ken was dead. He was piloting a plane on a training night flight near Chipping Warden in Oxfordshire when the plane crashed giving him no hope of survival. He was buried in Brookwood Military Cemetery. Ken Farnes was thirty years of age.

The tributes were warm and heartfelt. *Wisden* reported that "his death at the age of 30 came as a great shock to countless friends and the whole world of cricket." His figures (60 wickets in 15 tests, 690 first-class wickets in total) speak for themselves. But many recalled not only his cricket prowess and *Wisden's* view that he was the "natural cricketer", but the caring, kind personality of this most popular of cricketers. AA Thompson recalled how a seven-year-old boy had once queued outside the Essex pavilion in the hope of gaining Ken's autograph. Just as the disappointed boy was about to give up and leave Ken appeared, not only to sign the book, but with a soft and fizzy drink to reward the boy's patience. The young boy was DB Carr, later an England test player and Derbyshire captain. Stories such as this abound. What is in no doubt is that Ken Farnes, a man with so much more to give on and off the field, was one of the first losses to sport in the war and one of those most keenly felt.

George Macauley

Geoffrey Legge

CHAPTER 10
"A BOWLER WITH QUIVERING INTENSITY" AND "A BATSMAN OF GREAT SKILL"

The stories of George Macaulay and Geoffrey Legge

What becomes clear when researching sportsmen who made the ultimate sacrifice in World War Two is the variety of ways in which these losses occurred. In the Great War, our heroes were often lost on the battlefields of the Somme, in the mud of Passchendaele or on the beaches and cliffs at Gallipoli. It is true that some died away from the frontline but the image is one of our sporting heroes following, or in many cases leading, battalions 'over the top' into 'no man's land'. Not so in World War Two. Clearly, as we have already discovered, some sporting heroes died on the battlefield on D-Day, in the Italian campaign and in the deserts of Africa but many more died in situations that are not acknowledged with the same reverence and empathy. They were losses nonetheless. Two such losses are those of the Yorkshire and England bowler, George Macaulay and the Kent and England batsman, Geoffrey Legge.

George Gibson Macaulay was born on the 7th December 1897 in Thirsk into a keen cricketing family. His father, a publican, and his uncles were well known local players and it was no surprise when George showed interest himself. He was educated at the North Eastern County School, later known as Barnard Castle, an independent boarding school in County Durham. In later years, this school became better known for producing rugby players including England internationals Rob Andrew, the Underwood brothers, Rory and Tony as well as, more recently, Matthew Tait. Indeed, the school produced more rugby internationals between 1970 and 1995 than any school in the country. George confirmed himself to be a good all-round sportsman by swimming, playing golf and football as well as showing promise at cricket. On leaving school he worked as a bank clerk in Wakefield while continuing to play football and cricket both there and in nearby Ossett.

During World War One, the young George joined the Royal Field Artillery where he remained until the end of the war. He then returned to pursue his banking career and was based first in London and then Herne Bay where he became involved in club cricket. It was while playing in Herne Bay that he was spotted by both former Kent player, Sir Stanley Christopherson, and ex Yorkshire cricketer, Harry Hayley. Faced with a choice, George accepted a trial with Yorkshire. By now George was presenting mainly as a bowler who could bat, bowling at a fast to medium pace with a good action. Jim Kilburn, later the *Yorkshire Post* cricket correspondent, wrote that "his run-up was half shambling, his steps short and his shoulders swaying, but his feet were faultlessly placed and his aim was high at the instant of delivery."

George's arrival at Yorkshire Cricket Club was well timed. Following the death of both Major Booth on the Somme battlefield and Alonso Drake to illness, Yorkshire had lost the bowlers expected to spearhead their attack through the first half of the 1920s. By this time George Hirst was past his best and, although Wilfred Rhodes still had ten more years of first-class cricket in him, there was a need to introduce new bowlers. It was not long before George was given his chance. He played in two warm-up matches to the 1920 season where he took 12 wickets in three innings and he made his full debut on 15th May against Derbyshire. During the next two months, George played 10 matches for Yorkshire and took 24 wickets. But by the end of June, he had been dropped with *Wisden* concluding that George had "neither the pace nor the stamina required." There were also murmurings of a poor attitude to the game. It was the wily old professionals, Hirst and Rhodes, who took George in hand by telling him to reduce his pace, concentrate on bowling a good length and to try and spin and cut the ball as well as using his more conventional method. During the winter of 1920/21 George worked at perfecting his new style. The following summer his career really took off.

By 1921 George had settled for a style which incorporated both medium-pace deliveries, mixed with occasional off spin. He now had a short, bustling run, or "short, breezy run" according to Christopher Martin-Jenkins, often bowled from around the wicket. The results could be devastating. In the fourth match of the new season, he returned match figures of 10/65 and later took 6/3 as Derbyshire were bowled out for the measly total of 23. By the end of the season George had taken 101 wickets at the average of 17.33 per wicket, an excellent eye-catching return. Add to this a total of 457 runs at an average of 22.59 and it is easy to see why George could consider himself established. The following summer, 1922, was even better. Figures such as 6/12 against Glamorgan, 11/31 versus Northamptonshire and 5/31 when tormenting Middlesex led to his selection for the Players against the Gentlemen and, more importantly, contributing significantly to Yorkshire's championship victory, the first of four consecutive triumphs. When the MCC named its team to tour South Africa, where England were due to play five Test matches, it was no surprise that the name of George Macaulay was included.

On this tour George did confirm his value. He was not selected for the first test, which England lost, but he replaced Greville Stevens for the second at Cape Town on New Year's Day 1923. He took a wicket, that of George Hearne, with his very first ball in test cricket, only the third bowler to accomplish this feat. In South Africa's second innings he finished with figures of 5/64 giving him seven wickets in the match and he also hit the winning run in England's one wicket victory. One of his second innings victims was Cyril Francois whom George dismissed with a catch off his own bowling. Francois, who was a hard-hitting all-rounder, later served as an Air Sergeant in the South African Air Force during World War Two and was killed in May 1944 following a motor accident. He is buried at Thaba Tshwane Military Cemetery, Pretoria in South Africa.

After such a start it was inevitable that George would keep his place in the team as England went on to win the series 2–1 and George finished with 16 wickets at a cost of 20 runs each. *Wisden*, however, did not rate George's performance quite so kindly, stating that "he had neither the pace nor the stamina required." According to their report, no really effective bowlers emerged during the tour, a verdict that many in Yorkshire would dispute in later years as George went on to take more wickets for Yorkshire other than Rhodes, Hirst and Schofield Haigh. That summer he proved his effectiveness and versatility beyond question as he increased his season's haul to 166 wickets, including 7/13 against Glamorgan. *Wisden* relented and made him one of their Five Cricketers of the Year, despite expressing their opinion that George was "easily discouraged and did not respond when things went against him."

His good form continued into 1924 when George topped the national averages with 190 wickets but, surprisingly he was picked for only one test against South Africa that summer. Nevertheless, George continued to trouble the best opponents. Jack Hobbs fell to George's skilful bowling on five occasions in 1925 and, although Hobbs liked to attack his bowling from the first ball, this can be seen as a mark of respect or even a fear that George would bowl out most of the batting line-up. Examination of the number of occasions where George took 6, 7 or 8 wickets in an innings give credence to this view. The England selectors remained unimpressed and George was not chosen for the winter tour to Australia, despite Maurice Tate, England's leading bowler, needing some support. Why was this the case? Perhaps George's rather aggressive character had something to do with it. Yorkshire players were seen as somewhat difficult and undisciplined, a reputation that was cemented when four players were highlighted for poor attitude following a match against Surrey. George also developed a fondness for horse racing and Len Hutton remembered clearly having to communicate the result of the 2.30 at Thirsk during the drinks interval. More significantly, George had also been critical of the England captain Arthur Gilligan, not a move likely to win him friends in the MCC. Some of George's assets as a bowler could count against him when looking to build a successful team expected to tour together harmoniously for five months. The journalist Jim Kilburn described George as "passionate, hostile and fiery when bowling… believing that batsmen were his mortal enemies." Kilburn suggested that a deliberate use of the 'beamer' unsettled batsmen who, rightly regarded the tactic as unfair, illegal and contrary to the spirit of the game. Kilburn went on to say that,

"Should the batsman survive, he would be rewarded with a glare of concentrated venom calculated to stagger even the stoutest heart… Every scrap of his heart and soul went into every ball he bowled. He never gave up and his persistence was invariably triumphant sooner or later."

Laurence Le Quesne tells us that George bowled two full tosses straight at the head of England captain, Douglas Jardine, in 1932. Although often generous to his opponents, Bill Bowes said that when bowling he would glare and mutter underneath his breath, "filled with a devilish energy." Robertson-Glasgow confirms that George was a difficult man and that he was, "fiercely independent, witty, argumentative, swift to joy and anger. He had pleasure in cracking a convention or cursing an enemy… a cricket bag came between him and his blazer hanging on a peg and he'd kick it and tell it a truth or two, then laugh."

Colleagues like Herbert Sutcliffe confirmed that, although witty, you never knew what to expect from George. Bill Bowes confirmed that George could be cruel to teammates, especially if they made errors off his bowling. Perhaps it was this reason above all others that ensured his non-selection for the Ashes tour. Dudley Carew painted a clear picture of the contradictions in George's character.

"The whole man was highly strung, not nervous exactly, for he had too tough a kernel for that, but impatient and abrupt with repressed energy. He did not suffer fools gladly and could be devastating with a glance and an unacademic phrase, but he was a grand friend and a man who could do other things than play cricket."

Indeed, Carew goes on to tell us that George "had a passion for gramophone records, possessed a fine singing voice, and knew the Gilbert and Sullivan operas backwards." Nobody, says Carew, could mistake George for a "man of lazy tolerance and insufficient guts." Perhaps it was to be expected that the conventional, rather conservative selection committee would find it difficult to select such a man as a regular member the England XI.

Shrugging off the attitude of the England selectors, George played a very big part in Yorkshire's fourth consecutive championship win in 1925 by taking 211 wickets in the season. In one match, George snatched victory from the jaws of defeat when he came on to bowl with Sussex requiring only 40 more runs for victory and plenty of wickets in hand. In 33 balls George took the remaining 5 wickets for 8 runs, clinching victory for Yorkshire. In 1926, he was again selected for the Headingley test and helped to save the game for England by restraining his usual attacking batting style in order make a patient 76, sharing a partnership of 108 with George Geary in the process. Cricket historian Clive Porter described this innings as "his finest hour in his country's service." This is confirmation of George's ability as a batsman who was particularly good in a crisis. His bowling, however, was taken apart by Charles Macartney who became only the second batsman to score a century before lunch on the first day of a Test match. Allegedly, Macartney had requested permission from his captain, Herbie Collins, to "go after Macaulay."

During the latter years of the 1920s George's career began a slow decline. His batting skills in particular began to fade and, although he still regularly took 100 wickets each season, he was not the demon of old. Recurrent injuries did not help. Not that he had mellowed. In one match, Holmes, Sutcliffe and Kilner managed to drop three catches in one over off George's bowling. "When Madame Tussauds want a set of slips", he exclaimed, "I know where to find them." However, George did have something of an 'Indian Summer' in the early 1930s. Now bowling more off spin, Wisden tells us that "he recovered fully his length, spin and command over variations in pace." Yorkshire's bowlers in general improved and, now with Hedley Verity in the team, the title was won three years in succession from 1931. In 1933, he captured 148 wickets and found himself recalled to an England team, weakened by the 'Bodyline crisis', for the first test against the West Indies at Lord's. He kept his place for the second test in Manchester but achieved little of note. George's test career was now over having taken

24 wickets in his 8 Test matches, a record that belies his true ability and standing in the game. In the following two summers a finger injury and rheumatism caused severe problems so in 1935 he decided to call it a day in first-class cricket.

With an annual grant of £250, from Yorkshire George set out to be a businessman. This had been a long-held ambition. As long ago as 1924 he had gone into business with Herbert Sutcliffe running a sports' outfitters. However, he lost interest and Sutcliffe bought him out, going on to make the business a considerable success. In 1935, George attempted to market a patented rheumatic medicine but the business quickly failed. An athletic outfitting shop in Leeds went the same way and George was forced to file for bankruptcy in 1937. A disappointed, angry George accused Yorkshire of withholding his benefit money. A sum of £1,633 had been raised, a surprisingly small amount for such a good professional, but George had received only £530 as Yorkshire had invested the sum and released only the interest. The matter went to court where the official receiver found that the complaint against Yorkshire had no justification. George argued that the money was his as he had earned but accusations that he had spent too much time drinking in pubs and neglected his business did not help his cause. The result was that George had to return to the cricket field, this time in the Lancashire League with Todmorden and, later, in the Welsh League with Ebbw Vale.

This George did until the outbreak of war in 1939. He joined the RAF and trained to be a pilot officer where he was stationed at Church Fenton outside Leeds. However, tragically, George's war was a short one. He died of pneumonia, aged 43, on 13th December 1940 while on active service in Sullom Voe, an inlet between North Mainland and Northmavine on Shetland in Scotland. Sullom Voe was an airfield used by The Royal Air Force and the Royal Norwegian Air Force during World War Two and, sadly, it was to be George's last resting place. He was listed as one who died while on active service and was buried at Lerwick Cemetery, Shetland.

Following his death early in the war, and the nature of his passing, George has somewhat disappeared from memory. A memorial was unveiled in 1952 at Barkston Ash Church near Selby in Yorkshire and in 1973 a plaque was unveiled outside his birthplace in Town End, Thirsk but for a player who made such a significant contribution to Yorkshire cricket, he is overshadowed by Hirst, Rhodes, Sutcliffe, and later, by Hutton and Verity. Surely it is time that this impression is corrected. Although an underachiever at test level, George captured 1,838 first-class wickets at an average of 17.64 runs per wicket, took four hat-tricks for Yorkshire, a record that still stands and whose total dismissals for his county is greater than any bowler other than Rhodes, Hirst and Haigh. He deserves a significant place in the history of the sport. Cricket writers and historians can, and do, agree on that. The obituaries from the time, and the work of later cricket historians, are unanimous. In one of the most successful eras of Yorkshire cricket, the name of George Macaulay burns brightly. AA Thompson wrote that George "bowled with a kind of passion; he seemed to deny the batsmen's right to exist, not only at the crease but on the Earth, and there was a sort of uncontrolled fury in his attack." Thompson concluded that he bowled "with quivering intensity… with a dedication that was almost a lover's." On a rain-damaged pitch he was in his glory, almost unplayable, looking out on to the wicket as the rain fell thinking, as Thompson says, "of the seven left handers in the opposition team who were sitting where he could not get at 'em." The Yorkshire Post remembered him as "a great cricketer… not so much in mathematical accomplishment… as in cricketing character… who would be remembered for the fierceness of his enthusiasm when there was a fighting chance of victory." Even his personal shortcomings seemed to be forgotten. Robertson-Glasgow described him as "a glorious opponent, a great cricketer and a companion in a thousand." One of the earliest sporting casualties of a dreadful war, George Macaulay has to be seen as a huge loss to the game and a cricketer fit to take his place among the 'Yorkshire greats'.

Three weeks before George Macaulay succumbed to pneumonia, another England cricketer died who has, like George, disappeared into the mists of time. Geoffrey Bevington Legge was a Kent and England batsman who, for three years, had the honour of captaining his county. But this Oxford University educated cricketer, trying to balance a lucrative career in business with life as a stylish England amateur batsman, was a very different character to the intense Yorkshireman. Geoffrey's career, very much briefer, followed a different path to that of the professional Yorkshire bowler.

Born in Bromley on 26th January 1903 the eldest son of a 'paper agent', Henry B Legge and his wife Edith, Geoffrey was brought up in a house with five 'live in' servants. Following a move to nearby Baston Manor, Hayes, young Geoffrey was educated at Malvern School and it was here that his sporting ability came to be noticed. A good all-round sportsman who also showed promise on the football field, it was cricket that captured young Geoffrey's imagination. In the summer of 1922, he was made captain of the school XI and his performances began to attract the attention of *Wisden*. The performances of promising young, public school cricketers, were given great attention in this 'bible of cricket' and, in their review of public school cricket in 1922, Geoffrey was very much to the fore. He was described as a stylish batsman, particularly strong at off-driving and cutting, while his reliability as a slip fielder was also noted. *Wisden*, as well as enjoying his "beautiful off-side strokes", was particularly impressed with his captaincy. The writer concluded that, "Legge was an excellent captain who knew how to get the best out of his bowlers, and had a sound control of his eleven in the field." When Geoffrey was offered a place at Brasenose College, Oxford, it was probably seen as very likely that the elegant young Kent batsman would make his mark.

However, it turned out to be anything but a forgone conclusion. Promising young amateur batsmen, despite the losses during the Great War, were not in short supply and during the summers of 1923 and 1924 Geoffrey failed to make a single appearance in a first-class match for his university. He was finally given his chance in the fourth match of 1925 season when he was picked to play Worcestershire. Geoffrey did not waste this opportunity. He hit 120, reaching his century in two hours and followed this up with a creditable 40 in the second innings. Geoffrey was awarded his blue three weeks before the varsity match where, with some help from Geoffrey, a strong Cambridge side was held to an honourable draw. By the end of the season. Geoffrey sat at the top of the Oxford University batting averages. By the following summer, 1926, he was captain of the university team. Unfortunately, his tenure of this office was dogged by bad luck. Although Geoffrey once again topped the university batting averages, Oxford lost the varsity match while other early season fixtures were disrupted by the General Strike. On a personal note, Geoffrey suffered a hand injury when involved in a car accident. Although there is no evidence that Geoffrey was at fault it would be true to say that he did have a liking for fast cars.

Following university, it was predictable that Geoffrey would join his home county of Kent where he would attempt to make his mark on the county circuit. The Kent team of the 1920s was, as Gerald Howat puts it, "a side studded with elegance and style", a county of great amateur talent, personified by their glamorous England captain, Percy Chapman. But their most prevalent characteristic was inconsistency. The talented amateurs played when they could, or wanted to, preferring a warm summer's day at Canterbury rather than a damp May at Headingley. This could work with a squad that had depth which included a committed group of professionals but Kent had few professionals that fitted the bill. Two that did were the men who sustained Kent cricket as something of a force during this period — Frank Woolley and 'Tich' Freeman. Frank Woolley, a star before the Great War, was idolised throughout the 1920s. Tall and elegant with the bat, he was also a decent bowler, good enough to take 83 test wickets, and an impressive fielder, one of the true stars of the years between the wars. His total of 145 centuries over an exceptionally long career put him up with the greatest of batsmen, each hundred constructed in the manner of a great, stylish left hander in the David Gower mould. 'Tich' Freeman, with a style of spin bowling that was inviting to hit, took a career total of 3,776 wickets, second only to Wilfred Rhodes. His figures, which included the taking of 250 or more wickets in each of the six seasons between 1928 and 1933, are difficult to comprehend to the modern reader. He was the master of all batsmen except, perhaps, the very best, and this is probably the reason that he was not more successful at test level.

Despite the presence of these two superstars and the England captain, Kent flattered only to deceive. One of the best examples of their brilliance occurred in Geoffrey's first season and he was very much involved. Lancashire, the current county champions, had Kent struggling on 70/5 at Maidstone. Led by the brilliant Australian fast bowler Ted MacDonald, the Lancashire attack was blowing Kent away on a wicket that Neville Cardus described as a "flying wicket, drying after the rain." MacDonald was bowling at his best, a bowler that Cardus described as "one of the greatest, fastest and most beautiful bowlers ever seen." When Geoffrey joined Percy Chapman in two and a half hours of sensational batting, they turned the match on its head scoring 284 runs in two and a half hours. Geoffrey made 101 while the England captain and 'pin up' made 260. The story of Percy Chapman is one of English cricket's most tragic. A test player while playing Minor Counties cricket, Chapman took over the captaincy from Arthur Carr for the final test against Australia at the Oval in 1926. The four previous tests had been drawn but thanks to Rhodes and the debutant Larwood, England won to regain the Ashes. In the winter of 1928/9, Bradman's first in test cricket, Chapman took the England team to Australia and won the series 4–1. But as Bradman re-wrote the history books, Percy Chapman went into decline, dogged by a love of drink and the high life. A total of 26 tests, 17 as captain with only two defeats, counted for nothing as Chapman slipped into alcoholism and depression. He died, alone and lonely, in 1961 aged 61.

Geoffrey, meanwhile, continued with his promising career. In 1927, he averaged over 30 and the following summer he was made captain. Before that Geoffrey was picked for his first England tour to South Africa. Some of England's top players, including Hobbs, Hendren, Tate and Larwood, were unavailable so the tour was a good opportunity to blood some promising young players. Geoffrey made 120 against Orange Free State and was picked to make his test debut for the first test on Christmas Eve 1927. Batting on Boxing Day, Geoffrey got off to the worst possible start and was out, caught and bowled before he had troubled the scorers. *The Times* called this "a shaky start" and the unconvinced selectors agreed. England won the match by ten wickets so there was no further opportunity for Geoffrey to make amends. The selectors ensured that there were no further opportunities for him in the remainder of the series.

On his return to England, Geoffrey was able to begin his period captaining his county. With 'Tich' Freeman taking over 300 wickets, Kent finished second behind Lancashire who completed a hat-trick of championships. Geoffrey had a modest return of 800 runs at an average of 22, a figure that only rose to 929 runs at an average of 25 the following summer when Kent dropped to 8th. Nevertheless, it was enough to remind the selectors of his existence. Following his marriage on 19th September 1929 to the tennis player, Rosemary Frost, a player good enough to have defeated the great Suzanne Lenglen to win the tournament at Queens, Geoffrey was picked to tour New Zealand that winter. This was the winter when England undertook two tours, the other to the West Indies, simultaneously in an effort to spread the game.

The tour from Geoffrey's point of view was something of a mixed bag but contained one major highlight. After playing some first-class fixtures in Australia, the players moved on to New Zealand where they were scheduled to play three tests. The first test, with Maurice Turnbull making his debut, was won by 8 wickets. Heavy rain reduced the 3rd test at Eden Park, Auckland to one day so a fourth test at the same venue was added. Geoffrey did little of note in the first three tests but the added Test match saw his finest cricketing moment. Batting first, England made 540 of which Geoffrey contributed 196, his highest ever score. *The Times* was fulsome with its praise calling it a "considerable measure of batting success" and concluding that he was very unlucky to be given out when just short of a double hundred. England drew the match to win the series 1–0. Although Geoffrey was bowled for a duck in the second innings, few would have guessed that this would be his last Test match. He had scored 299 test runs at an average of just under 60 and had even taken wickets on this tour bowling leg spin. Figures of 6/24 against Southland and nine wickets in the match against Manawatu hint at some untapped bowling ability.

On his return from the tour, Geoffrey found himself overlooked by the selectors. Australia were the visitors and it was decided that it was vital that England selected their biggest stars if they were to retain the Ashes. With batsmen of the calibre of Hobbs, Sutcliffe, Hammond, Woolley, Leyland, Duleepsinhji, Chapman and Hendren it is hardly surprising that Geoffrey was overlooked. Despite this array of talent

England lost the series 2–1 with Bradman running amok. A century at Trent Bridge, double hundreds at Lord's and the Oval as well as a triple century at Headingley proved too much for England. Moreover, Geoffrey averaged only 14 during the season. His test career, and soon after, his first-class career, was over. Geoffrey played his final first-class match for Kent against the touring New Zealanders, victims of his proudest moment, at Canterbury the following summer.

Following his retirement at the age of 28, not particularly young for an amateur cricketer with a career to pursue, Geoffrey went back into the world of business. In keeping with his glamorous image, he bought an aeroplane which he sometimes flew to business meetings around Europe. It was no surprise, therefore, that with the outbreak of war, as a Royal Naval Volunteer Reserve, he joined the Fleet Air Arm, the flying arm of the Royal Navy. By mid-November 1940, Geoffrey had been made Lieutenant Commander attached to the Royal Navy Air Station St Merryn, HMS *Vulture*. This was an aircraft training centre for training airborne observers and aircraft carrier flight manoeuvres, skills that would prove to be of great importance in the coming years. Geoffrey's participation in the war effort beckoned. Tragically it was not to be. Just six days later, on the 21st November 1940, Geoffrey was killed in a flying accident at the age of 37. He was buried in St Merryn Churchyard in North Cornwall near Padstow. He is one of 29 World War Two burials mostly from the Royal Naval Air Station where Geoffrey was based.

With his death, Geoffrey Legge fades into history, largely forgotten. Although his first-class batting figures (147 matches, 210 innings and just under 5,000 runs at an average of 25) don't jump out as being particularly noteworthy, it is wrong to forget his contribution. In a period where great England batsmen carved out their place in the history books, Geoffrey managed to play in five Test matches averaging just under 50. It was true that he did not bat against the strongest bowlers of the day but, given the opportunity, he might have achieved more. *Wisden* concluded that "in everything he attempted he showed skill at the game" and for this alone he should be remembered.

More significantly, we should think of Geoffrey Legge like we should of George Macaulay, as a brave sportsmen prepared to give his life for his country.

Herbert Roberts

CHAPTER 11
THE GUNNERS AT WAR: THE STORY OF ARSENAL FC AND WORLD WAR TWO

As we have already seen, by 1939 football was the most popular spectator sport in Britain. It was inevitable that the sport would suffer losses but it would be true to say that the number of high-profile losses were fewer than that suffered by cricket and rugby union. There were no footballers with the profile of Alexander Obolensky or Hedley Verity killed in World War Two and some of those players who were well known to the public did not necessarily die on the battlefield. Not that this lessens the tragedy of their loss but it does result in their demise being 'less of a story' and more likely to be lost to history. Nevertheless, most clubs did experience losses. While no one club suffered to the extent of the Edinburgh club, Heart of Midlothian in the Great War, where seven first team players died before the Armistice and others had their lives shortened by the effects of the conflict, the whole of the football world was hit hard by the impact of war.

One such club was Arsenal, the club that had enjoyed more success than any other during the 1930s. For Liverpool in the 1970/80s, Manchester United 1990/2000s and Manchester City in recent years, read Arsenal between the wars. Managed for the most part by the legendary Herbert Chapman, Arsenal won five league titles and two FA Cups during the 1930s establishing themselves as the premier team in the country and one which set the standard for others to follow. Chapman, appointed in 1925, had won two consecutive league titles with Huddersfield — the hat-trick of titles was completed in 1926 under his successor — so the appointment was seen as something of a long-term project to make Arsenal England's premier club. And so it proved. By Chapman's death in 1934, just before Arsenal won their second consecutive title, he had built a formidable team. One year after

Chapman died, Arsenal became only the second team, after Huddersfield, to win three consecutive titles.

The war, however, hit the club hard and nine of the players on Arsenal's books in 1939 were killed. Twenty-two-year-old Leslie Lack, a reserve team player, was killed by friendly fire when returning from a mission in his Spitfire in March 1943 while Bill Dean, a goalkeeper who played in wartime fixtures, thereby fulfilling his stated lifetime dream of playing for Arsenal, died in March 1942 while serving with the Royal Navy. His ship HMS *Naiad* was hit by a torpedo. Hugh Glass, 23 years old, of the Royal Fusiliers was drowned at sea in November 1942 while 25-year-old Cyril Tooze, who was also in the Royal Fusiliers, was killed by a sniper in Italy in January 1944. Others who were killed were RAF personnel. Flying Officer Sidney Pugh died in April 1944 aged 24, William Parr, a 26-year-old sergeant in the RAF who was shot down during a mission to hunt a German U-boat in March 1942 and Sub-Lieutenant Harry Cook who died in February 1943 aged 22 while training to land a plane on an aircraft carrier. They were not first team players and were largely unknown to the public.

One particularly sad case, a player who might have gone on to be a household name, is that of young Bobby Daniel. Bobby was the older brother of Welsh international Ray Daniel who was later to win the league title with Arsenal in 1952. Bobby was born in Swansea, the son of a steelworker, and was brought up in a house, now demolished, on the site of what is now the Liberty Stadium. A schoolboy international at the age of 16, a great future was predicted for the young Welshman. During the war, he became a Flight Sergeant gunner with the RAF serving as part of a seven-man crew on a Lancaster bomber, a particularly dangerous way of serving your country. The life expectancy of a crew member of a Lancaster was 22 days of flying, somewhat similar to that of an infantry officer in the Great War, and nearly 75% of crewmen flying Lancaster crews were killed in World War Two. The Lancaster crews played a very big part in the Allies' eventual victory. Berlin and Hamburg were bound to be as difficult 'nuts to crack' as the Luftwaffe had found London to be in 1940 and at first results were disappointing. On 30th May 1942, 898 air crews dropped 1500 tons of bombs which resulted in 474 German lives being lost, as well as 291 British airmen. Berlin was badly damaged between March 1943 and March 1944 when the bombing was stepped up. Raids in July and August 1943, in particular those on Hamburg, Berlin and the Ruhr Valley, adversely affected German morale. This success did come at a cost, and tragically Bobby was one of those lost. He was killed on the night of 23/24th December 1943 while on a bombing mission to Berlin, the crew never found. Like Leslie Lack, Bobby is remembered on the Runnymede Memorial along with another 20,000 airmen with no known graves.

Not all Arsenal players were involved in active service during the war. One of their biggest stars, the winger Cliff Bastin, had an interesting story. Bastin was deemed unfit for active service due to increasing deafness so he became an ARP warden in London. Not that this prevented him being named as a war casualty. In 1941, Rome Radio reported that Cliff Bastin was a prisoner of war in Italy although he had never actually left the country. Two other big stars did, however, give their lives, although not on the battlefield. The clubs centre half, Herbie Roberts and forward, Jack Lambert were key players during Arsenal's golden period and both were casualties of the war, casualties indeed that confirm that the dangers faced by people in wartime are not only present on the battlefield.

Herbie Roberts was born in Oswestry, Shropshire on 19th February 1905, the son of John Owen and Margaret Ann Roberts. On leaving school, Herbie trained as a gunsmith who spent his spare time playing amateur football for Oswestry Town where he soon made his mark. With his thick red hair combed back to reveal a high forehead, Herbie was a very noticeable figure and it wasn't long before professional clubs began to show an interest. At this time Herbie was an effective right half and quickly impressed the relatively new Arsenal manager Herbert Chapman. In December 1926, Chapman got his man, by now nearly 22 years old, for the bargain price of £200. Patrick Barclay, in his excellent biography of Chapman, describes this signing as "verging on theft", a verdict that would become indisputable in the years that followed as Herbie proved himself to be one of Chapman's best ever buys. Not that Herbie had the most straightforward introduction to top division football. He made his first team debut against Aston Villa, another giant of the English game, on 18th April 1927 but, although Arsenal won 2–1 in front of 38,000 fans, this was one of only five first-team appearances in his first two years. The turning point for Herbie came when Chapman decided to introduce a new formation, one which would change the face of football for decades to come. A change in the offside law in 1925, which made the law more relaxed, encouraged Chapman to experiment with a new system involving the centre half. He decided to use the centre half as a 'stopper' between the two full backs. The full backs were now deployed to mark the opposition wingers with the centre half dropping back into the resulting space. One of the inside forwards was deployed to drop back into the midfield area and provide the link between defence and attack. Arsenal trainer Tom Whittaker gave credit to Charlie Buchan who, he said, first suggested the ploy to Chapman. A 7–0 defeat to Newcastle United convinced Chapman that he needed to do something radical so the new system, later known as the "WM" formation, was given a trial. At first the role was given to England defender Jack Butler but, although intelligent and willing to agree to his bosses' wishes, Butler was not the man for the job. By early 1929 Herbie had made the position his own and his success soon became the talk of football. Flanked as he was by England international full backs Tom Parker (later George Male) and Eddie Hapgood, this system proved successful if not universally popular with rival fans. Herbie seemed born to the role, completely unruffled by the controversy around him and totally resistant to the barracking that he received in many opposition grounds. His role as "Policeman Roberts" made him one of the most unpopular players in the country but as his club mate Cliff Bastin said, "as an all-round player he may have had his failings, but he fitted in perfectly with the Arsenal scheme of things." In hindsight it appears that maybe the Arsenal website, which has no picture of Herbie and only the bare statistics of his career, has not given full credit to his achievements. There is no doubt that, as the first really successful centre half in the game, this shy and unassuming man helped to change the face of football. Tom Whittaker was in no doubt as to his significance when he states that "Roberts's genius came from the fact that he was intelligent, and even more important, that he did what he was told."

Success on the field followed quickly once the system had bedded in. In front of this new defensive line-up Alex James, the diminutive Scottish inside forward, ran the show ably supported by David Jack, at a cost of around £11,000, more than twice the highest ever transfer fee. Further forward Joe Hulme and Cliff Bastin raided down the touchlines and Jack Lambert, followed later by Ted Drake, converted many of the resulting goal opportunities, the most formidable side to emerge in the interwar years. Arsenal's first success under Chapman came with victory in the 1930 FA Cup Final over the manager's previous employers, Huddersfield Town, but, unfortunately, Herbie missed the final through injury. Arsenal was probably relieved that his absence was not more costly. In another game that Herbie missed shortly before the final, Arsenal drew 6–6 with Leicester City, hardly a reassuring defensive performance. Herbie was soon to make up for this disappointment. In 1931, 1933, 1934 and 1935 Arsenal were champions and in each of these seasons Herbie was a regular playing between 30 and 40 league games each season. *The Times* described his contribution as most important, using his height and strength to good effect, "His heading is the bugbear of all the forwards… He always seems to be in the way. He is the stumbling block for all kinds of attack."

The FA Cup had proved less successful than the league championship for Herbie. Not only had he missed the 1930 final through injury but when he did play, in 1932 against Newcastle United, Arsenal lost a controversial match 2–1. The 1936 final against Sheffield United provided happier memories as Arsenal, with Herbie at centre half, won a disappointing match 1–0 against their second-division opponents. Prolific centre forward Ted Drake scored the only goal in a match that saw the BBC use sports commentators for the first time. This had been a relatively poor year for Arsenal in the league where they finished 6th. Indeed, in a move that runs contrary to modern-day thinking, Arsenal played a weakened team in league matches, saving their strongest XI for the FA Cup. Such a tactic cost the club a £250 fine but the Arsenal board probably thought it a small price to pay as the Cup looked down at the directors in the boardroom.

Herbie's brilliant career was, however, coming to an end. In October 1937, in a game against Middlesbrough, Herbie broke his leg. It was his thirteenth league appearance of the season, one short of the number required in order to be awarded a medal if the team won the championship. Almost inevitably, Arsenal did win the title and Herbie, as in 1930, had to watch from the sidelines as his teammates collected a major trophy. Not that Herbie need have worried too much as sandwiched between these two disappointments were four league-title-winning medals and one FA Cup. Add to this his solitary England cap, won against Scotland in March 1931, and Herbie could look back on a marvellous career during which he played a total of 335 matches for Arsenal scoring 5 goals. Despite deserving of more England caps, Herbie could rightly consider himself an Arsenal legend and somebody whose significance in the game went further than that of winning medals and international caps.

Following his enforced retirement from the playing field, Herbie's contribution to Arsenal's continued success was not over. The following season, 1938/39, he took on the job of reserve team trainer but his time in this role was to be short-lived. With the outbreak of war Herbie joined the Royal Fusiliers (City of London Regiment) where he rose to the rank of lieutenant. Tragically he died of the skin disease, erysipelas, on 17th June 1944, aged 39, when many of his fellow soldiers were landing on the beaches of Normandy in the ultimately successful attempt to liberate Europe. Herbie was buried in Southgate Cemetery, his loss described by Patrick Barclay as,

"a fate unbefitting one of Chapman's most likeable, modest and restrained characters: a polite man who, for so diligently carrying out the role of destroyer allotted by Chapman, had been booed and jeered on every away ground and not seemed to mind a bit. He was the most prominent of nine players registered with Arsenal who perished amid the conflict."

The death of Herbie Roberts reminds us that soldiers were not only at risk on the battlefield and that the dangers they faced were not only in combat. The death of Herbie's teammate, Jack Lambert, reminds us that it was not only members of the armed forces who were at risk. In his global study of World War Two, *A World At Arms*, Gerhard Weinberg tells us that 33,000 British civilians were killed in air raids, a number which has been amended to 40,000 by the online family history website 'Ancestry'. This website breaks down the numbers by giving the total losses in many of the worst-hit cities. London, unsurprisingly, suffered most with 17,500 deaths, 14,000 by the end of 1940 alone. This was followed by Liverpool with 2,677. Other cities referenced were Birmingham, Bristol, Hull, Plymouth, Coventry, Portsmouth, Belfast and Glasgow. Witnesses have vividly described the horror of these events. Evelyn White, a nurse, recalled standing on the roof of the nurse's home and seeing the dome of St Paul's Cathedral ringed by fire, part of the 2,500 fires said to have been burning around London after this particular attack. Another witness, Peter Bennett, a Surrey schoolboy, was with his father filling up with petrol when he thought he saw the sunset. Peter soon realised that it was the London docks on fire. Meanwhile Eric Hill, a young eight-year-old schoolboy, remembers being in Bassett watching the city of Southampton being 'dive-bombed' and set alight. Many Londoners took to the tube stations during the Blitz and by the end of September 1940 177,000 Londoners were sleeping on the bedding arranged on station platforms. By now, many children had been evacuated for the second time. In the cities people tried to maintain morale, not an easy task in a city like Coventry where there were 1,400 casualties and 100 acres of the city destroyed. In Clydebank, 12,000 houses were destroyed and 35,000 people left homeless. Nevertheless, morale was maintained, possibly helped in London by the Luftwaffe bombing the whole city rather than particular pockets, a tactic which tended to pull Londoners closer together in their determination to hold out. Inevitably well-known sportsmen were among those affected. Arthur Bacon was an inside forward who, after trying his luck at Manchester City and Derby County, found success in the lower divisions of the Football League. His goal scoring record is impressive with 44 league goals in 69 games for Reading which included 6 in one game against Stoke City in a 7–3 victory in 1930/31, an achievement that remains a club record. At Coventry City this ratio was even better with 16 goals from 17 games. Bacon was killed in an air raid in Derby while working as a special constable in July 1942. As he was wearing a uniform, it was deemed to be appropriate that Bacon, and others lost in this way, could be commemorated and acknowledged as 'a war dead'. Chesterfield, one of Bacon's other clubs, included him in their memorial garden ensuring that he be remembered as laying down his life for his country.

Jack Lambert, the prolific centre forward of the Chapman years, killed in a motor accident during the blackout, was not given the same recognition. Subsequently he is not among the nine Arsenal players honoured as having given their lives for their country but his story is nonetheless very significant. Jack was born in Greasbrough near Rotherham on 22nd May 1902. The big, burly centre forward was turned down by Sheffield Wednesday in 1922 and joined his home club, Rotherham. Later that year, he moved to Yorkshire rivals Leeds United, where he stayed until 1925, before moving to another Yorkshire club, Doncaster Rovers. During this time Jack attracted the attention of Herbert Chapman, at that time managing yet another Yorkshire club, the League champions Huddersfield Town. When Chapman moved to Arsenal, he took the opportunity to sign Jack and he made his debut against Bolton on 6th September 1926.

Jack's Arsenal career got off to something of a slow start with only 1 goal in his first 16 appearances and the supporters were unconvinced of his ability. On one occasion, Chapman appealed to supporters to stop their jeering at Jack's efforts and threatened to have them removed from the ground. During these early years at the club, Jack was lucky to play 16 first-team games a season. Unsurprisingly he was omitted from the team to play Cardiff City in the 1927 FA Cup Final, a defeat which meant that the trophy left England for the only time to date. However, during 1929/30 Jack became a regular in what was now a formidable team, scoring 18 goals in 20 league appearances for his club. Not that this ensured him a place in that team for the 1930 FA Cup Final against Chapman's former club, Huddersfield Town. On the Monday before the final, Jack missed the game against Leicester City, a match which finished as a breathtaking 6–6 draw. Jack, nursing an injury, watched his replacement Dave Halliday score four goals and make a late claim for a place in the final. Halliday was a player to be reckoned with, topping the 1st division goal scoring list with 43 league goals in 1928/29. He had been signed from Sunderland for the fee of £6,000, three times that which Chapman had paid for Jack. Halliday's goal record at Sunderland was most impressive, 156 goals from 166 league appearances, and remains the third highest scorer in their history. Sunderland was a top club themselves, finishing 3rd in the league in 1926 and 1927, so Jack must have half expected to miss the final. Chapman, however, kept faith with his now fit again bustling striker. The move paid off with underdogs Arsenal winning 2–0 with Jack clinching the victory by scoring the second goal in the 88th minute after Alex James had given the London club an early lead. Receiving the ball from James in the centre circle, Jack ran half the length of the pitch before beating the goalkeeper from the edge of the penalty area. This Cup Final might be best remembered for the arrival of a 776-foot Graf Zeppelin passing over the stadium or for it being the first final where the teams walked on to the pitch side by side. But for Jack, the match signified the start of a glorious period, the peak years of his career.

The following season was even better. Before the 1930 Cup Final *The Times* had described him as a hard, fearless player who "takes his knocks in good part and never seeks to avoid them." These qualities were now shown in abundance as the forward line made up, as we have seen, of wingers Joe Hulme and Cliff Bastin supplied by inside forwards David Jack and Alex James, created enough opportunities for Jack to score a club record 38 goals in 34 matches, including a remarkable 7 hat-tricks. Arsenal won the title and effectively replaced Huddersfield Town as England's premier club. In 1931/32, Arsenal reached the Cup Final again but this time lost 2–1 to Newcastle United. Rather like Herbie Roberts, Jack did not play particularly well in this controversial final and the centre forward was guilty of missing a few good chances. Newcastle equalised with a disputed goal after the ball had, clearly, gone out of play, a verdict confirmed by photographs published later. No matter, Arsenal proceeded to win the league title in each of the following three seasons. In 1932/33, Jack contributed 14 goals to the title success but, now in his thirties, his time at the very top was coming to an end. In October 1933, after 109 goals in 161 games, he moved to Fulham where he spent the next two seasons. His importance to Arsenal was not forgotten however and when Chapman died on the eve of the 1933/34 title success, Jack was one of the pallbearers at the funeral. Along with the captain, Eddie Hapgood, he joined the other members of that title- and cup-winning forward line in carrying out this sad duty. Following his time at Fulham, Jack moved to non-league Margate, where he soon became player-manager, before returning to Arsenal in 1938 and joining Herbie Roberts as a coach with the club.

Jack was not called upon to serve on the outbreak of war but he quickly became a victim, albeit rather indirectly. Blackout regulations had been imposed in Britain two days before the declaration of war. As well as covering all windows and doors with heavy curtains or paint, all external lights such as street lights were switched off, or at least, dimmed and shielded to deflect light downward. Traffic lights were given slotted covers to deflect their beams down to the ground. From September 1939 only sidelights could be used by motor cars, although later on dipped headlights were permitted as long as the driver had headlamp covers with three horizontal slits. Moreover, a 20mph speed limit was imposed on all night drivers. Railways were also blacked out with blinds remaining closed at night and all light bulbs being painted blue. During air-raids all lights were extinguished on trains and stations had no lights whatsoever, a potentially dangerous practice for all passengers some of whom left the train at the wrong station while others left their carriage to leave where there was no station at all. The cities themselves were often in complete darkness. The MP Harold Nicolson described the situation in his diary. "When I go down to the House of Commons at 5.30, they have already darkened the building and lowered the lights... When I leave... I am startled to see a perfectly black city."

As well as annoying much of the population these regulations, enforced by civilian ARP wardens, changed people's lives more than any other single feature of the war. Angus Calder, in his book *The People's War: Britain 1939–45*, tells us that the regulations proved dangerous, as people walked into canals, fell down steps, plunged through glass roofs and toppled from railway platforms. Calder quotes a Gallup Poll published in January 1940, which showed that by that stage around one person in every five could have sustained an injury, albeit usually minor, as a result of the blackout. It was particularly dangerous for drivers and pedestrians out after nightfall. Indeed, it is now known that car accidents doubled from 1939, largely as a result of blackouts and the ban on the use of headlights. And to what end? The King's surgeon, Wilfred Trotter wrote an article for the *British Medical Journal* which argued that the blackout did more to help the Luftwaffe than protect British citizens. He warned that "by frightening the nation into blackout regulations, the Luftwaffe was able to kill 600 British citizens a month without ever taking to the air, at a cost to itself of exactly nothing."

On the evening of December 7th, 1940, Jack became a tragic victim of the blackout when he was killed in a traffic accident at Enfield in north London. He is not listed as a war dead as only civilians killed by enemy action, such as Arthur Bacon, are remembered in this way. For World War Two, the Commonwealth War Graves Commission list 67,000 Commonwealth Civilians who died as a result of enemy action. Jack is afforded no such recognition. Yet it can be argued that the 38-year-old ex-Arsenal centre forward, hero of two league titles and two FA Cup finals, should be remembered if only as an example of one of the many different sacrifices made by ordinary men and women in the war against fascism.

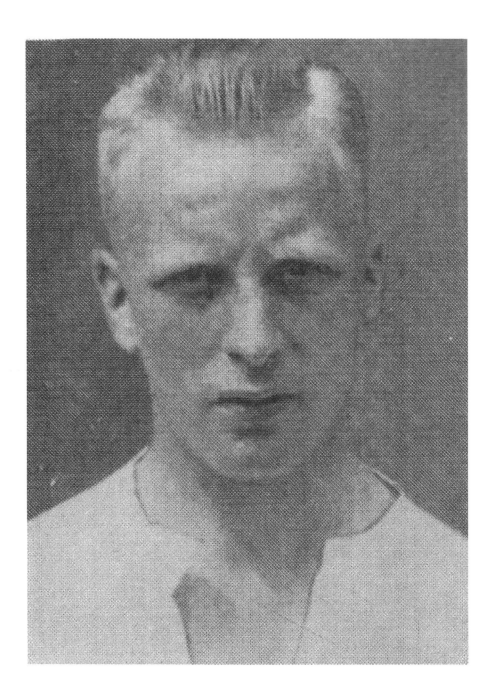

Thomas Cooper

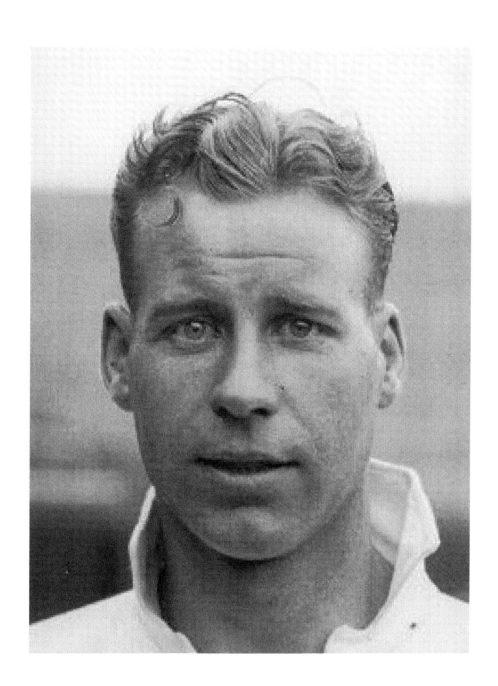

Harry Goslin

CHAPTER 12
INSPIRATIONAL LEADERS: ENGLAND FOOTBALL CAPTAINS AT WAR: HARRY GOSLIN AND TOM COOPER

For many sportsmen the war must have had a very unreal quality. For many, their initial training at least was done in various parts of Britain and some never left the shores of their homeland. Towns where training took place became very lively with thousands of would-be soldiers, sailors and airmen descending on places where many of the young men were away and women left at home. Blackpool in particular was the place for these young men to be where, according to Eamon Dunphy, every pub operated as if it were New Year's Eve. Men, aware that their future might be bleak, lived very much for the present and were determined to make the most of what Blackpool had to offer. As we saw in an earlier chapter, Dunphy tells us that "all the scum, all the prostitutes, all the villains came to Blackpool... There were 80,000 airmen there and at least as many Yanks." And not a bomb fell on Blackpool during the duration of the war. Other towns, although not as notorious as Blackpool, had a similar experience. While these men partied, unsure of their future or even their survival, some sportsmen were lucky in being given work which kept them away from the firing line, often as physical training instructors or other non-combative roles. It was thought by some, that footballers in particular, were 'looked after' in this respect.

Although many footballers were found roles which kept them away from the firing line, this was not the case for every player. All three services, the Army, Royal Navy and RAF saw professional, highly respected, footballers killed in action. Alan Fowler was a schoolboy international and an accomplished striker, first for his hometown club of Leeds United and then Swindon Town for whom the diminutive five feet six inches forward scored 102 goals in 224 appearances. Quick thinking with good ball control, this natural sportsman remains the twelfth highest scorer in Swindon's history and topped the club's scoring chart for three of the six seasons spent at the club. Fowler began the war impressively by joining 'The Dorsets', part of the 43rd Wessex Division, and by saving the lives of three fellow soldiers when priming grenades. In 1944, he was made a sergeant and was involved in the D-Day landings. On July 10th, 1944, 37-year-old Alan Fowler was killed in the attempt to liberate Martot and Eterville, part of the wider effort to capture Hill 112 and control Normandy. It appears that he was tragically killed by British fighter planes dropping two bombs on their own men. His grief-stricken father, Joseph, an assistant groundsman at Swindon's County Ground, died three years later still mourning the loss of his talented son. Joe Coen, a Scottish goalkeeper, joined Luton Town from Celtic in 1934 and played 153 times for his new club. A bright boy who had studied to join the Civil Service before committing to football, Joe trained to be a pilot when war broke out. Tragically 29-year-old Joe Coen was killed on 15th October 1941, two months before he was due to qualify as a fully trained pilot, when he was involved in a mid-air collision. The Royal Navy too could point to the loss of a footballer, albeit one who had retired from the game. Charlie Sillett had been a dependable full back with second division Southampton, whom he captained in the 1937/8 season, eventually appearing 183 times for the club. Enlisting as a gunner, Charlie Sillett died when the SS *Corvus*, part of a convoy attacked by two German U-boats, was hit by a torpedo seven miles from Lizard Point, Cornwall. He did, however, leave a footballing legacy. Both his sons, Peter and John, played for Southampton and Chelsea. Peter won the league title with Chelsea in 1955 and played three times for England in that year. John, not as accomplished a player, was also part of Chelsea's first title-winning squad but is best remembered as the manager of Coventry City's FA Cup winning team of 1987. Like Charlie Sillett, Harry Goslin was a one club footballer who had a solid career followed by a dangerous war that was to end in tragedy. Harry was born in Willington, Cheshire on 9th November 1909. Playing at right half, Harry was spotted by Bolton Wanderers while with Boots Athletic, a team based just outside

Nottingham. A fee of £25 was agreed and Harry joined one of England's oldest clubs. Moreover, Bolton were a club with a recent record of success having won the FA Cup three times in the 1920s. Indeed, for the most part, Bolton Wanderers have remained a club to be reckoned with having spent 72 years in the top division of the Football League, the longest run of any club yet to become champions. The current plight of this great club is not one which reflects their proud history.

However, when Harry joined them Bolton's period of pre-eminence was coming to an end. The signs were there from the outset with the team losing 7–2 to Liverpool on Harry's debut. In 1932/3 season, the club hit a new low when they were relegated to the second division. Harry was playing regularly and becoming one of the mainstays of the team, one which looked to a quick return to the top tier. In 1933/4 they finished third, just missing out on promotion, but the following year they made no mistake finishing second behind Brentford to return to the top division. Harry played in every game that season and made a huge contribution to the club's success. This was recognised in 1936 when he was made club captain. After narrowly avoiding relegation in 1937, Harry led Bolton to seventh and eighth in Division One in the next two seasons. Playing in every game in the 1938/39 season, Harry was generally regarded as one of the best defenders in the country. He was also somebody who looked to the future and, realising that his career would quickly come to an end once he moved into his thirties, Harry opened a sports shop in Bolton with the intention of it providing financial security in later years.

However, during the 1938/39 season, matters other than consolidating his club in the top half of the table and ensuring the success of his sports shop were occupying Harry's mind. Harry was aware of the dangerous international situation and was one of the first sportsmen to act on his concerns. In 1939, before the end of the season, Harry joined the territorials and did his utmost to ensure that others joined him. On April 8th, 1939, as the football season was drawing to a close, Harry addressed his home crowd at Burnden Park before the game against Sunderland. He left the supporters in no doubt as to where their duty lay.

"We are facing a national emergency. But this danger can be met if everybody keeps a cool head and knows what to do. This is something you can't leave to the other fellow, everybody has a share to do."

Harry's words, reminiscent of the attempts at recruitment on the outbreak of the Great War, were not delivered in vain. He persuaded fourteen other Bolton players to join the territorials and before the hostilities were over, 32 out of 35 Bolton Wanderers players were in uniform with the remainder involved in other, war-related work. As for Harry himself, once war began in earnest, he found himself a sergeant in the 53rd (Bolton) Field Regiment, Royal Artillery.

Not that this unofficial recruiting and subsequent enlisting brought an immediate end to his football career. During the early years of the war, Harry guested for Leeds United, Bradford City, Norwich City and Chelsea as well as playing for Bolton Wanderers when he was available. More impressively, Harry made a belated appearance on the international stage. In December 1939, he was selected to play at right half for England in the unofficial wartime international against Scotland. He was named as captain and successfully led his country to a 2–1 victory. Harry faced the same opposition in both May and October of 1941, games which were won by England 3–1 and 2–0 respectively. Later in October 1941, Harry played his part in the 2–1 victory over Wales. Unofficial as these games were, they gave just a taste of the service Harry might have given to the English national side in peacetime had he been allowed the opportunity. His leadership qualities came to the fore, something that was to be confirmed in the heat of battle.

However, Harry's war had little to do with football. His first significant contribution was to come during the evacuation of Dunkirk in May/June 1940. Here he played an important role in the rescue of over 338,000 troops between 26th May and the 4th June. Following this, Harry was promoted to lieutenant and sent to East Anglia to patrol possible German landing sites. Returning to France, Harry was credited with destroying four enemy tanks on 12th May 1941. By now a seasoned and experienced war veteran, in the summer of 1942 Harry set sail for Egypt where he was to experience more action in a very different, but equally significant, theatre of war.

On arriving in Egypt, Harry and the 53rd Field Regiment came under the command of Lieutenant-General Bernard Montgomery and the Eighth Army. Here, between 23rd October and 11th November 1942, in the Egyptian desert, they would take part in one of the most famous battles of the war, The Battle of El Alamein. Their first task was to repel Field Marshall Rommel's attack on Alam el Halfa thereby preventing the Axis from advancing further into Egypt. This they did between 30th August and 5th September and so, on 23rd October, Montgomery launched 'Operation Lightfoot', a very heavy attack which initially the Germans resisted. Then, on 2nd November, Montgomery launched 'Operation Supercharge' which would attempt, following aerial bombardment, to draw Axis troops out into the open. By the 4th November they had succeeded in this objective and by 12th November Harry, with the 8th Army, had recaptured Tobruk. The cost had been enormous for both sides and Harry was lucky to survive. The British had lost 13,500 casualties and 500 tanks, although 350 were repaired and returned to battle later. The Germans suffered more and approximately half of Rommel's 100,000 strong army was killed, wounded or taken captive while they also lost 450 tanks and 1,000 guns.

Following the success of El Alamein, Harry was moved to Baghdad, Kirkuk and Kifri where he was based for a total of five months. From here the 8th Army, including the 53rd (Bolton) Field Regiment, Royal Artillery, moved to Italy to face some of the most difficult fighting of the war. Back in Britain, the exploits of British soldiers fighting in Italy was often underrated and even overlooked but in subsequent years historians have attempted to put right this misconception. Not that the difficulties were apparent on arrival in Italy as progress towards the Sangro River in the autumn of 1943 was relatively straightforward. But the battle to cross the Sangro River was anything but straightforward. These battles in Italy were the last fought by Montgomery as commander of the 8th Army and they were to test him to the full. It was the aim of the Allied troops to capture Rome, with the 5th Army attacking from the west and Montgomery's 8th Army moving in from the east. The German army was determined to halt the advance and fighting began around the Sangro River. Starting on November 20th, at first the British had some success and, supported by 652 guns and the Desert Air Force, they crossed the river and severely damaged the German 65th Division. After weeks of heavy fighting, the Germans withdrew north of the Moro River. The Moro River runs from the central mountain spine of Italy to the Adriatic coast south of Ortona. The German defences here were a centrepiece of their Winter Line. It was Montgomery's intention to punch through the Winter Line, capture Ortona, then Pescara and advance to Rome. On the 4th December, the offensive began and it was here that Harry was tragically killed.

Throughout the next week the German positions were attacked and several bridgeheads were established. Both sides were pinned down by continuous combat operations, the British being held up in a narrow pit called 'The Gully'. The conditions faced by the troops were dreadful and reminiscent of those associated with 1917 rather than 1943. One Canadian soldier said that the land beyond the Moro River was "a landscape that seemed almost lunar in its desolation where men lived and died in unremembered ways." The New Zealand Commander, Brigadier Kippenberger, thought that "I had not seen men so exhausted since Flanders. Their faces were grey." The winter rain and swollen streams had turned fields into "mud soup" as vehicles slid around on greasy tracks. The river became a 1000-foot-wide torrent which washed away bridges and destroyed anything in its path. It was here, after a week of fighting with the Germans having retreated to higher ground, that Harry was hit by splinters from a shell. This shell had exploded in a tree above the 'slit trench' where Harry was taking shelter from shells or bombs exploding on the ground. These trenches could be effective protection but not from shells exploding overhead, even when it was caught up in a tree. Harry battled for four days in an effort to survive but on the 18th December 1943 this highly respected, much-loved footballer succumbed to his injuries. He was 34 years old.

Despite the casualties, the Eighth Army carried on with vicious hand-to-hand fighting taking place in the streets of Ortona. The heavily bombed streets had become a debris-filled maze and were littered with mines and booby traps, a most dangerous place to wage war. But when

Ortona and Ville Grande were captured by the end of December it looked as if the Eighth Army only needed to strike one more blow at Orsogna to complete the breakthrough and move on to Rome. However, it was not to be. By 26th December, the Eighth Army was exhausted. A blizzard quickly set in and the conditions became impossible as drifting snow, sleet and biting winds ensured that communications were almost impossible. Montgomery realised the hopelessness of the situation and advised General Sir Harold Alexander, commander of the 15th Army Group, to call off the offensive. This he did on the last day of 1943. The capture of Rome would have to wait until after the final Battle of Monte Cassino in May 1944. It was only then that future Liverpool manager, Bob Paisley, and his colleagues could enter the city in their tanks.

Harry was the only Bolton Wanderers footballer to be killed in World War Two and, as such, received much well-deserved recognition. The Wartime Wanderers captured the essence of his appeal to the club's supporters and to football supporters throughout the country.

"Goslin was a tall, athletic, ramrod-straight man with piercing blue eyes whose physical presence combined with his pleasant but firm personality made him an ideal choice for club captain. Under his astute leadership the club's fortunes improved."

At the time of his death, Harry's reputation and the respect in which he was held appeared to be secure. He left a wife and two young children to preserve his memory. His son, Bob, continued to do this in a way that might well have pleased his father, serving as a senior police officer in Bolton. Bob later became Assistant Chief Constable of South Yorkshire Police Force and then Deputy Chief Constable of Cambridgeshire. Yet it seems that as a true war hero, Harry Goslin has been somewhat overlooked. Perhaps *The Bolton Evening News* can remind us of the man who still lies buried in the Sangro River War Cemetery.

"Harry Goslin was one of the finest type of professional football breeds. Not only in the personal sense but for the club's sake, and the game's sake. I regret his life has had to be sacrificed in the cause of war."

Fine and much-loved footballer though he certainly was, Harry Goslin cannot lay claim to being the best-known professional footballer to lose his life in World War Two. That distinction must surely go to the Derby County, Liverpool and England full back and captain, Tom Cooper. Even today, eighty years after his death, Tom can be considered to be one of England's greatest full backs, certainly if you consider only those playing in the interwar years. In the era of Herbert Chapman's stopper centre half, Tom was a reminder that defenders, too, could play cultured football. Although one of the toughest tacklers in the league, Tom was much more than just a 'stopper'. He was a good passer of the heavy ball on pitches that sometimes resembled a paddy field, particularly when playing in the depths of winter on a wet Saturday afternoon.

Tom was born on the 9th April 1904 in Stoke-on-Trent, the seventh of eight children born to Stephen James and Sarah Ann Cooper. The family originally lived in Fenton, part of the county borough of Stoke-on-Trent where his father worked as a bricklayer. Although he didn't originally plan to be a professional footballer, especially when his studies took him away from playing, Tom did play locally, first for Longton and then Trentham. In August 1924, the twenty-year-old defender signed for Port Vale for the sum of £20, a bargain for the second-division club. Over the next two seasons, Tom played in 32 league games and the club finished a very creditable eighth on both occasions. In March 1926, before the season had ended, fellow second-division rivals Derby County paid £2,500 to lure Tom to the Baseball Ground. Originally Derby had offered £2,000 which was refused so they began to look elsewhere. Having no luck with their approach to Hull City's Jock Gibson, County returned for Tom, a decision that they never regretted. Just a few months after Tom's arrival, Derby were promoted as runners-up in Division 2 and over the next few years, they consolidated their position in the top division by finishing 12th, 4th and

6th before securing the runners-up spot behind Wednesday (later Sheffield Wednesday) in 1930.

By 1931, Tom had been made captain and over the next three years he led the team to respectable positions in the table without ever threatening to win the title. In all Tom made 267 appearances for 'The Rams' consolidating his reputation as England's best full back, an opinion which was strengthened by his performances at international level. Tom made his international debut at Windsor Park, Belfast on 22nd October 1927 where he played at right back in the 2–0 defeat. The 521st footballer to represent England, Tom was informed of his selection in a way that seems quite bizarre today. He received a postcard which congratulated him on his selection followed by the words "bring your own soap and towel." Tom was to win a total of 15 caps for his country, an impressive total given the number of international fixtures at this time, and it would surely have been more but for two serious knee injuries which resulted in both cartilages being removed. Tom tasted success in these games as England won the Home International Championship in 1931/32 and shared the title in his last international season, 1934/35. Indeed, for his last four internationals Tom was given the highest accolade, that of captaining his country. A 3–0 victory over Scotland at Wembley in April 1934 and a 4–0 win against Wales at Ninian Park the following September were played either side of two defeats in Eastern Europe during May, both with 2–1 score lines, to Hungary and Czechoslovakia.

His international career over and injuries beginning to take their toll, one could be forgiven for thinking that Tom was coming to the end of his career. After all, he had reached the dreaded age for sportsmen of 30 years. But it was at this point that Liverpool, another first-division club, contacted Derby County with an offer. A fee of £7,500 was agreed and, in December 1934, Tom was on his way to Anfield. This was not a vintage Liverpool side. His first two seasons were spent successfully fighting against relegation but in both 1937/38 and 1938/39 he was able to help Liverpool to an eleventh-place finish. Tom's contribution was noted by the fans and he quickly acquired the nickname 'Snowy', due to his blond hair. The club acknowledged his importance to the team in their programme notes, confirming that his signing was, "… the event of the season. His fee is a record one for a full back. Cooper is a back who, although on the robust side, is one of the fairest men in the game. He is 'fair' in a double sense being silvery thatched — 'Snowball' some of the fans call him." With Cooper and Blenkinsop in the side, Liverpool will possess the most distinguished pair of backs in the land. Well done, Liverpool!!"

Away from the football field, Tom confirmed his all-round sporting ability. There is no argument that, in the north of England, he was the best golfer in the football world. He won the Merseyside Professional Association Footballer's Golf Championship three years running, completing the hat-trick in October 1938. This was an impressive achievement given the competition but by the time that the next golf championship was due to take place more serious matters were afoot. Tom played his 160th and last peacetime game for Liverpool, as he had his first, against Chelsea. The results reflected Liverpool's improvement during Tom's time at the club, a 4–1 defeat at Stamford Bridge in 1934 and a 1–0 victory at Anfield in 1939.

With the outbreak of war, Tom became a sergeant in the 9th Battalion, The King's Regiment (Liverpool), and served with the Military Police. This did mean that Tom was available, in part, to play in the regional wartime leagues set up when the professional leagues ceased at the start of the war. He played a total of 9 wartime fixtures for Liverpool in the Western Division, the last being a 6–3 victory over Crewe in March 1940. Tom also guested for Wrexham during this period but his wartime duties took precedence. Tragically, this service was not to last long. On 25th June 1940, when riding his despatch motorcycle, Tom collided with a lorry, or possibly a double-decker bus, in Aldeburgh and was killed outright. Following this tragic death of a well-known footballer, an enquiry found that from this point onward it was compulsory that despatch riders wear a crash helmet.

Tom was buried in Nottingham Road Cemetery, Derby, with a Commonwealth War Grave headstone. A total of 76 Liverpool FC players and staff enlisted during World War Two and Tom was the only one to be killed. Nevertheless, Tom had the unfortunate distinction of being the first recorded footballer fatality of the war. With a total of 459 appearances in league and cup, most at the highest level, we should try to ensure that this fine footballer and man not be forgotten.

Julius Hirsch

CHAPTER 13
FOOTBALL AND THE HORRORS OF THE HOLOCAUST:
THE STORY OF JULIUS HIRSCH

When historians, writers and film makers look back on World War Two, one event stands out, defining the horror of this particular war and setting it apart from any other conflict, however dreadful. This event was the Holocaust of which so much has been written but which still leaves us in a state of disbelief when we learn of the horrors faced by Jewish communities in the years leading up to, and during, World War Two. A now generally accepted figure of six million Jewish men, women and children put to death in camps that, when referred to today, eighty plus years after the outbreak of war, still has the capacity to shock us to the core. Names such as Auschwitz, Bergen-Belsen and Dachau are fixed in the public consciousness, rightfully reminding us of our responsibility never to allow such an event to occur again. There were other mass killings in history's bloodiest century, each one contributing to the horrors of warfare, but nothing chills the public mood quite like the Holocaust. A genocide carried out through the use of pogroms, mass shootings, labour camps and extermination in gas chambers across Germany and German-occupied Europe resulted in the deaths of around two-thirds of Europe's Jewish population.

It is instructive at this point to examine more closely what this actually means in raw figures. By 1939 there were Jewish communities all over Europe, as there had been for centuries. Indeed, some communities dated back more than 1,000 years, and there had been previous attempts to persecute Jews in many European countries. The figures confirming the number of Jews in some European countries in 1939 are approximately as follows: Poland 3,225,000; Germany 554,000; Russia 1,300,000; Romania 796,000; France 320,000; United

Kingdom 345,000; more than 20,000 Jewish communities, large and small, were destroyed between 1940 and 1945. Hitler's policy towards these communities should have come as no surprise as justification for his actions were clearly expressed in *Mein Kampf* in 1925. In this book he stated that "My conduct is in accordance with the will of the Almighty creator… In standing guard against the Jew, I am defending the handiwork of the Lord." Despite further efforts at 'mass ethnic cleansing' in other parts of the world during the post-war years, they have done nothing to lessen the horror of Hitler's 'Final Solution'.

The loss of many European sports stars as a result of these dreadful events has, understandably, given the scale of the losses, led to many of their names being almost forgotten by the general public. Historians have tried to rectify this. One such historian is Agnes Grunwald-Spier in her book *Who Betrayed the Jews? The Realities of Nazi Persecution in the Holocaust* in which a number of Jewish footballers are referenced. We are told of Jozsef Braun, a right sided midfielder or half back who won 9 championships and 2 cups with MTK Budapest in the Hungarian League. Winner of the Hungarian Player of the Year when only 19 years old, Braun went on to win 27 caps for Hungary, scoring 11 goals, 2 of which came in a remarkable 7–1 victory over Italy in 1924. This was an Italian side managed by the great Vittorio Pozzo, the manager who was to lead Italy to two World Cup triumphs in 1934 and 1938. Later a successful coach, Braun died in a forced labour camp in Kharkiv, Ukraine on 26th February 1943. Another Hungarian, Arpad Weisz, was a former international who managed both Inter Milan, twice, and Bologna to the Italian championship. He and his family perished at Auschwitz in 1944. Poland gained their first ever international victory in Stockholm when the hosts were defeated 2–1. The scorer of Poland's first goal was the tall, rangy defender Jozef Klotz, one of Poland's first football stars, who played for both Jutrzenka Krakow and Maccabi Warszawa. Klotz was shot by Nazis in the Warsaw Ghetto in 1941 but has recently (2019) been remembered in a ceremony prior to a European Championship qualifying match between Poland and Israel with the presentation of a signed shirt to his nephew. Also playing in Poland's first ever international match alongside Klotz was the tricky, fast-footed winger, Leon Sperling who was shot in 1941, this time in the Lwow Ghetto in Lviv, Ukraine. Another compatriot, Antoni Lyko, a striker for Warsaw Krakow, although not a Jew but somebody seen as a political opponent, was shot in the head by the Nazi guard at Auschwitz, also in 1941. This notorious camp also saw the death in a gas chamber, in April 1943, of Eddy Hamel, the first Jew to play for AFC Ajax. Those conducting these dreadful deeds were not immune from retribution. The French national football team captain, Alexandre Villaplane, worked actively with the Gestapo and rose to become an SS lieutenant. He was executed by the Allies in December 1944.

Perhaps the greatest soccer-playing Jew of them all was Bela Guttmann. Guttmann played for Hakoah Vienna, champions of the world's first professional soccer league in Austria in 1925 and the first foreign side to win on English soil when they defeated West Ham United 5–0 in 1923. When Guttmann made his international debut for Hungary in 1921, he was one of six Jews in the team. Indeed, both the Austrian and Hungarian national teams, the dominant forces in European football in the 1920s, relied heavily on its Jewish contingent. When his successful playing career was over, Guttmann turned to management. Once again, like many other Jewish managers at the time, he proved to be a great success. He was the last manager to manage Hakoah before the club was shut down by the Nazis in 1938. Guttmann then moved to Ujpest FC where he guided his club to the Hungarian league title and the Miltropa Cup, a competition contested by clubs from the states previously part of the Austro-Hungarian empire and one of the first international club cup competitions. After the war, he managed in Brazil, Portugal and Hungary winning trophies in each, before guiding Benfica to consecutive successful European Cup trophies in 1961 and 1962 — a team containing, among others, the great Eusebio. Guttmann was the leading light among a group of Jewish managers revolutionising football in Europe. The fact that Bela Guttmann was able to achieve this is remarkable given the dangers that he faced during the war. Dave Rich, in his article, 'How The Holocaust Swept Away European Jewish Soccer' published in 'Forward' in 2018, tells us that during the spring and summer of 1944, when the Nazis deported over 400,000 Hungarian Jews to their deaths, Guttmann was hiding in an attic above his future brother-in-law's apartment on the outskirts of Budapest. He later escaped from a forced labour camp to avoid deportation and almost certain death. His family were not so lucky. His father, sister, nephew and other members of his extended family were all murdered in the Holocaust.

One event that specifically links the game of football with World War Two, the use of concentration camps and the Holocaust was the notorious 'Death Match' which took place on 9th August 1942 and involved both Russian and German soldiers. Following Germany's declaration of war and the subsequent invasion of the USSR, the city of Kiev was captured along with approximately 600,000 soldiers. There was a total and strict occupation which included the shutting down of schools and universities and the use of males of fifteen years and upwards as forced labour. However, the German commander, Major Eberhardt, decided that Kiev was a difficult place to police so he decided that it was necessary to placate the city's population. He therefore decided that a football team be formed from the top division championship team Dynamo Kyiv and Locomotive Kyiv from the third tier of competition. Three players were selected from Locomotive and the rest from Dynamo, mostly professional footballers who had hitherto been working at the City Bread Factory Number 1 whilst under occupation. This team was to be called FC Start, meaning 'the start of something new'.

The new team got off to an impressive start and during June and July 1942 they played a total of seven matches winning them all with a goal ratio of 37–8. On August 6th, a match was arranged against Flakelf, a team made up of German Luftwaffe air defence and artillery footballers. FC Start did immense damage to the idea of a German 'superior race' by winning 5–1, thereby ensuring the need for a rematch. This time Flakelf were taking no chances against their opponents who they referred to as *"untermenschen"*, meaning subhuman, and strengthened their team considerably.

What actually happened in this return fixture, played in front of approximately 2,500 spectators on August 9th, is unclear. Soviet authorities later claimed that the referee was an SS officer who ignored fouls committed by the German team and disallowed perfectly good goals scored by the Kiev players. Another SS officer, during the half-time break, allegedly threatened FC Start players with death if they did not allow the German team to win. Soviet authorities later claimed that after the match all the Kiev players were shot by the SS and this version became the accepted truth following the USSR re-taking of Kiev in the autumn of 1943. Novels and even a film, *Third Time*, seen by 32 million people in the USSR, were based on this account. Other versions of the events following the game included tales of players being tortured, executed or being sent to concentration camps. Two players were even reported as having escaped, although details of how and where is unclear. During the Brezhnev era, the event was used for propaganda purposes and the emphasis was on Soviet heroism. Details were given of four players who had been killed and they were posthumously awarded the 'Medal for Courage' while surviving players, of whom it was now admitted existed, were awarded the 'Medal for Battle Merit'. Monuments were put up in the city and the Zenit Stadium was renamed FC Start Stadium. By 1985, this story had evolved further with the result now given as a victory for FC Start following a penalty shoot-out while confirming the execution of some players and the involvement of a referee who was a member of the Gestapo. Following the fall of communism, the story changed yet again and on the 50th anniversary of the match, the use of SS/Gestapo officers as referees was denied and, although there were up to five murders in the coming five months, these players were arrested nine days after the match. The football match itself was played in a spirit of fairness with no heavily armed soldiers or dogs in attendance.

What was the truth? Recent research, including that carried out by Andy Dougan for his book *Dynamo: Defending the Honour of Kiev*, does conclude that there were guard dogs at the game; a red shirt was part of the kit worn by FC Start in order to highlight their communist beliefs, and that the fixture was something of a revenge match where the Nazi salute was given before kick-off. But it would appear that the dreadful executions took place a short time later. Following the game, at an after-match party, the players mixed and drank together, and on the 16th August, FC Start played another match, this time against Rukh, which they won 8–0. Two days later, the horrific events began to unfold. The Gestapo arrested eight of the FC Start players and they were forced to spend three weeks in a Gestapo prison before being sent to Syrets Concentration Camp on the outskirts of Kiev. Here they were given hard labour for the next eighteen months before at least three were shot. The original story does still, however, resurface from time to time. John Huston's 1981 film, *Escape to Victory*, is based on the Death Match. Even as late as 2012, the film *Match* by Russian director Andrei Malyukov was based on the original version, ignoring eyewitness accounts. Perhaps the real significance of this event is that it confirms how sport can be used in the propaganda war as two totalitarian states fought leading to mass slaughter on an unprecedented scale. One survivor, Makar Honcharenko, was of the opinion that those who died did not do so because of football but as part of a grand-scale massacre. In that respect, the demise of these footballers was no different from any of the other deaths in this worldwide catastrophe.

The fate of some Jewish footballers in World War Two is particularly well illustrated by the story of Julius Hirsch, the first Jewish footballer to represent Germany at international level. Along with his club and international teammate, Gottfried Fuchs, they are the only German Jews to represent Germany on the football field. By 1918 both were football and war heroes but by 1939 they had been forgotten, wiped out of history by the Nazi regime, in Julius' case, a probable victim of the Auschwitz concentration camp. Only since the 1990s has Julius Hirsch been rediscovered, helped by the author Brian Blickenstaff in his book *War, Auschwitz and the Tragic Tale of Germany's Jewish Soccer Hero*. More recently Werner Skrentny has produced a biography which became the basis of an article written by respected *Daily Telegraph* football journalist Sam Wallace, an article which appeared in the *Daily Telegraph* in January 2020. Such is the recent interest in his story that a mural containing his image has been constructed on the West Stand at Stamford Bridge, the home of Chelsea FC, a club formed only a few years before Julius' football career began. Julius is one of three names engraved on the memorial alongside fellow prisoners of war, Ron Jones, a member of the 1st Battalion, Welch Regiment of Newport,

South Wales and Arpad Weisz, a Hungarian Jewish footballer who played for and coached, among others, Inter Milan. Jones, a goalkeeper while a prisoner, survived both Auschwitz and the 900-mile Death March, to eventually return to Wales where he became known as 'the oldest poppy seller' in the country. He died in September 2019 at the grand old age of 102 with the award of a BEM and the respect of everybody who knew him. Weisz was not so lucky. His wife and two sons were murdered on their arrival at Auschwitz in 1942 while Weisz was kept alive only to be exploited as a worker for the next 18 months. He died in the camp in January 1944.

Julius Hirsch was born on 7th April 1892, the seventh and last child of Jewish textile merchant Berthold Hirsch and his wife Emma, a hatmaker. The family were part of a thriving working class in Karlsruhe and lived in the Akadamiestrasse area in the heart of the city. Emma suffered with serious health issues following fourteen pregnancies, seven which resulted either in still birth or infant deaths. The result was that Emma suffered a stroke and the early onset of an early form of dementia which led to her being admitted periodically to a mental institution in Achern. Indeed, Julius was born at the Hospital and Sanatorium Illenau. Despite this difficult start to his life, it was clear that the young Julius had a particular talent on the football field. By the time he was ten, his local club, Karlsruhe FV (KFV), a club founded by a Jew, Walther Bensamann, had secured a commitment that Julius play for them. Football was an amateur sport in Germany until 1945 but under the table payments and generous expenses were commonplace. Sam Wallace tells us that, once Julius became a German international, he was paid 10 Deutschmarks a day and complimentary second-class rail tickets. Nevertheless, it was imperative that footballers had another trade or profession so Julius became an apprentice in a leatherworks company which specialised in furniture.

Julius made his debut for KFV at the age of 17 in 1909 and the following year his club won the German championship. Playing alongside Julius in a legendary attacking formation were fellow Jew, Gottfried Fuchs, three years older than Julius, and the Karlsruhe-born Friedrich 'Fritz' Forderer. According to Blickenstaff, film excerpts exist of KFV playing the reigning champions, local rivals Phoenix

Karlsruhe, and both Julius and Gottfried Fuchs are clearly visible with Julius playing as usual on the left side of the attack, running in his distinctive, head-down, rather stooped style. A crowd of around 8,000 is watching the rival clubs clash, both based in the same city, one of only three cities to boast two championship-winning clubs, Berlin and Munich being the others. At this stage of his career, Julius was being guided by the English manager, William Townley. Townley had been a footballer of note in England and was the scorer of the first hat-trick in FA Cup Final history when he achieved this feat for Blackburn Rovers in their 6–1 victory over The Wednesday (later renamed Sheffield Wednesday) in 1890. He scored again the following year when his team defeated Notts County 3–1. Only Ian Rush, with five, has scored more goals in FA Cup Finals than Billy Townley. Capped twice for England, he joined Manchester City but was forced to retire with a head injury. Townley then turned his attention to coaching and soon became a well-known figure in continental football in the early years of the century before being imprisoned in Germany during the Great War. As well as KFV, he coached SpVgg Furth, Bayern Munich and, in the 1924 Olympics, the Dutch national team. A left-sided player himself, Townley quickly recognised Julius' ability to slice through defences and his lethal left-foot shot, a shot which led to Julius being nicknamed 'Juller'.

In 1911, Julius made his international debut, the first of seven appearances for his country for whom he scored on four occasions between 1911 and 1913. Seven might not seem a great number but the German record in 1918 was only eighteen as so few international matches were played during this period. The war, of course, brought international football to a temporary halt and Julius' friend and fellow German-Jewish footballer Fuchs played in only six internationals while Fritz Forderer played in only two. Along with his two colleagues, Julius did play in the 1912 Olympics where Germany lost to Austria and Hungary but did beat Russia 16–0 with Fuchs scoring a remarkable ten goals. Julius nearly missed the Olympics as he was due to complete a year of compulsory military service at that time. His most memorable appearance came in March 1912 in the 5–5 draw with the Netherlands. Julius scored four of the goals with Fuchs scoring the other, a huge contribution from Germany's two Jewish players. By now the two friends were playing a crucial part in the football boom that was taking place in Germany, one of the last European countries to experience this enthusiasm for the sport.

In 1913, Julius left his home city and signed for SpVgg. This was seen as a good fit as, not only was he joining a successful club who won the championship in Julius' first season, but it was a town in which many Jews had settled and they were, at least on the surface, welcomed. Furth had been a refuge for Jews since 1528 when many were expelled from Nuremberg. This became even more significant after the Thirty Years War and, by the early years of the nineteenth century, the town had seven synagogues with Jews making up one fifth of the population. Julius probably felt at home here as the Jews in the town were a tight knit group, middle class but socially and culturally distinct. They were not second-class citizens and had been assimilated successfully in pre-1914 Germany. Jews could both serve as magistrates and vote in all elections whether local, state or national and many were leading figures in medicine, the law and in teaching. Football itself had a liberal attitude regarding race and culture. Physical fitness was paramount to the Prussian image in the nineteenth as well as the twentieth century and so football was encouraged as an approved pastime for all young males. Yet underneath this façade there was a less palatable picture. The historian Niall Ferguson talks of "the sneer in the streets", the "scornful look" and "recurrent contempt." He quotes the author, Jakob Wassermann, who, although born in Furth, saw himself "as only a guest." In 1921, Ferguson tells us, Wassermann predicted that Germans already "want a scapegoat."

The club went on to great success following the Great War, winning the German League in 1926 and 1929 as well as the German Cup on four occasions between 1923 and 1931. The club could count among its most devoted supporters the young Heimat Kissinger, later better known as the USA Secretary of State Henry Kissinger. Kissinger's biographer, Niall Ferguson, tells us of the SpVgg rivalry with Nuremberg, steeped in the history of the area, which he, as a proud Scotsman, sees as something akin to that of the Glasgow clubs, Celtic and Rangers. Ferguson also describes in detail Kissinger's love of football tactics and defensive formations, so much so that young Henry's parents eventually banned him from attending matches. Kissinger himself recognises the importance of football to the people of his home town saying that "Furth was to soccer as Green Bay was to American Football." For Julius, the 22-year-old German-Jewish left winger, already the holder of two championship titles, life must have appeared full of promise until war severely interrupted his career and set off a train of events that was to end in tragedy.

The Great War itself was a period of very mixed emotions for Julius. He joined the German army in 1914 and served in the Royal Bavarian Landwehr Infantry Regiment No 12, 5th company throughout the war. Julius even succeeded in winning the Iron Cross, (second class) in 1919, an honour that, although relatively common at this time, does indicate a high level of bravery and commitment to the German war effort. Indeed, besides Julius, his three brothers, Leopold, Max and Rudolf, each won the Iron Cross. Tragically, Leopold was killed at the Battle of Kemmel Ridge in 1918. Returning from the war, Julius decided that it was time to return home so, in 1919, he re-joined KFV where he continued playing until 1923. He later said that he was more proud of what he and his brothers achieved in the war, than of anything that he achieved on the football field. Following his retirement, Julius continued to work with KFV as a youth coach and married Ellen Hauser, a Christian, with whom he raised two children. During this time, along with his brother Max and Fuchs, Julius tried to convert the family textile business into a sports goods company but, as Sam Wallace tells us, the business failed and they were forced to file for bankruptcy.

The remainder of the 1920s passed relatively quietly for Julius but the situation in Germany was changing rapidly. Following the economic crisis of the early 1920s, the German economy had settled down. The 1929 Wall Street Crash and subsequent Depression was to change all that. By the end of January 1933, Adolf Hitler was in power and on the 10th April, southern German football clubs announced the banning of all Jews. The writing was well and truly on the wall. In a letter to the club, Julius reminded officials of the sacrifices that people of the Jewish faith had made for Germany. He detailed in his letter, not only the efforts and sacrifices made by himself and his brothers, but also his father's participation in the Franco-Prussian War of 1870. All to no avail. By the end of the year this loyal servant could not even enter the stadium at KFV, although a former KFV player and local businessman, Lorenz Huber, did succeed in smuggling Julius into some games. He even provided the family with food.

By now the banning of Jewish goods in the city meant it was unlikely that Julius would be able to revive his business career. He therefore joined, at the age of forty-two, one of the many newly formed Jewish football clubs, Turnclub 03 Karlsruhe. In 1935, they won the Baden Regional Championship. Following this brief moment of success, Julius moved around working in a combination of various football coaching roles and the sale of textiles. By 1937, he was working for a paper company in Karlsruhe but the following year it too, was 'Aryanised' so Julius was working as forced labour in the municipal works within the city. With his coaching career effectively over, Julius, without his family, set off for Paris, arriving on 5th August 1938, where he moved in with his sister Rosa and her husband. This was situated in a rather well-to-do area, just across the River Seine, near the Eiffel Tower. On the surface this might appear to have been a good move but things in Paris were difficult, especially for those of foreign nationality moving into the city. Failure to find a job meant that by November 1938, with the Munich Treaty already signed, Julius headed back to Germany.

Attempts to get back to Germany failed disastrously. Thinking that his family had been killed back in Germany, Julius suffered a breakdown and attempted to take his own life. Luckily, he was found in a rock quarry, covered in blood but alive. He was placed in a French mental hospital from which he attempted to escape in June 1939 but on the 20th of that month he was discovered and returned. Julius was released on 1st September 1939, the day that France and Germany declared war. Ellen, still alive despite Julius' fears, arranged through her brother that her husband be brought home. A few months later, those inmates who had been in the mental hospital with Julius were taken to Grafeneck Euthanasia Centre and gassed. It is thought that

100,000 people, many of whom were children, thought to be too mentally weak or physically disabled to 'merit' life were gassed.

Back in Karlsruhe there was a plan being hatched to save both of Julius' children. By October 1940, Jews were increasingly rounded up and sent to camps. Both of the Hirsch children were considered to be *'Mischling'*, a subcategory of the Jewish race or a 'half-breed', which meant that they were not taken immediately. The plan was that Julius and Ellen divorce so that the children could be baptised as 'Christian'. On 1st March 1943, however, Julius and his 15-year-old daughter Esther were seized. They were taken to a train where Julius was made to board while Esther, probably benefitting from her status as a *'Mischling'*, was sent back home. Two days later, she received a birthday card from her father, apparently now in Dortmund. Julius was never heard of again.

So what happened to this brave and loving husband and father? There are conflicting stories in existence but it seems probable that Julius was intended for Auschwitz. Yet his name doesn't appear on any surviving lists. Blickenstaff disputes that he ever made it to the camp but his date of death is given officially as the 8th May 1945, VE Day, and the date given to those who perished in the camps where no actual, accurate date is recorded. The remainder of the family were more fortunate. On 14th February 1945, both children were transported by train to Theresienstadt, now a part of the modern Czech Republic but then known as Terezin and sent to a camp. Fortunately, they both survived. Ellen, who had taken her original name of Hauser, reverted back to Julius' surname, Hirsch, and lived until 1st March 1966, twenty-three years to the day after Julius' forced departure. Max, one of Julius' brothers went with the children to Terezin and also survived.

The story of what happened to Julius fellow club and international teammates is one to contemplate. Fellow Jew and World War One hero, Gottfried Fuchs, escaped first to England and then to Canada in 1940. He died on February 25th, 1972, at the ripe old age of 82. Their colleague, Fritz Forderer, the third member of the attacking trio, like Julius, became a coach following his retirement but his war experience was very different. One of his teams became members of the Third SS Death Head Unit while Forderer himself joined the Nazi Party in 1942. He died of natural causes ten years later aged 64. As for Julius himself, he has been rediscovered for history. During the 1990s historians discovered evidence of his impressive career and his important contribution to German football history. So Julius has at last been recognised in his home country. Since 2005 the German Football Federation (DFB) has awarded the Julius-Hirsch-Preis which recognises outstanding examples of integration and tolerance within German football. The award is a result of a 300-page report, written in book form, and commissioned in 2001. It was written by the University of Mainz lecturer, Nils Havemann, and it confirms that the DFB had no difficulty in becoming an ally of the Nazi regime. Indeed, even before 1933, the DFB had behaved in an inappropriately nationalistic way towards foreign players. Post 1945 the DFB was eventually forced to face its past. The result was an acceptance that thousands of Jews had been forced out of all levels of football and that some, like Julius, were murdered. The DFB state that the prize should be given to those who represent "the sanctity of human dignity and an opposition to anti-Semitism and racism" and now attempts to expose the exclusion of people and promote diversity in the game. Wholly appropriately, Andreas Hirsch, Julius' grandson, is a member of the jury that decides the winner of this award. Finally, the plight of Jewish footballers in Nazi Germany has been acknowledged and Julius Hirsch allowed to take his rightful place in German football history.

Victor Perez

CHAPTER 14
WORLD CHAMPION BOXER VICTOR PEREZ AND THE DEATH MARCH

The story of Julius Hirsch is only one of many tragic tales that are now coming to light concerning the fate of Jewish sportsmen and women. We have already made reference in earlier chapters to how the German-Jewish fencer Helene Mayer and the high jumper Gretel Bergmann were used for propaganda purposes by the Nazi regime. They were the lucky ones. Other Jewish Olympic competitors did not survive the dangers of war or the horrors of the concentration camps. The Olympic Sports Website lists 565 names of those Jewish competitors who were missing in action or confirmed as dead as a result of the two World Wars. We are told that 68 Olympians were interned in concentration camps. Of these, 49 died in the camps and that only 19 Olympians survived. It would appear that at least seven of those who died were Hungarian while sixteen Dutch Olympians died between 1942 and 1944, the greatest sacrifice of any country.

Although most European Jews who took part in the 1936 Olympics did, like Helene Mayer, survive, the losses are many and important to study. Lilli Henoch, a German-Jewish athlete, was the holder of four world records and ten German records in four different disciplines, the discus, shot put, long jump and 100 metres relay. Henoch was prevented from entering the Olympics in the 1920s as Germany was not readmitted to the Olympic family until the early 1930s but she was a very high-profile German athlete. Nevertheless, because of her Jewish background, Henoch was prevented from participating in the 1936 Olympics. More tragically, along with her mother and brother, she was deported to occupied Latvia where she was taken to the Riga Ghetto before being machine gunned, along with her mother, by a Nazi mobile killing unit. Her brother disappeared without trace. Equally tragic was the story of Estella Agsteribbe, a Dutch gymnast who won a gold medal as a member of the Dutch gymnastics team in the 1928 Olympics, which had been held in her native Amsterdam. She, her husband, six-year-old daughter and two-year-old son all died at Auschwitz on September 17th, 1943.

One sport that has yet to be discussed is that of boxing, a sport which, given its popularity between the wars, inevitably has its share of victims, some of whom were of Jewish origin. Following the end of the Great War, many new Jewish sports clubs were set up all over the world, often offering young people the opportunity to develop skills in such sports as gymnastics, fencing and boxing. The clubs were set up by the Maccabi World Union (MWU) from 1921 and this organisation succeeded in uniting many of these clubs, spreading its influence throughout the world. The MWU stated with the utmost clarity that "The goal of the Union is the physical and moral rejuvenation of Jews for the sake of restoration and existence of the Jewish land and its people." That the MWU made an impact is beyond doubt; for example, between the wars, Jewish boxers dominated, so much so that between 1910 and 1940 thirty world titles were won. Perhaps the best-known Jewish boxer and victim of the Nazi regime, certainly the best known at the time, was Victor Perez, a former Flyweight World Champion. Victor's story is as instructive as any in helping us to appreciate the suffering of the Jewish race during these years.

Victor Perez was born one of five children in Dar-El-Berdgaria, the Jewish quarter of Tunis, Tunisia, on the 18th October 1911, the son of Khmanssa Perez, a household goods salesman, and his wife Khanlou Rene Perez. At the age of fourteen, encouraged by his older brother Benjamin, the diminutive Victor became interested in boxing. His boxing idol was Louis Phal, known as the 'Battling Siki', who was an American-Senegalese world light heavyweight champion who had been murdered in 1925. Louis Phal had served in the French Army during the Great War and had been decorated for bravery, something that was bound to impress Victor who, as a Tunisian, lived under French rule. It is unclear whether or not Victor was aware of Phal's notorious lifestyle of partying, frequenting nightclubs and his love of Champagne but he was an inspiration to the young would-be boxer. At sixteen, after training in the Maccabi organisation, Victor won his first fight. Following this success, in December 1927, Victor headed for Paris intent on a career in the boxing ring.

On arriving in Paris, Victor initially made his living selling shoes but he had the good fortune to meet Joe Guez, the man who would become his trainer. During his free time Victor worked hard at perfecting his boxing skills and by the end of 1928, he was showing real promise. There is some conflicting evidence as to whether it was 1930 or 1931 that Victor won the French Flyweight Title. He still measured only five-foot one inch in height and weighed only one hundred and ten pounds but Jewish publications state that he defeated Kid Olivia, a fighter from Marseilles, in Paris during 1930. However, the boxing historian, Mike Silver, in his book *Stars in the Ring: Jewish Champions in the Golden Age of Boxing* says clearly that the first title fight was against Valentin Angelmann on June 4th, 1931, and that it was Victor's 54th professional fight. Given Mike Silver's status as a boxing historian, it is probably safer to accept his research as the more reliable. What is not in doubt is that on October 24th, 1931 'Young Victor', as he was now known, won the International Boxing Union World Flyweight crown when, in front of around 16,000 fans, he knocked out Frankie Genaro in the second round. This was a most significant victory. Genaro had won an Olympic gold medal at Antwerp in 1920 just two days before his nineteenth birthday and he went on to have an extremely successful career—a career that saw him ranked as one of the greatest flyweights of all time, always placed between 3rd and 13th in any list of all-time greats at the weight. He had won the world title in 1928, lost it, but immediately regained the crown. Genaro's loss to Victor finished his career as a top boxer and he retired in 1934, living until 1966. Victor, meanwhile, was the youngest ever world champion at barely twenty years of age.

Following his world title win, Victor returned to his home country of Tunisia where an enthusiastic crowd of approximately 10,000 people met him at the port. On his return to Paris, his victory parade down the Boulevard Jules Ferry, the main thoroughfare through the capital, saw even greater numbers as upward of 100,000 delirious supporters thronged the route. The future could not have looked brighter for the young boxer. It was not to last. A passionate affair with the notable and glamorous French actress Mireille Balin resulted in Victor neglecting his training. Balin was born in Monte Carlo, the daughter of a journalist and brought up in a comfortable middle-class family. Educated in Paris and Marseilles and fluent in Italian, German and English, Balin was considered one of the finest French cinema actresses of the 1930s and it isn't difficult to see why Victor was so attracted to her. But the relationship did him no favours. Following the conclusion of their affair Balin met the singer and actor Tino Rossi to whom she became engaged. Then she met the love of her life, Birl Desbok, a German officer in the Wehrmacht. In 1944, they were arrested by the Free French near Nice and he was probably executed. Balin was beaten, raped and then imprisoned before she was released in January 1945. Although Balin made one more film following her release, now very frail, she was unable work successfully. Mireille Balin's fraternisation with the Nazis had ruined her career. She died in 1968, in poverty and forgotten, at the age of 59.

Victor's inability to prepare properly during his affair with Balin cost him dear. In 1932, he lost his title to the English fighter Jackie Brown at the King's Hall, Manchester following a technical knockout in the 13th round. Victor had struggled to make the 112-pound weight limit so he did not seek a rematch preferring instead to move up to the 118-pound bantamweight limit. By 1934, Victor had regained his ambition and won the right to challenge another 'Brown', Arthur 'Al' Brown from Panama. Al Brown, boxing's first Hispanic world champion, is a most interesting fighter. Standing at five foot ten inches, the tallest man ever to hold the bantamweight crown, Al Brown stood a full nine inches taller than Victor and with such a long reach advantage was always the favourite to win. And win he did, defeating Victor in round 10, although Victor claimed that he was stopped by an illegal punch. Al Brown continued with a hugely successful career and retired in 1942 with 123 wins, a superb boxer and heavy puncher who, in 162 fights, was never knocked out. His personal life was notable for a 'gay' relationship with Jean Cocteau, the French writer, designer, playwright, artist and film maker, not a lifestyle associated with many high-profile boxers of the first half of the twentieth century. However, as with many boxers of this era, his later years were difficult. He died in 1951, penniless in New York after contacting tuberculosis.

As for Victor, he settled in Paris, a far from obvious move as the city was already witnessing the growth of anti-Semitism. This applied to Tunisian Jews as much as to any of the Jewish faith. Indeed, during the war, around 100,000 Tunisian Jews were forced, like all those of the Jewish faith, to wear a yellow star in public. This badge denoted that the wearer was a religious or ethnic outsider, in effect it was a badge of shame. Victor had never disguised his Jewish background, quite the reverse, as he wore the Star of David on his shorts and displayed the Star on his suitcases. When he travelled to Berlin in November 1938, he displayed his courage for those who chose to see which way Germany was heading. At this point Victor finally retired from boxing at the relatively young age of 27 with an impressive record of 92 victories, 26 defeats and 15 draws. It had been a career that had touched the heights, although one could be forgiven for thinking that in some respects Victor had fallen short of his massive potential.

With the fall of France in May 1940 saw Victor decide that his best option was to leave Paris. He didn't get far and was forced to return. Following this failure, it appears that Victor kept a low profile and managed to stay out of trouble. This was not the experience of many fellow Jews. During the war, a total of 73,853 French Jews were seized in France alone and taken to holding camps such as Drancy, a north eastern suburb of Paris where detainees were later sent to Auschwitz. Of these, only 2,500 survived. A total of 11,400 French Jews killed at Auschwitz were under 16 years of age. Years later, in 1976, Shlomo Selinger, a sculptor, created a 'Memorial to the Deportation at Drancy' to commemorate the French Jews held there. Clearly Victor's safety could not be guaranteed and on 21st September 1943, following his denunciation to occupation authorities, he was arrested in Paris. Like thousands before him, Victor was detained in the Drancy internment camp before being transported to Auschwitz. He arrived at the camp on 10th October as part of 'Transport 60', a group of 1,000 prisoners from the Drancy Internment, so named due to it being the 60th transport to leave that particular camp. Once there, Victor was placed in the Monowitz camp which, since its creation in October 1942, was one of the three main camps in the Auschwitz camp system. This particular camp held around 12,000 prisoners, most of whom were Jewish although there were also non-Jewish prisoners described as being "not up to par with German work standards."

Once in the camp, like everybody else, Victor was subjected to hard manual labour. But it was not long before Victor was recognised and the Nazi guards soon had additional plans for their celebratory guest. Show fights were often arranged by the guards on which they would then place bets. The winner of these contests would be given an extra ration of food while the loser faced the possibility, even probability, of execution. Victor, of course, had a distinct advantage in these contests and it is said that he won 140 fights in a fifteen-month period, 139 by a knockout. The cruelty of these contests is unimaginable. Fighters, usually Jewish, were expected to fight until one of them dropped to the ground, either from a punch or from exhaustion. The Nazi guards were not happy until they saw blood.

Victor was one of the lucky ones, at this stage of the war, at least. His skill as a boxer enabled him to survive in this most cruel of environments but the war was beginning to take a different turn. The Red Army was advancing towards, first Austria, and then Germany. From the middle of 1944, just as the Allies were taking their first steps into France in the west, concentration camps based in Eastern Europe, in particular Poland, were having to be abandoned and the inmates moved to camps within Germany itself. By January 1945, it was even more crucial that the prisoners were moved. Although some did leave by train many were forced to cover the distance on foot. These were known as 'The Death Marches' where it is estimated that around 100,000 Jewish men, women and children lost their lives. The killing started even before the first painful steps were taken. Any prisoner considered to be too weak to march was shot. Once the march had begun, no mercy was shown to those who found the journey too difficult. A survivor, Israel Gutman, was quoted by the Holocaust historian Martin Gilbert as saying that "anybody who had to sit down for a few minutes was shot" and their bodies thrown into ditches on the side of the road. In case it be thought that those travelling by train were relatively safe it is important to learn that, at Leszczyny in Poland, 250 prisoners attempted to jump from their train and make their escape. None made it and all were shot, their bodies dumped unceremoniously in ditches at the side of the track. The chances of surviving the move to a new camp were severely unlikely by whichever means it was undertaken. A group of 1,000 women were marched from the Neusalz camp in Poland but 42 days later only 200 reached the camp in Flossenburg alive. These were then sent to Belsen where their chances of survival were minimal. For Victor too, the end was tragic if inevitable. The story is told that Victor was forced to walk on a death march that headed into Upper Silesia in southern Poland. On the 22nd January 1945, near Gilwice, he attempted to help a fellow prisoner by giving him a piece of bread, a paltry amount no doubt, but a huge act of kindness to a fellow human being. For this act of humanity, Victor Perez, the former world champion boxer, was shot. He was 33 years old.

Even after Hitler's death on 30th April 1945, the death marches continued. A survivor, Hugo Grym, is later quoted by Martin Gilbert as saying that, "For the Nazis, the destruction of Jews had an unchanging function until the very end of the war; it was the only thing about which they have never changed their policies. I have never ceased to be amazed by the priority they gave it, even when everything was collapsing."

As we have already seen, many of the Jewish sporting icons so inhumanly treated in World War Two were forgotten and disappeared from public consciousness. This is not quite true of Victor Perez. In 1986 he was inducted into the 'Jewish Sports Hall of Fame'. In 1997 the 'Institut National des Sports' in Paris named its boxing arena after Victor 'Young' Perez and unveiled a plaque in his memory.

Perhaps even more significantly, in November 2013 a film, *Victor "Young" Perez* was shown in Israel and France. The film, written and directed by Jacques Quaniche and starring Brahim Asloum (Victor), Steve Suissa (his brother Benjamin) and Isabella Orsini (Mireille), had been made in 2009 and was nominated for both Best Feature Film in the Sao Paulo International Film Festival and Best International feature at the Santa Barbara International Film Festival. Although it did not win at either festival, the film was well-received. Quaniche did take some liberties with the film and not every scene could be said to be historically accurate but it provides an entertaining, if ultimately tragic story. Mireille Balin is portrayed as an extremely ambitious actress who uses Victor to further her career. She shows Victor a good time in Paris with plenty of glitz and glamour and this predictably leads to the boxer spending less and less time in the gym. This interpretation has more than a grain of truth as does the portrayal of the passionate Mireille being something of a party girl. But the scene showing Victor knocking her German boyfriend to the floor while questioning Mireille's loyalty to France — an action which resulted in Victor being arrested and sent to the concentration camp — is unlikely to be true. Certainly, there is no evidence come to light as yet to support it. The role of his brother Benjamin is also questionable. In the film Benjamin, a fellow boxer known as 'Kid' Perez, leaves Tunisia for Paris in order to find his much-loved younger brother and encourage him to see sense over the effect Mireille was having on his career. After failing in his efforts, Benjamin too is arrested and ends up in the same camp as Victor. Once again there is no evidence to confirm this story. Benjamin, the flyweight champion of North Africa in 1928, had probably returned to Tunisia before the Nazi invasion of France. The Nazis didn't carry out their policy of 'ethnic cleansing' in Tunisia so it is very likely that Benjamin, in fact, survived the war. There is evidence of a 'Kid' Perez becoming a trainer after the war and this is likely to be him.

What we can be sure of is that the tragic story of Victor 'Young' Perez tells us as clearly as any the horrors of the Nazi concentration camps and 'Death Marches'. The life, but particularly the death, of the youngest ever world champion boxer, humiliated in the camps and brutally murdered when displaying a simple act of human kindness, stands today as a stark reminder of the Jewish experience in World War Two.

Eric Liddell

CHAPTER 15
"AS CLOSE TO A SAINT AS ANYONE I HAVE EVER KNOWN": THE STORY OF ERIC LIDDELL

One of the best known, possibly the best known, of all the British sportsmen to die during World War Two did not serve in the Army, Navy or RAF. Nor was he killed by the many bombing raids which rained down on many British cities. Indeed, he did not participate in the armed conflict at all. His contribution was that of a missionary who became a leader and organiser in a Japanese internment camp in the heart of China where he was to die five months before the end of the war in the Far East. This remarkable man was Eric Henry Liddell, Olympic 400-metre champion and Scottish rugby international, the man of whom his biographer, Duncan Hamilton, says "proved that heroism in war exists beyond churned-up battlefields." Not that any of this gave Eric Liddell immediate recognition as a war hero. His journey to this status has taken longer than the length of his remarkable life but his name has finally taken its place in as a 'WW2 Civilian Deaths, 1939-1945' on the online 'Ancestry' records. More importantly, he joins the 68,873 names listed by the Commonwealth War Graves Commission as British Civilian War Dead. This belated recognition demands that the story of Eric Liddell be told in this book.

Eric Henry Liddell was born on 16th January 1902 in Tientsin, China, the son of the Reverend and Mrs James Dunlop Liddell, both of whom were missionaries with the London Missionary Society. Eric's parents had met in China and married in October 1899, at the start of the Boxer Rebellion, a particularly dangerous time for Christians in that country. Eric was his parent's second son and a further brother and sister arrived in due course. Eric began his education by attending school in China while in the family home the emphasis was on the importance of service, religion and missionary work. When Eric was six years old and his brother, Robert, eight, the boys were enrolled together in Eltham College in the suburbs of London, a boarding school for the sons of missionaries. With no history of sporting achievement, or even interest in sport, in his background, there was no sign of Eric's future prowess in rugby union or athletics. Eric's time at Eltham College appears to have been unhappy in many respects and he often looked to Robert for support. He felt that he had been orphaned, the only relief coming on the rare occasions when his parents returned home and the whole family, mother, father and four children could be together in Edinburgh. Eric, however, found his solace on the sports field in Eltham. By the age of fifteen, he was a successful member of both the 1st rugby XV and the cricket first XI teams which he later went on to captain. He also succeeded in winning the Blackheath Cup, the trophy given to the 'athlete of the year'. Despite this success, Eric's main character trait was already coming to the fore. His headmaster, George Robertson, described Eric as being "entirely without vanity."

Following his time at Eltham College, Eric was offered a place at Edinburgh University where he enrolled to study for a BSc in Pure Science. In the autumn of 1920, Eric set off to Edinburgh in order to join his brother Robert who was already studying there. It was while studying in Edinburgh that Eric really began to make his mark as an exceptional sportsman and it was as a very fast winger with a sharp eye for the try line that gave him his first national recognition. In the autumn term of 1921 Eric, by now a star of the university First XV, was selected for the Scottish trial. His performance in this trial was nothing short of sensational and he left the field having scored five tries, his selection for the full Scotland XV assured. A few months later, on 2nd January 1922, Eric made his debut for Scotland in front of 37,000 spectators in Stade Colombes, Paris. The result was a 3–3 draw, a disappointing result against an ordinary French side. But Eric had done enough to keep his place and a month later Scotland faced Wales at Inverleith where the result was another closely fought draw, 9–9, but on this occasion a more creditable result as it prevented Wales from achieving their first post-war Grand Slam. In the game against Ireland Eric had the distinction of scoring his first international try, the winning score, as Scotland won 6–3, once again at their home ground of

Inverleith. Eric missed the defeat to England at Twickenham but the following season he was back. And a very impressive return it proved to be. The first three matches were all won, France 16–3, Wales 11–8 (the first ever Scottish victory at Cardiff Arms Park) and Ireland 16–3. Moreover, Eric scored a try in each of these matches, proving what a lethal finisher, he could be. Following the final whistle in Cardiff, both Eric and another try scorer and ex pupil of Eltham College, the captain, Leslie Gracie, were carried shoulder high from the pitch. This set up a Grand Slam decider against England at Inverleith in what would prove to be Eric's last international appearance, at least on the rugby field. Both sides scored two tries but a conversion by England front row forward William Luddington, a naval officer later killed in Sicily, made the difference as his team won their fourth Grand Slam 8-6. Scotland had lost only two matches in the two seasons that Eric played but a first Grand Slam still eluded them. This feat was finally achieved in 1925 but by then Eric had moved on to sporting greatness in a very different arena.

The major reason for Eric's decision to concentrate on his other sporting love, sprinting, was quite clear and perfectly understandable. Then, as now, the risk of serious injury playing such a physical contact sport was easy to see. If Eric was to reach the very top in the competitive athletics' arena then he needed to be in perfect condition and not battered and bruised by confrontation on the rugby field. It was already felt by many that Eric could become, if he was not already, the fastest runner in Scotland. At the same time Eric had been spotted by the renowned coach Tom McKerchar, the man who had advised Heart of Midlothian FC and who regularly coached students from Edinburgh University. McKerchar was seen as an innovative coach, very much in the mould of Sam Mussabini who was destined to prepare Harold Abraham for Olympic success in 1924. McKerchar was among the first coaches to use massage and physiotherapy as part of his coaching regime while he also believed strongly in self-discipline. He had his work cut out with Eric who refused to change his ungainly running style with his head held back, pumping arms and high knee lift. Eric's habit of arriving late for training due to his attendance at a Bible class was also frustrating. But McKerchar, keen to find a successor to the

Scottish Olympic 400 metres champion Wyndham Halswelle who was killed at Neuve Chapelle, Laventie in 1915, could not ignore Eric's potential. Once he became convinced of Eric's character and his commitment and loyalty, McKerchar had no problem in taking on the job. Three years and two months later, having run 146 races, Eric was an Olympic champion.

Once Eric had made the decision to concentrate on athletics rather than rugby there was a significant improvement in his performances. In 1923, he won the AAA Championship in both the 100 yards (in a time of 9.7 seconds, not equalled for another 23 years) and the 220 yards (21.6 seconds). Eric was clearly a potential gold medallist for the 1924 Olympics due to be held in Paris. McKerchar had accepted that it would be counter-productive to change Eric's running style, so he worked on maximising the natural ability through thorough preparation. Not that the strong team from the USA, containing the great sprinters Charley Paddock and Jackson Scholz, thought that Eric posed much of a threat. The *New York Times* insisted that he "did everything wrong" and that his appearance, an eleven stone frame, five foot nine inches in height with short legs, did not give the impression of a well-proportioned sprinter. The strong American team was not losing sleep over Eric, despite his newly acquired nickname of 'The Flying Scotsman'.

There was also another complication that threatened Eric's bid for Olympic glory, that of his religious beliefs. It was already clear that Eric was a devoted Christian and that his long-term future would eventually lie in this vocation. Despite not having spent much time with his missionary father, there is evidence to suggest that from early on in his life Eric wanted to be like him. While a student in Edinburgh Eric was quickly involved in Christian activities, speaking and preaching at religious meetings. His fame drew large crowds to neighbouring Glasgow where he spoke at the Glasgow Students Evangelistic Union and it became clear that Eric was beginning to place more importance on his religion than he was on his running. By 1924, he had decided that, on completing his Science degree at Edinburgh later that year, he would study Theology at Congregational College, also in Edinburgh. This commitment to his faith was to result in Eric making decisions about his participation in the Paris Olympics, decisions whose results would be portrayed in an Oscar-winning film, *Chariots of Fire*, nearly sixty years later.

As the 1924 Olympics approached, the British Olympic Committee hardened its determination, that the British team would have a successful games. Success for them meant defeating the USA and winning some of the major, more glamorous events. Following the conclusion of the Great War, the USA was quickly establishing itself as the major power in the world. Britain had borrowed heavily from the USA to finance the war and, coupled with the resulting economic difficulties being suffered in Europe, Britain was no longer looking like the world power of pre-1914. Many in the British establishment saw the USA as something of an upstart threatening to take Britain's rightful place in the world. Defeating the brash young Americans in the Games would be a big boost for British self-confidence. Among the events which could help achieve this was the 100 metres where the American Olympic champion of 1920, Charley Paddock, was expected to be challenged by his fellow countryman Jackson Scholz and the British stars Harold Abrahams and Eric Liddell. The problem was that the heats for the 100 metres were to be run on a Sunday and to participate would go very much against Eric's belief that the Sabbath was not a day for sport. The British Olympic Committee were devastated and tried desperately to persuade Eric to run. But Eric was not one to compromise, particularly on an issue such as this and, when reminded that he needed to be patriotic, Eric replied that he answered to a higher authority. In the film, the committee were seen trying to persuade Eric to run on the journey to Paris. Even the Prince of Wales is seen using his undoubted charm to affect a satisfactory outcome. This is not how it happened. Eric and the committee were aware well before the Games of the athletics timetable and a solution was found months in advance of the team's departure. Although the committee did not withdraw him from the 100 metres until five weeks before the games started it was agreed that Eric would run in the 200 and 400 metres and adjust his training accordingly. Not that anybody thought that he had much chance of winning. Despite being the AAA champion at 440 yards his time of 49.6 seconds was modest by world standards and he had only run the distance competitively on ten occasions in his life. A remarkable 440 yards run at Stoke in 1923, where Eric fell thereby giving the field a twenty-yard lead before overhauling them to win by six yards, had been forgotten by all except McKerchar and Eric himself. Eric's decision was not universally accepted and for a time he was, as one friend put it, "the most unpopular man in Britain." In April 1924, months before the games, Eric journeyed to the University of Pennsylvania to test his preparation by running some races. He achieved only modest results. The Americans saw nothing to fear.

Nevertheless, the British travelled in good heart. The strength of British running was built around Oxbridge athletes such as Abrahams, Henry Stallard, Evelyn Montague, David Cecil, Guy Butler and Douglas Lowe. Once again, *Chariots of Fire* is not entirely accurate in its telling of the story. Montague (known as Aubrey, his middle name, in the film), was a graduate of Oxford not Cambridge; Cecil (Lord Lindsey in the film) did run in 1924 but achieved little in these games, winning his gold medal in 1928 while Stallard was affected by injury which meant that a bronze in the 1500 metres and 4th place in the 800 metres was the best that he could do. Lowe, a Cambridge man who isn't referenced at all in the film, surprisingly won the 800 metres, a title that he successfully defended in 1928. Butler, another unreferenced Cambridge man and relay gold medallist in 1920, did win two bronze medals in Paris. Abrahams, although criticised for employing a professional coach, Sam Mussabini, gloriously won the 100 metres, beating Scholz into second place with Paddock fifth. Eric watched from the side-lines.

The 200 metres, totally unacknowledged in the film, came next. Here Eric gained a bronze medal, with a display of that *The Times* called "fine running", three places ahead of a tired Abrahams but behind the gold medallist Scholz and Paddock. The 400 metres was a very different story, one in which Eric, played sympathetically and accurately by Ian Charleson, was to create the legend. This event, expected to be a battle between the Americans Horatio Fitch and John Coard Taylor, had produced headlines even before the final had been run. The world record for the event was broken in the heats by the Swiss athlete Josef Imbach only for Fitch to break it immediately after. In the semi-final, Eric served notice of his potential by beating both

Taylor and Imbach but Fitch remained the favourite, beating Butler in the other semi-final. There was no hint of what was to come when Eric was drawn in the outside lane and running blind. The usual tactic at this distance in 1924 was to run it more as a middle-distance race: run hard on the first bend, coast the back straight and sprint to the finish. Eric, with no idea of what was happening behind him, sprinted the whole way, finishing in a World and Olympic record time of 47.6 seconds, six yards ahead of the American champion Fitch. Guy Butler finished a distant third. Taylor and Imbach were blown away, the former pulling a muscle in a vain attempt to gain a medal while the latter fell. It emerged later that an American masseur had slipped Eric a quotation from 1 Samuel 2:30 — "Those who honour me I will honour" — but the media were unaware of this as they went into raptures over Eric's performance. *The Times* described it as "the most dramatic race ever seen on a running track" and "the most memorable day that the Olympics had ever seen" turning from the "dullest of days" in less than a minute. All was forgiven and Eric was a hero—despite his costly absence, once again due to his refusal to run on Sundays, to run either the 4x100 relay where Great Britain gained silver or the 4x400 where a bronze was won.

The media coverage was low-key when compared to today's frenzied reaction to Olympic success, but both Eric and Harold Abrahams were received as heroes. Although *The Times* covered Abraham's success in a column of only 888 words, which included all the athletics of that particular day, the newspapers do give a flavour of the excitement that these young men had generated. Thousands of people turned up to welcome them back to Victoria Station while Eric was met by thousands more at Waverley. Six days later, Eric received his degree and was carried shoulder high from the ceremony by his fellow students. This modest man, who maintained that Henry Stallard's bronze medal, won while carrying an injury and competing against the legendary Paavo Nurmi, was of greater value than his own gold medal, was now seen by Reuters as "the most popular man in Paris." Following his win, Eric was now the toast of the athletics world and something of a 1920s 'poster boy'. And Eric proved that his triumph was no fluke by defeating Fitch in a relay at Stamford Bridge despite receiving the baton a full ten yards behind his American rival. The American champions, expected to defeat the British, had been banished back across the Atlantic, at least they had in the eyes of the British media.

The opportunity for Eric to capitalise on his newly won status was not long in coming. Along with Abrahams and Lowe, he was offered the chance to tour the USA where his clean-cut image appealed to the public as a contrast with the more questionable images of Walter Hagen, Jack Dempsey and Babe Ruth and where he could exploit his fame financially. This, however, was not the way for these British athletes. Armed with their newly obtained degrees, they looked to more conventional middle-class professions where they could earn a living. Abrahams, a lawyer, was injured in 1925 so pursued a career in journalism, broadcasting and sports administration and was soon on his way to becoming 'the father of British athletics and a regular radio commentator. As well as adopting two children during the war he and his wife, Sybil, took in two Jewish refugees, a German boy and an Austrian girl. It is said that, when he died in 1978, Harold Abrahams still wondered what might have been the outcome if Eric had run in that 100 metres final. Stallard and Lowe became an ophthalmic surgeon and barrister respectively while Evelyn Montague, the grandson of the legendry CP Scott, the renowned editor of *The Manchester Guardian*, evolved into a highly respected war journalist. While covering the Italian campaign Montague contacted tuberculosis, which resulted in his death in 1948.

What of their American rivals? The most interesting, and ultimately tragic story is that of Charley Paddock, gold medallist in the 100 metres and the 4x100 relay in 1920 and the silver medallist in the 200 metres in both Antwerp and Paris. The man known as 'the World's Fastest Human' raced successfully throughout the 1920s and, following his retirement, Paddock, like Montague and Abrahams, went into journalism. He became a successful publisher and editor as well as vice president and general manager of three newspapers owned by his father-in-law, Charles H Prisk. The USA entry into World War Two did not phase Paddock as he already had an impressive war record. During the Great War he had served in the US Marines as a lieutenant of field artillery so it was no surprise that he wished to make a significant contribution to the next conflict. Paddock was asked to serve on the personal staff of Major General William P Upshur, a holder of the Medal of Honor, in the Royal Marine Corps where he concentrated on public relations. Tragically both Major General Upshur and Captain Paddock were killed on 23rd July 1943 in a military plane crash near Sitka, Alaska. Paddock is interred at the Sitka National Cemetery.

Eric, despite winning all three sprints in the Scottish AAAs in 1925, had decided his future, one that was very different from that of his fellow Olympians. "God", he said, "had made me for China." Throughout his life. Eric had an unbroken bond with China. He regarded China as home and, as Duncan Hamilton tells us, missionary work was considered to be "the family business." In 1925, he returned to Northern China, to Tianjin where he taught in an Anglo-Chinese college for wealthy Chinese students. Eric's hope was that the students would become influential in China and spread Christian values but this was easier said than done. China had felt very let down by broken promises following the Great War, particularly when Shandong Province was given to Japan despite it having been promised to the Chinese. Resentment began to build against Britain and France and the newly formed Communist Party of China, founded in 1921, was able to capitalise on this. To be Christian, many felt, was to be anti-Chinese. Disorder and lawlessness followed, so much so that Eric felt that he could not possibly leave China at this time. In 1928, there were attempts to coax Eric into running in the Amsterdam Olympics (he was still only 26 years old) and he did run against, and beat, members of the French and Japanese Olympic teams. Some felt that now Eric was a stronger, more mature athlete, one who could develop into a great 800-metre runner and two years later, he won the North China Championship. Eric was clearly still a force but he refused all offers. Instead, he helped to design and build the Minjuan Stadium in Tianjin, a copy of Stamford Bridge, his favourite running track.

Following his father's stroke in 1929, Eric decided to reconsider his plans. Eric joined the London Missionary Society soon after and returned to Edinburgh in 1931 to study further in order to become ordained as a congregational minister. This he did in June 1932, a year before his father's death, and so he was able to return to China fully fledged and committed to his missionary work in China. Another major life-changing event was also about to happen. In 1926, Eric had first met the fourteen-year-old daughter of a Canadian missionary, Florence Mackenzie. Romance followed when Florence reached adulthood and the couple married in Tientsin (the previous name for the place now known as Tianjin) Union Church on 27th March 1934. Two daughters quickly followed, Patricia born in 1935 and Heather in 1937, but by now China was a precarious place for the family to be living. The Sino-Japanese War began in 1937, a war which was to claim anywhere between 10–20 million lives. During August 1937, 2,526 bombs fell on Shanghai, killing around one million people while the Nanking massacre claimed another 300,000 lives. This was the China where Eric and the family lived and worked but none of this deterred Eric. In the autumn of that year Eric and his brother Rob were posted to Siaochang but the London Missionary Society refused to let Florence and the girls travel to such a dangerous area. They were right. On the journey Eric was twice robbed at gunpoint. The conditions were dreadful with cholera rampant and Eric's missionary work being carried out with the sound of Japanese guns rumbling in the distance. Wounded Chinese soldiers were rescued and the sick were visited, but every time that Eric went out, he risked being shot. In 1939, there was some relief when Eric was allowed to return to Scotland and Florence and the girls joined him from Canada, where they had been living, the following summer. During this family reunion, Florence fell pregnant and it was agreed, following the family's return to China, that it was too dangerous for the new baby to be born there. Florence therefore took the girls with her to Toronto where another baby girl, Maureen, was born in September 1941. Eric returned to Tientsin, destined never to see baby Maureen.

The situation for Eric was by now even more serious. Following the Tripartite Pact of 27th September 1940 and the Japanese attack on Pearl Harbour on December 7th, 1941, he was pretty much trapped in China. During the following year, for a short time, Eric did have hopes of the Missionary Society arranging a posting in Canada as there was talk of repatriation for missionaries. In the end it was only small numbers of rich businessmen who were able to bribe their way out of China and this would never have been Eric's way. Missionaries were finally refused a safe passage, instead destined to be held in a camp where few soldiers would be needed to watch over them. Eric's immediate future was to be taken to a Civilian Assembly Centre in Shandong Province called Weihsien Interment Camp, a dreadfully run-down former Presbyterian mission. Here, in what is now the modern city of Weifang, Eric found a camp that had no running water, no heating, vandalised toilets and limited electric lighting. A grey eight-foot-high wall surrounded the camp to which was later added electrified bands of barbed wire. Searchlights had been placed on the corner towers while guards with dogs patrolled the camp. Hamilton describes it vividly — "filthy and insanitary, the pathways strewn with debris and the living quarters squalid." The meals usually consisted of nothing more than bread and soup, hardly a diet to ward off sickness. The inmates' reaction to being made to live in such conditions was predictable enough with countless disagreements and arguments often resulting in fights. When Eric arrived in Weihsien with his few possessions in March 1943, we can only try to guess how hopeless the situation must have looked.

Dreadful as it must have been, Eric was not one to give in easily. It was not long before he became a leader and main organiser in the camp by trying raise the morale of the 1,600 inmates through a variety of activities. This was by no means a straightforward task. The camp consisted of a variety of nationalities ranging from western European countries such as Belgium, Holland, Switzerland and the Scandinavian countries as well as from countries outside Europe, such as South Africa, Australia and the USA. Their backgrounds were also very different, ranging from bankers, businessmen and lawyers to drug addicts, alcoholics and thieves. To pull all this together and to reduce the squabbles and the physical confrontations that took place required remarkable skill which Eric alone seemed to possess. Before long, Eric was what Duncan Hamilton called "the conscience of the camp", known as 'Uncle Eric' to many of the younger men and the man who became involved in every activity in the camp, from playing chess to building models, teaching science and, of course, organising sporting activities. The holding of Bible classes too became a key part of Eric's huge contribution. Norman Cliff, a writer of religious books and somebody who spent time at Weihsien, described Eric in his book *The Courtyard of the Happy Way* as "the first Christian gentleman it has been my pleasure to meet. In all my time at the camp, I never heard him say a bad word about anybody." Another Protestant theologian, the American Langdon Gilkey, left a particularly detailed and moving recollection of Eric's importance and impact.

"Often in an evening I would see him bent over a chessboard or a model boat, or directing some sort of square dance — absorbed, weary and interested, pouring all of himself into this effort to capture the imagination of these penned up youths.

He was overflowing with good humour and love for life, and with enthusiasm and charm.

It is rare indeed that a person has the good fortune to meet a saint, but he came as close to it as anyone I have ever known."

It is difficult to imagine a more fulsome tribute or a more deserving recipient.

Such a reputation is not won without a cost and it is with his health that Eric paid the price. It became clear, even to those who saw him daily, that Eric was deteriorating physically during his two years at Weihsien. He became slow in movement, cheekbones and chest sunken, a shadow of the athlete the world revered in 1924. It was not surprising. Fellow inmates depended on him for everything: comfort, the completion of numerous jobs needed to be done around the camp and, of course, the teaching. This was enough to sap the strength of any man but the presence of a brain tumour, undiagnosed until it was far too late to treat, made the tragic end to Eric's life inevitable. The first signs of the onset of his illness appeared when his memory, revered for his ability to remember word for word huge chunks of the Bible, began to be affected, although Eric attributed this to overwork, malnourishment and stress. In his last letter to Florence, he revealed that he was having a nervous breakdown. In fact, Eric was dying. On the 21st February 1945, to the despair of every one of his fellow inmates, he passed away. Six months later, on the 17th August, just over a week after two atomic bombs dropped on Hiroshima and Nagasaki, effectively ended World War Two, the camp was liberated. Not that the end of the war was the end of China's misery. Following the Japanese surrender, China dissolved into renewed or continued civil war between the Nationalists led by Chiang Kai-shek and Mao Zedong's Communist Party. The struggle continued until the Nationalists collapsed and Mao established The People's Republic of China in 1949.

The story of Eric Liddell does not end in Weihsien although the immediate years brought less recognition than one might expect. Florence did not know of Eric's death until 1st May 1945 by which time media interest centred on the closing days of the war in Europe and Hitler's death a week later. His funeral at Weihsien was described as "the most moving event in the whole of camp life" by one of the inmates. Even the guards kept a respectful distance from the ceremony. Of course memorial services were held, particularly in Scotland, but following his burial behind the Japanese officers' quarters in the grounds of what is now a school, Eric disappeared from public consciousness. Even Florence, devoted to Eric as she undoubtedly was, realised that life had to go on. She made a successful second marriage in 1951 to Murray Hall, a cousin, and four years later gave birth to a fourth child, Jeannie.

Eric's return to claim his rightful place in the first rank of British sporting heroes took another thirty-five years to gain momentum. Perhaps it began when Alan Wells, another proud Scotsman and Olympic champion, was asked on winning the 100 metres gold medal in the 1980 Moscow Olympics if he had won it for Harold Abrahams, the last British winner of that title. "No," replied Wells, "I did it for Eric Liddell." *Chariots of Fire* was nine months away from general release but the heroic story of Eric's Olympic triumph and the events surrounding it was about to emerge from the darkness. The 'Eric Liddell Centre' in Edinburgh opened in 1980 honouring his belief in community service, supporting people of all ages and cultures. In 1989, the location of the grave but not the grave itself, was rediscovered. A monument, seven feet high and two and a half feet wide and built using an enormous slab of granite from the Isle of Mull, stands in the vicinity of the grave which disappeared following the liberation of the camp and subsequent building on the site. In 2002, Eric became the first inductee in the Scottish Sports Hall of Fame while his triumph was even recognised by the Chinese. As the 2008 Olympic Games to be held in Beijing approached, only a six-hour drive from where Eric is buried, the Chinese claimed Eric to be China's first Olympic champion. Due to his birth and death in their country, China maintains this to the present day. The Chinese even sought to enhance his reputation by claiming that Eric sacrificed a possible prisoner exchange, approved by Churchill, to allow a pregnant woman to take his place. Impossible to confirm and a total surprise to the family but further evidence, if any is needed, of the respect and affection in which Eric is held.

Perhaps the final word on Eric should go to Stephen Metcalf, a fellow internee and a keen young athlete to whom the Olympic champion became something of a mentor. So much so that Metcalf later became a missionary in Japan where he worked for the Overseas Missionary Fellowship between 1952 and 1990. Following Eric's death, his disciple wrote passionately,

"He gave me two things: One was his worn-out running shoes, but the best thing he gave me was the baton of forgiveness. He taught me to love my enemies, the Japanese, and to pray for them."

Perhaps it is this even more than his remarkable achievements on the running track, the essence of his character captured so well in *Chariots of Fire*, which places Eric Liddell at the pinnacle of sporting heroes.

Keith Miller

CHAPTER 16
SURVIVORS 1: THE AIRMEN

There is no disguising the horror of World War Two and the damage that it inflicted both to the infrastructure and, much more importantly, to those involved in the conflict. As we have already seen, exact numbers of losses are difficult to confirm but one can confidently state that at least 383,700 British military personnel lost their lives along with around 67,200 civilians. This is around half of the number of British military losses during the Great War but the country suffered many more civilian deaths in the second conflict. But it is also true that, just as in the Great War, most soldiers returned home. Psychologically and physically scarred maybe, but they returned home nonetheless. Just as in the years following the 1918 Armistice, returning soldiers had no wish to glorify their achievements, this being particularly true of those who had witnessed the worst of atrocities. Many played down their part in the war, happy to tell the occasional anecdote and enjoy with their families some of the countless World War Two films 'doing the rounds' in hundreds of cinemas throughout the country. By the 1960s and seventies they could enjoy, if they wished, TV comedies such as *Dad's Army*, *It Ain't Half Hot Mum* and *Allo 'Allo*, all of which give us an amusing, if not always historically accurate, picture of events. These comedies highlight the important and necessary comradery between the participants, and the often-amusing attempts to maintain morale and make sense of the appalling situation in which they were involved. As a result, the true horrors of these momentous years, has sometimes been lost. Indeed, as suggested in the introduction to this study, the survivors from the sporting fraternity have not been acknowledged as readily as they might have been. This situation needs to be remedied and we can go at least part of the way to redress the balance by examining the stories of some high-profile sporting heroes who survived the conflict.

There are, of course, numerous stories that could be told. Stan Mortensen, the famous Blackpool and England centre forward started the war as an eighteen-year-old wireless operator. He was the only survivor when his RAF bomber crashed, thereby having the opportunity to become one of the best-known footballers in the country. He played in three post-war FA Cup finals and scored the only hat-trick ever scored in the final when Blackpool beat Bolton Wanderers 4–3 in 1953, the 'Matthews Final'. Bert Trautmann was a German paratrooper in the Luftwaffe for most of the war, winning five medals including an Iron Cross. He was captured by both the Russians and the French, escaping on each occasion, before finally being captured by the British. He was imprisoned in several camps in Britain before being interned in Ashton-in-Makerfield. He was finally released in 1948. Deciding to stay in Britain, Trautmann became a professional goalkeeper for Manchester City where he was to become the hero of his club's 1956 FA Cup Final victory over Birmingham City. Trautmann finished the game with a broken neck, not discovered until three days after the match, and became an instant footballing hero, the 1956 Footballer of the Year. Or we could examine the story of Leo Goldstein, a Polish-born Jew, who survived the concentration camps to become a FIFA referee who worked at the 1962 World Cup in Chile. The stories are many, far too many to consider in a single book. Some, however, are worthy of greater examination.

Perhaps the first place to begin this process is by looking at the stories of some of the Allied fighter pilots. We have already seen the horrific losses suffered by the crews of Lancaster bombers with their life expectancy of twenty-two flying missions. Spitfire pilots in the Battle of Britain fared no better with an average of approximately four weeks' action before they too came to grief. In the Battle of Britain alone, a total of 554 British RAF pilots died. Churchill's oft repeated quote, "Never in the field of human conflict was so much owed by so many to so few", even eighty years later, has left a powerful imprint on the nation's consciousness. For those airmen who did survive it did something else. It gave many of those men a devil-may-care, live for the moment, attitude which followed them back into civilian life and influenced their actions for the rest of their lives. This is particularly true of two cricketing fighter pilots, the Middlesex and England batsman Bill Edrich and his Australian all-rounder, friend and rival, Keith Miller.

William John Edrich was born on 26th March 1916 in Lingwood, Norfolk, a member of a big cricketing family. His brothers, Brian, Eric and Geoff all played first-class cricket while his cousin John became one of the most successful England opening batsmen of the post-war years. While only five feet six inches in height, Bill was packed full of sporting talent. A good enough amateur footballer to play for both Norwich City and Tottenham Hotspur, Bill quickly made his mark when he represented Norfolk, aged only 16, in the Minor Counties Championship. It was as a batsman that he caught the eye but it was soon apparent that, bowling at fast/medium pace, Bill could be more than just a change bowler. By 1937, he had qualified for Middlesex and he set out on one of the most interesting, if somewhat inconsistent, cricketing careers. Bill's first season at Middlesex was an instant success as the twenty-one-year-old batsman scored 2,000 runs. The following summer, 1938, he became one of only eight batsmen to have scored 1,000 runs by the end of May. This places Bill in exalted company which includes Grace, Hammond and, of course, Bradman who is the only player to have achieved the feat twice — a remarkable achievement given that 'The Don' only played four summers in England during his career. A test career clearly beckoned and surely enough, Bill was selected to make his test debut on 10th June 1938 in the Ashes test at Trent Bridge, Nottingham, England's 300th test player. Unfortunately, Bill achieved little in this series, once again dominated by Bradman and also by Len Hutton's record-breaking 364 at the Oval.

Despite this less than impressive start to his test career, Bill was selected for the MCC tour to South Africa the following winter. Once again, the expected runs failed to materialise. With Hutton injured, Bill opened the batting in the first test but made no impact. *The Times* voiced an opinion held by many observers that Bill lacked the necessary technique required to see off the new ball and called him an "enigmatic" player but even when he dropped down the order, success eluded him. Only his bowling kept him in the side, surprisingly given that he had been described by Alec Bedser as having "negligible quality", lacking class and "something of a slinger." Despite this uncomplimentary analysis, which view was not held by Bedser alone, Bill opened the bowling in three tests with the established Ken Farnes. Finally, in the fifth and final test at Durban, Bill fulfilled his potential. The story is that this dramatic change of fortune owed everything to Bill's preparation. Earlier in his career his captain, Lionel Tennyson, that most accommodating of leaders, warned Bill that excessive drinking and socialising was forbidden. Heeding this advice, Bill tried to restrain himself with early nights and a self-imposed reduction in his drinking and smoking. Given his lack of success so far, Bill decided before the final test that he would revert to 'normal' preparations. Although he scored only one in the first innings, Bill helped to save the series for England. As we have already seen, the position of the teams in the series, with England leading 1–0 with one test to play, required that this final test be played to a finish. England were set the mammoth task of scoring 696 in their second innings in order to win the test. It was Bill who made this almost impossible task achievable with a brilliant innings of 219, leaving England only 250 runs short when he was finally out. Others took up the challenge and England reached 654/5, only 45 runs short when play was finally halted on the 10th day. England had a boat to catch. After 99 timeless tests, this was the last to be played.

Although he was surprisingly dropped for the 1939 series against the West Indies, at last Bill could be considered a Test match batsman, confirmed when he was named as one of Wisden's Five Cricketers of the Year. The war was to seriously interrupt this progress but Bill had no hesitation in deciding how he could make his contribution. He had always wanted to fly so he joined the RAF Physical Training Branch as a quick route in. After discussing his future with his old Middlesex captain and England leg spinner, Walter Robbins, he managed to get a transfer to Cranwell where he gained a commission and a year's operational training on the Blenheim aircraft. He was then posted to No 2 Group, Bomber Command and on 21st May 1941, he reported to 107 Squadron at Little Massingham, Norfolk. Within 19 days, Bill was promoted from Pilot Officer to Acting Squadron Leader, an indication of the heavy losses as much as his ability to lead. Nevertheless, it quickly became apparent that Bill could lead and that he was a man who others would follow anywhere. Ernie Hope, a colleague for whom Bill later became best man at his wedding, confirmed this. Ernie later said, "Bill was a great man and he flew his aircraft in the same cavalier spirit as he played his cricket." This was a view shared by all his colleagues, both pilots and cricketers.

Although Bill had missed the Battle of Britain in 1940, he was not long in seeing serious action. Although Hitler's plans to invade had been thwarted, due in no small part to the skill and bravery of the RAF pilots, the danger was far from over. As Bill went into action, he was fighting with a backdrop of 43,000 civilians having been killed in air raids over Britain in the previous twelve months. His first action was to attack a heavily defended enemy convoy moving from Hamburg down the Dutch coast to Rotterdam and he was soon flying through an intense barrage. Bill was lucky to survive. Although he did manage to release his four bombs after jinking and rolling to distract defending gunners and succeeded in leaving the ship in flames, a huge segment of the aircraft rudder had been shot away in the attack. Bill himself recognised the danger and recounted that during the attack he had "experienced an extraordinary feeling of claustrophobia, trapped in the goldfish bowl of the cockpit."

Despite this experience, Bill had gained confidence in his aircraft. He never had as much faith in any machine as he had in the Blenheim and, despite the Germans having superior firepower, Bill didn't lose that confidence. On August 12th, he was involved in what the *Daily Telegraph* called "the RAF's most audacious and dangerous low-level bombing raid" when the Blenheim bombers attacked power stations in the area around Cologne, the first daylight raid deep into the German industrial heartland. Bill led a section of the squadron in which each plane carried four 250-lb bombs with eleven second fuses. This time lapse allowed the three boxes of six aircraft to follow each other through the target area at the lowest possible height and for the last aircraft to steer clear by the time the first bombs exploded. This was an extremely risky venture, so much so that 12 of the 54 aircraft failed to return. It was for a very good reason that Churchill claimed that "the exploits of our daylight bombers can be likened to the Charge of the Light Brigade at Balaclava."

Bill's efforts and his leadership qualities were quickly recognised and he was awarded the DFC following this mission. The citation described the dangers that he faced and the skill required, concluding with the following words,

"Squadron Leader Edrich led his formation in at exactly the right height and time, all aircraft dropping the bombs in the centre of the target area. By carrying out his orders with the greatest exactitude and determination, he must be given credit for a large part of the success of the attack."

Air Marshall Sir Ivor Broom, who was also on the raid with his 114 Squadron, later remembered Bill's contribution:

"Bill's dynamic and cheerful leadership imparted tremendous confidence in those who followed him. The immediate award of the DFC brought great pleasure to his many RAF friends who so admired and loved him."

This was just the beginning for Bill. Soon he was leading low-level raids on enemy convoys in the North Sea and English Channel. These raids were carried out on convoys which were escorted by anti-aircraft ships, which could zero in on the bombers with their heavy and light guns. Bill and his colleagues were often attacking the convoy at a maximum height of between ten and twenty feet, an extremely dangerous operation. The cricket biographer, Alan Hill, tells us that Brian Edrich, Bill's brother who was also serving in the RAF, clearly spelled out the risks to the RAF pilots.

"The Blenheims attacked the ships by coming straight at them, just lifting over the top, and then releasing their bombs into the sides of the vessels. At the speed they came in — around 250mph — they were fairly easy targets. The hazards were heightened by the lack of manoeuvrability of the slow and cumbersome Blenheim bombers, which had been developed from civilian aircraft. Evasion tactics had to be learned by bitter experience."

Clearly Brian had less confidence in the Blenheims than his brother but Bill was not alone in his appreciation of this particular aircraft. Following a raid on the Cherbourg docks, one Flight Intelligence report described the sight of the Blenheim aircraft,

"The sea-coloured camouflage on the top surface of the Blenheims was so effective that the first we saw of them as they flew out from the target was their wakes in the water."

Even so, the pilots needed luck and Bill had his share. On returning from one raid, he was intercepted by a group of Messerschmitts. A number of direct hits had left the Blenheim in a bad way and evasion was the only hope. Bill failed to shake off one of the Messerschmitts but miraculously it had run out of ammunition. The German pilot flew alongside Bill, looked at him, shrugged and flew off. They gave each other a goodbye wave.

One would think that escapes like this would leave the nerves shattered. But Bill was quick to point out the exhilaration that he experienced when flying. Once again, Alan Hill supplies the quotation,

"Flattened low on the water, tucked in as close as I dared to the leader, I felt an exhilaration that swamped all other emotions. Low flying did not bother me. I loved it. It gave me an illusion of speed and security. Two hundred knots may not be much by 'sound barrier' standards but with the sea racing by 30 feet below it seems incredibly fast."

But the war had affected Bill deeply. Years later he reflected that "in four months in 1941 I experienced the heights and depths of emotions — supreme elation like the effects of good wine and profound remorse at losing so many fine friends." It did give him a sense of perspective on life which was to remain with him and, despite accusations by some, less well versed in the daily dangers faced by pilots, of being rather juvenile, Bill was determined to live each day as if it was his last. His father, Bill senior, has recounted an anecdote that serves to highlight the remarkable life being led by these airmen. "Carried out an early morning raid on Westerland, the fighter airfield on the island of Sylt. At ten a.m., soon after he got back, there was a report of a German convoy in the North Sea. Needed somebody to lead it so Bill volunteered. Was due to play cricket that afternoon but was on a raid so turned up late — 3 Blenheims went on the raid and only 2 returned. Bill was one of them but was shaken. By two thirty, he was back and batting 1st wicket down. Turned up in his tatty England sweater which he wore on raids for good luck. Drank a quick beer before he batted. Made 80 in 30 minutes before getting run out so he could rest."

The day was summed up by Alan Hill, "A sortie before breakfast; an enemy vessel destroyed by nine a.m.; desperate air battle over the Channel by eleven a.m.; a riot of runs in the afternoon; a rendezvous with a handsome village girl that evening." It is no surprise that having experienced days such as this it was difficult to settle to 'normal' civilian life when the war ended.

By 1943, it was decided that Bill needed a break from the constant stress of being a fighter pilot so he was sent on a course at Army Staff College at Camberley. Subsequently he was employed on RAF Group Operations at Wallingford helping to prepare for the D-Day landings. Following this success an exhausted Bill was able to relax, safe in the knowledge that his astounding bravery had made a real contribution to the outcome of the war.

A year later it was over and, after expressing his "immense relief that he had survived the war", Bill attempted to return to 'normality'. As well as driving his car in the same manner as he flew aircraft, this, of course, meant cricket and 1947 was to prove to be his greatest of years. Although by now their twenties were behind them, Bill and his 'Middlesex twin' Denis Compton ran riot. Bill scored 3,539 runs that summer while his 'twin' scored 3,816, the two highest totals ever scored in an English season. He also hit centuries in Test matches in the immediate post-war years: one against Australia in 1946/7, two against South Africa in the summer of 1947, one more against the unbeatable 1948 Australians and finally against New Zealand a year later. It makes one wonder what figures he might have achieved, if he hadn't had lost six summers fighting fascism. Nevertheless, along with Compton, Bill helped to put the smiles back on people's faces. The great cricket writer Neville Cardus wrote movingly that he had never been,

"So deeply touched on a cricket ground as I was in this heavenly summer when I went to Lord's to see a pale-faced crowd, existing on rations, the rocket bombs still in the ears of most folk, to see this warm, dowdy crowd watching Compton and Edrich."

The 1950s saw a steep decline and the perception prevailed that Bill couldn't play the West Indian spinners Ramadhin and Valentine. But he played his part in the 1953 Ashes success and it was Compton who hit the winning runs at the Oval with his mate Bill undefeated at the other end. A fitting climax to a wonderful career and, although he played in five further tests, four on Hutton's tour to Australia, the Oval was his last great moment. When Bill left first-class cricket in order to play in the Minor Counties Championship with home county Norfolk, he had scored 36,965 runs at an average of 42 and 2,240 runs at 40 in Test matches. A colourful personal life, which included five marriages and numerous parties, awaited him but by the time of his death on 24th April 1986 following a fall, his reputation as one Britain's war heroes and most colourful cricketers was secure. In 1991, two new grandstands were opened at Lord's, the Compton Stand and, most fittingly, the Edrich stand, a permanent reminder of a remarkable career.

It is, perhaps, inappropriate to have favourites when researching and then writing about sporting heroes and their war service. But it is very difficult not to be attracted to the character and thrilled by the exploits of the great Australian all-rounder Keith Miller. Keith was one of the 'larger than life' characters of twentieth century cricket, the man whom Neville Cardus called "The Australian in Excelsis", whom *Wisden* listed in 1998 as the 17th greatest player of all time and the man who was possibly the greatest of Australian all-rounders. The journalist Ian Wooldridge wrote that he was "the golden boy of cricket... who was more than a cricketer... He embodied the idea that there was more to life than cricket." Wooldridge hints at a love of life that matches the attitude and exploits of Bill Edrich, an idea supported by the BBC cricket broadcaster and writer Christopher Martin-Jenkins who wrote that the length of Keith's run-up depended largely on how he had spent the previous evening. Ray Robinson, a premier cricket writer of his generation, gave an Australian perspective on Keith in 1951.

"Long before Keith Miller gets near the wicket you can tell that something extraordinary is going to happen. The erect set of his capless head on his square shoulders, the loose swing of his long legs, the half-smile on his handsome face and his general ease of manner all signify that no ordinary cricketer approaches."

Robinson described him as an "Olympian god among mortals" who "brings boys' dreams to life... the cricketer they would all like to be." Robinson painted a vivid picture of a player "as masculine as Tarzan, whose style suffuses his cricket with glowing power, personality charges it with daring and knocks bowling and conventions sky-high." Great praise indeed!

Comparing cricketers across eras is a risky business but there is no doubt that Keith, although not as prolific or versatile as Gary Sobers, belongs in the same company as Ian Botham, Kapil Dev, Imran Khan, Richard Hadlee and Jacques Kallis. Perhaps, of Australian all-rounders, only Richie Benaud comes near. Being bowled by Keith when he was in his pomp was worn as a badge of honour by some. The renowned cricket writer AA Thompson, borrowing from the novelist Thackeray, likened such an event to "being kicked downstairs by a Duke." With such a press it is scarcely surprising that Keith, with his matinee idol looks and flowing black hair, is seen as one of cricket's most glamorous personalities. Add to that the war record of a brave fighter pilot and you have the complete package.

Keith Ross Miller was born in Sunshine, Victoria, a western suburb of Melbourne, the youngest of four children, three of whom were boys. His Christian names were a tribute to the Australian pilots Keith and Ross Smith who were in the process of making their historic flight from Britain to Australia when Keith was born, an interesting choice of names given his later war service. All three boys showed ability on the cricket field, following their father who was a good local player and who ensured that each of the boys developed a faultless technique along the lines of the great Bill Ponsford. At first, despite his father's love of cricket and his success in playing for an Under 15s team at the age of 12, it seemed that Keith, rather small for his age at this point, was more likely to become a jockey. Success in gaining a place at the selective Melbourne High School soon changed that. Here, his Maths teacher was the 1930s Australian captain, Bill Woodfull, who immediately saw Keith's ability as a cricketer. The man who had captained an Australian side containing Bradman and Ponsford and who had faced, on and off the field, the pressures of the 'Bodyline' tour was somebody not easily impressed. Keith, however, was in the First XI by the age of 14 and he was on his way. Playing for South Melbourne, Keith was also able to impress Lindsay Hassett and Ian Johnson, both of whom later captained him in the full Australian side.

Before much longer, Keith had a growth spurt and, on reaching the height of six feet two inches, needed to abandon any thoughts of becoming a jockey. He left school, became a clerk and concentrated on playing cricket for VCA Colts where he had great success, especially with his batting. In the late summer of the 1937/38 season Keith made his debut for Victoria in the 'friendly' match against Tasmania where he made 181. In the 1939/40 season Keith really arrived and made his Sheffield Shield debut against South Australia at the Adelaide Oval. His appearance was memorable for his running out of Bradman and he did enough to keep his place. In the return match, he scored 108 batting against the great leg spinner Clarrie Grimmett. Despite representing St Kilda and the Victorian State team in Australian Rules football and being a useful footballer for Brighton, Victoria, cricket was by now definitely Keith's major sport. A great future awaited him. Then came the war.

On the 20th August 1940 Keith joined the Militia (army reserve) and was assigned to the 4th Reserve Motor Transport Company. Here the confident, rather brash, Keith quickly clashed with authority and he was fined for "using insulting language to a superior officer." Such was his ability to get into fist fights, or what were commonly called 'dust-ups', that Keith acquired the nickname 'Dusty' during this period. He then tried to join the Navy but when a close friend's application was rejected, Keith's response was to tear up his own paperwork. He went to the RAAF recruiting office instead where, following the Japanese bombing of Pearl Harbour, it wasn't long before Keith was called to prepare for active service. He began his training at Victor Harbour in South Australia where he was given his 'wings' in late 1942 and promoted to Flight Sergeant early the following year. This now required him to set sail for Europe and it was on this journey, while stopping over at Boston, New England, where he first met his future wife, Peg Wagner. On arriving in England, Keith was invited to join the RAAF cricket team and played for the Warner XI at Lord's. The opposition included Bob Wyatt, 'Gubby' Allen, Trevor Bailey and Alec Bedser, a pretty formidable set of opponents, but Keith made his mark and for the first time in England began to gain some media attention. It was also at this time, the summer of 1943, that he met Denis Compton for the first time. This was a friendship that was to last the rest of his life.

By the end of the summer Keith was based in Gloucestershire and made an impression, but not in a way set to endear himself to his superior officers. After threatening to punch his commanding officer, Keith was given a three-week course of hard labour as a punishment. Following this, he was sent to Newcastle where he trained in the use of radar. While in Newcastle, Keith also managed to injure his back in a wrestling bout, an injury which did affect his bowling from time to time throughout his career. His batting, however, did not seem to suffer. Playing for the RAAF again in the summer of 1944, Keith scored a century at Lord's just as a V-1 flying bomb landed. He later scored 85 in 100 minutes against an England XI and took 6/28 against the West of England.

It was while he was doing damage to the reputations of England's finest bowlers and batsmen in August 1944 that Keith finally obtained his commission as a pilot officer. He was sent first to Grantham and then to Cranfield in Bedfordshire, although a night of drunken revelry nearly saw him discharged. Keith escaped, fortuitously, with a fine. On 4th November 1944, Keith achieved his promotion to a flying officer and was assigned to 169 squadron flying Mosquito fighter bombers, taking part in missions over mainland Europe. These included attacking

V-1 and V-2 production and test launch sites in the North Sea, attacks on German installations in Flensburg, Denmark and, like Bill Edrich, an attack on Westerland Airfield on the island of Sylt. On this occasion Keith was very lucky. He was forced to land when the bomb stuck to the plane and failed to drop. Fortunately, it didn't explode.

This wasn't the only narrow escape that Keith had during the war. Indeed, while training with Bristol Beauforts, Beanfighters and Mosquitos, he had several near-death experiences. On one occasion a mechanical problem with his Beaufighter saw Keith forced to make an emergency landing. The next time that particular plane was used the pilot was killed in an accident. On another occasion, Keith avoided hitting a hangar by centimetres. Keith's love of a party is well-documented but on one occasion he was actually forced to miss a social engagement. Tragically, the venue was hit by a V-1 bomb and many of the guests were killed. On another evening, Keith went AWOL in order to see a concert. This absence led to him being discharged, only to be reinstated after agreeing to play cricket. His narrow escapes were not confined to his flying adventures, as one particular incident took place at sea. Keith was ordered to take part in an exchange programme which required him to sail on a Royal Navy destroyer. The destroyer became engaged in a battle with a German U-boat which only ended when the latter was sunk.

Despite these adventures, Keith did survive the war and returned to a job at Vacuum Oil. Before doing so, one of his final tasks before leaving the RAAF was to fly Air Force personnel over Germany to report back on the success, or otherwise, of the Allied bombing. He found that the work at Vacuum Oil was seen by some as demeaning and this left him frustrated. He considered playing professional cricket in the Lancashire League where he could earn good money but he realised that this would scupper his hopes of playing for Australia. And it was test cricket that he set his mind on. From now, and for the next decade, test cricket was to dominate his life as Keith became 'the golden boy of cricket', giving rise to his new and long-lasting nickname of 'Nugget'. In the first Victory Test of 1946, Keith bowled to Bill Edrich, his fellow fighter pilot, for the first time. By the time these five Victory Tests had been completed, Keith topped the batting averages and had taken 10 wickets. He had, at the age of 26, truly arrived on the international stage. And it was his bowling partnership with Ray Lindwall that first caught the public's imagination. Len Hutton, even years later, confirmed that the Lindwall and Miller opening bowling partnership was the most hostile that he ever faced, Lindwall with his smooth, controlled action and Keith, more unpredictable, with his lethal slower ball and his fastest delivery bowled off a shortened run. Between them they caused havoc in the immediate post-war years, key members of Bradman's 1948 touring team to play England, 'The Invincibles', possibly the greatest cricket team in history. At this stage even Bradman was an admirer, praising Keith's aggressive batting, although lacking judgement, his dangerous bowling and calling him the best slip fielder in the world. Keith's ability to bowl sides out is confirmed by his taking of 170 wickets in 55 tests but it is only part of the story. A very powerful striker of the ball, capable of batting as high as three, four or five in the order, Keith was also an excellent fielder anywhere in the field but, as Bradman had said, especially in the slips where he took many acrobatic catches. By 1948, Keith was the most glamorous of cricketers with only his 'mate' Compton to challenge him.

Neville Cardus leaves a clear and vivid picture of the man, "handsome in a sun and windswept way", never completely happy unless he was attacking.

"I like to see him walking out to bat, looking about him so as not to miss anything, the legs moving easily but no part of the upper body moving at all. Once when he was coming through the pavilion gate at Sydney on the way to face the England attack in a Test match, a small schoolboy ran after him through the pavilion gate, defying red-faced authority. He asked the boy to hold his bat while he wrote an autograph for him."

Keith finished his test career with seven centuries and 2,958 runs at an average of nearly 37 while his 170 test wickets came at a cost of just under 23 per wicket. A total of 29 of his 55 tests were against England with very few played against the weaker test playing nations.

It would be easy, and very tempting, to recount in detail Keith's achievements after the war. But the real appeal of Keith Miller is that personal figures meant little to him. What was important was his love of the game and the contest, winning in the right spirit, all influenced no doubt by his wartime experiences. He deplored Bradman's ruthless attitude to crush the opposition. The best example of this came when the brilliant 1948 Australians were playing Essex. On their way to a score of 721 made in one day, Keith came in when the scoreboard read 364/2 and he was promptly out first ball. Not for him the pleasure of grinding a weak county side into the ground. Besides, as he once said, "I had a good hand of cards waiting for me" or perhaps he needed to hear the result of the 2.30 at Newmarket. His relationship with Bradman was always tense, the Roundhead against the Cavalier, and it is probably this relationship that cost him the opportunity to captain Australia. Bradman became a selector and his was the voice that mattered in Australian cricket. Stories such as the one that told of Bradman knocking at Keith's hotel door one night in the middle of a Test match only to find his star player in his dinner suit. "Well," said Keith, "I was in at the curfew like you requested but now I'm going out." Bradman was not amused. Going out for Keith also meant meeting up with Compton and Edrich, two kindred spirits, but fraternising with opponents to this extent was also frowned upon. Keith himself told the story that, in the Ashes series of 1946/7 in Australia, when Bill Edrich arrived at the wicket on a pitch that was bound to cause him trouble, even injury, he decided to 'go easy' on his old mate and fellow pilot. Bradman was not amused and told Keith to bowl quicker. Keith said that he never felt the same about test cricket after that. Nor did Bradman ever feel the same about Keith. After bowling three consecutive bouncers to Bradman in a testimonial match in 1948/9, dismissing him with the third, Keith was omitted from the Australian team to tour South Africa. This despite Keith clearly being the best all-rounder in the world at the time.

The pressure on modern-day sportsmen and women playing top level international sport is fiercely debated these days, especially the effect that competing continually at a high level has on the performer's mental health. Modern-day sports stars are often compared unfavourably to heroes of the past who often had a different set of pressures with which to contend. Participation in one or other of two World Wars certainly comes into this category and there is no doubt that Keith's war experiences influenced his attitude to sport. Perhaps the best example of this is one that is often told, most recently in Duncan Hamilton's biography of Neville Cardus. On being interviewed by the master of the one-to-one interview, cricket fanatic, journalist and BBC personality, Michael Parkinson, he was asked about the pressures of Test match cricket. "Pressure?" I'll tell you about pressure, scoffed Keith. "Pressure is a Messerschmitt up your arse. Playing cricket is not." Although Keith was always a true competitor, perhaps within this quote we can see the root of a rather carefree attitude to his cricket. But it would be wrong to see Keith as some adventurer, only interested in a good time. He always played to win while maintaining an interest in a very wide range of activities. He had a love of classical music, Beethoven in particular, so much so that while on a bombing mission he broke away from his squadron in order to fly over Beethoven's birthplace, Bonn. Cardus tells us that, while standing in the slips waiting for the next delivery, Keith, relaxed and conversational, is as likely to be dismissing with a wave of the hand somebody's tip for the 3.30 as whistling a phrase from a Beethoven piano concert. It would be dangerous to see Keith as a one-dimensional character.

When Keith eventually retired from first-class cricket, he was awarded the MBE for services to cricket, later to be followed by the honour of Member of the Order of Australia. He worked as an often-controversial journalist with the *Daily Express* during the English summer for the next 20 years, worked for Vernon's Pools, owned by the millionaire horseracing entrepreneur Robert Sangster, and then as head of a lobby group in promoting Australian Rules. He had married Peg in 1946 following three years of separation due to the war but there were always rumours of affairs, one with a beauty queen and another, unsubstantiated relationship, with Princess Margaret. He had four sons and fell out with each of them, although they did reconcile before his death. A glamorous character for sure but Keith was not the easiest 'family man', being much more at home at the cricket or at the races. He finally divorced Peg in 2002 and married Marie Challman with whom he had been living since 1999. Ill health had plagued Keith since 1991 and his problems included having a stroke, hip injuries which put him in a wheelchair and finally, possibly as a result of his refusal to ever wear a hat, skin cancer. This remarkable cricketer and man finally passed away on 11th October 2004 aged 84, much to the dismay of his many friends, teammates and former opponents. Keith's home state of Victoria gave him a State funeral which was broadcast live on radio with hundreds left outside a packed cathedral. In later years, Keith became one of only four Australians to have their portraits hang in the Long Room at Lord's, the others being Bradman, Victor Trumper and Shane Warne. Unsurprisingly, Keith became one of the ten inaugural members of the Australian Cricket Hall of Fame, a player who perhaps better than anyone achieved greatness without ever losing sight of the true place of sport in society. A game to be enjoyed but kept in perspective. Serving as a pilot in the most dreadful of wars had taught him that and it was a lesson that he never forgot.

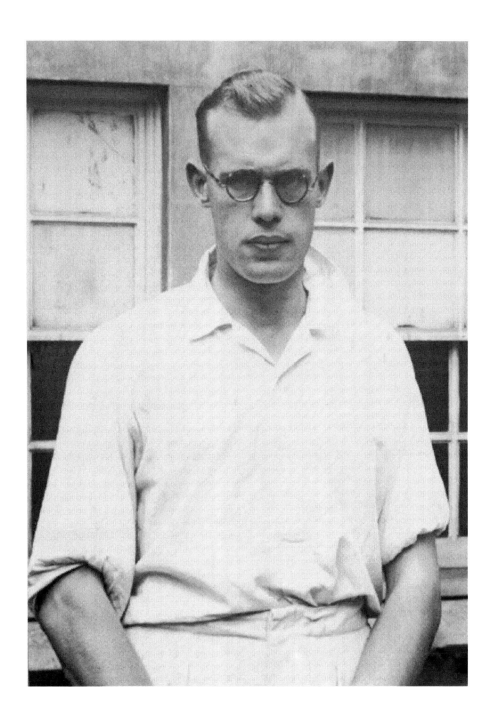

Bill Bowes

CHAPTER 17
SURVIVORS 2: PRISONERS OF WAR

The fighter pilots who were lucky enough to have survived the war maintained an aura and glamour for the rest of their lives, their bravery and skill never in doubt. For other survivors, the experience was very different, much less glamorous but often one of unimaginable hardship. Few, if any, would echo former USA President Donald Trump's assessment of his political rival and Vietnam War veteran John McCain's wartime experience as a prisoner of the North Vietnamese when he said that he, Trump, questioned whether being captured made McCain a hero. But there is no doubt that there has been less recognition for the ordeal suffered by prisoners of war than there might have been. A study of the Yorkshire and England fast bowler Bill Bowes and his experience in a German prisoner-of-war camp confirms exactly the hardships faced by these captives.

William Eric Bowes was born on 25th July 1908 in Elland, Leeds, the son of John, a railwayman with the Lancashire and Yorkshire Railway Company. The six foot four inches tall right-arm fast-medium bowler with the big heart developed into one of the popular and respected players of his generation, playing in 372 first-class matches between 1929 and 1947 and taking 1,639 wickets at an average of 16.76, an astonishing average for the time. Bill's 15 Test matches resulted in him taking 68 wickets at 22.33, a perfectly respectable performance in an era when the bat tended to dominate the ball.

Living in Yorkshire and having a father keen on the sport, Bill, in his own words "just slipped into the game." He, like many boys of his generation, played both in the street and at school; in Bill's case, Armley Park Council School and, later, West Leeds High School. Bill also joined Kirkstall Educational Cricket Club and during his spare summer days watched his local team, Armley. By 1924, Bill had left school and, ignoring his mother's wish for him to train as a schoolteacher, joined an estate agency. While playing for Kirkstall during this period, Bill began to make his mark and attracted the interest of several league clubs prepared to offer him a professional contract. However, tempting this might have been, Bill decided to remain with Kirkstall and hope for something better—perhaps even the dream of playing for Yorkshire.

No offers were forthcoming at this point but the bespectacled Bill, who looked more like a university professor than a fast bowler, impressed some influential watchers. He was serious about his cricket from the start, although this could be deceptive as he sometimes appeared somewhat indifferent. Dudley Carew observed that "fate, the batsman and the weather-cock on the pavilion seem all one to him." Bill was not without humour, always willing to indulge in a spot of leg-pulling. In 1927 he was invited to Lord's in order to have a trial for the MCC. The MCC were planning fixtures against all the counties the following summer so it was imperative that they recruited new players. Pelham Warner, hugely influential at the MCC, was sufficiently impressed and Bill was offered a job on the Lord's ground staff. By now Warwickshire were also showing interest but it was too late and Bill headed to St John's Wood. Yorkshire quickly woke up to what they might be missing and in 1929 it was agreed that Bill could play for Yorkshire on those occasions when he was not required by the MCC.

Bill, 20 years of age, made his Yorkshire debut on 8th May 1929 against Oxford University followed soon after by his first County Championship appearance against Essex. And what intimidating company for a young cricketer to keep. Wilfred Rhodes, Emmott Robinson, Herbert Sutcliffe and Maurice Leyland, all Yorkshire legends, were part of that team while before long Percy Holmes and George Macaulay had returned to the side. However, playing with such experienced players in such a good side, had great advantages. Yorkshire were not at all bothered that Bill was a rather limited fielder and a genuine tail-end batsman. His job was to get wickets and, Rhodes and Robinson in particular, helped him to do this by protecting him as much as possible, nursing him through those early games.

By 1930, Bill was established in the Yorkshire team and that summer he took 100 wickets for the first time. Indeed, Bill was to achieve this feat every year during the 1930s with the exception of 1937 when he suffered an ankle injury which reduced his number of appearances. With Hedley Verity now also established in the side, Yorkshire were looking extremely strong. In 1931 they won their first championship since 1925 and retained the title a year later when Bill took 192 wickets, a superb return for a fast bowler. At least some of this success was the result of advice offered by the ex-Lancashire and England fast bowler Walter Brearley who taught Bill to reduce his run-up and to concentrate on moving the ball, both by mastering the late away swinger but also by developing a late in swinger. Bill mastered this without any noticeable change to his bowling action. Rhodes and Robinson also helped this development, often during away fixtures sitting with Bill and Hedley Verity in their hotel bedroom and analysing the performance of their young protégés. These sessions took place regardless of the number of wickets the young bowlers had taken. There was always room for improvement. It was the Yorkshire way.

Bill's bowling action was the subject of much comment among cricket writers. In typical style, Neville Cardus referred to Bill having "a somnambulistic gait, bowled as though sleep was still drowsily soothing his limbs." Robertson-Glasgow was of the opinion that Bill was "the most difficult fast-medium bowler in England" who did not make the mistake of bowling too fast but rather opted for control, realising that his deliveries came off the pitch much quicker than the batsman expected. Perhaps it was Robertson-Glasgow's assessment which gives us the clearest picture of Bill's bowling action.

"Bill's run-up is a leisurely business. I sometimes wonder if he is going to get there at all. His whole approach to the supreme task in cricket suggests, quite falsely, indolence, negligence, almost reluctance. But he is just keeping it all for the right moment... If you watch closely, you will see the full use of great height, strong shoulder and pliant wrist. His direction is unusually accurate; he varies his pace to suit the pitch; he can swing even a worn ball very late from leg; and often with an awkward kick."

Leisurely Bill's action might have been but he quickly got results. In the summer of 1932, he experienced the most memorable performance of his career when, at Scarborough, he took 9/121 against Essex and was only denied all 10 wickets when a catch was dropped off his bowling. The *Yorkshire Post* concluded that Bill had performed well enough to have bowled two sides out in a day. It couldn't have been that the wicket helped the bowlers to any great extent. When Essex bowled, the Yorkshire batsmen, Sutcliffe and Leyland destroyed Ken Farnes by taking 66 runs off his first four overs. The up-and-coming Farnes was put to the sword by two great players determined to put him back in his place. The kindly Bill consoled his future England teammate afterwards and advised him not to bowl so many bouncers at players of the calibre of Sutcliffe and Leyland.

Such performances did not go unnoticed by the England selectors and Bill was selected for the only test of the 1932 summer. Opening the bowling with Bill Voce, he took six wickets in the match thereby booking his place on the infamous 'Bodyline Tour' of 1932/3. As a bowler who knew how to use the bouncer and supporting the front three pace attack of Larwood, Voce and Gubby Allan, the Australians knew what to expect. However, with Larwood and Voce having such success backed by Allan (who as an amateur player, born in Australia, refused to bowl 'Bodyline'), Bill was only picked for one Test match. This was the second test played at Melbourne when he bowled Bradman first ball. Bradman, however, had his revenge in the second innings, making an unbeaten century which resulted in Australia's only success in a series that they lost 4-1. Bill did regain his place when the tour party moved on to New Zealand. With Larwood injured and exhausted by his efforts in Australia, Bill took 6/34 at Auckland, a match in which Walter Hammond made a world record test score of 336 not out.

On returning from the Southern Hemisphere, Bill's career continued to go well at county level, although he was not selected for the test series against India in 1933. He took another 159 wickets that summer as Yorkshire completed a hat-trick of titles. In 1934, the title was lost to rivals Lancashire but Bill had some consolation in the 1934 series loss to Australia where he bowled well in the two tests in which he played at Leeds and the Oval. Now, with Larwood out of the picture following his refusal to 'apologise for his bowling in Australia', by 1935 Bill was one of the prime contenders to be part of England's regular pace attack. That summer, Yorkshire won the title back with Bill taking a remarkable 193 first-class wickets. This included 8/17 and 8/18 against Northamptonshire, 7/58 against Essex in the next match and 6/16 and 6/83 at Bradford in the Roses match. The Test matches, however, were a disappointment. England were beaten 1–0 by South Africa and, other than taking 5/100 in the fourth test at Old Trafford, Bill had a quiet series and lost his place in the England team. The ankle injury which kept him out of action in 1937 prevented any chance of a return to the test scene but in the 1938 Ashes series Bill did play in the 4th and 5th tests with some success. Although not selected, once again, for an overseas tour, Bill did play in the final series before the war against the West Indies and took 6/33, his best ever test performance, in the 2nd test at Old Trafford. Despite his rather inconsistent test career, by 1939 *The Times* thought Bill "the best bowler you could ask for" able to move the ball in any direction. Their reporter wrote that "he would, in fact, be a member of any English team during the last 50 years." Then came the war.

Bill, along with Hedley Verity, was quick to join up. In 1933, Bill had married his wife, Esme, and two years later their son Tony was born. With Esme expecting a second child, Vera, in the very near future, Bill initially joined the ARP as soon as war broke out. It wasn't long before he received an infantry commission and was on his way to serve as a Gunnery Officer in North Africa. Here he served successfully until the disaster of Tobruk in June 1942. Tobruk, a port in Libya, North Africa, was to become synonymous with one of the great Allied disasters of the war. In late 1940 and early 1941, after routing the Italians, British troops had established control of Tobruk. This was a real boost for the British troops as the Italians were superior in number. The Germans, however, were determined to win it back by sending Rommel to reinforce the Italian troops and from then on, the war in this theatre became very intense. Bill says nothing about his experiences until the day of the British surrender but we do know from other accounts how dreadful the conditions were. Private Peter Salmon of the

2/28 Battalion, Australian Army, tells of the flat landscape which, unlike the Sahara, had little sand, the acute shortage of water and the bitter cold at night. More graphically, Sergeant Harold Atkins of the 2nd Battalion, Queen's West Surrey Regiment, describes having to clear up after the almost continuous bombing. This included bringing in the dead and, as Atkins tells us, some were in bits. "You have to remember that some of these bodies had been lying out there for four, five, six, seven days and the sun had got to them, so they had deteriorated terribly — green, bloated, limbs hanging off, half or no heads, half a body — goodness knows what."

Bill says nothing in his autobiography about any of this until, following an eight-month siege, he is one of those captured by the German Army and its panzer division at Tobruk Aerodrome on the early morning of June 21st, 1942. Here, he was one of 30,000 prisoners, along with 2,000 vehicles, 2,000 tons of fuel and 5,000 tons of rations to be captured by Rommel. Bill was now to spend the remainder of the war, the next three years, in captivity, an experience, he tells us, that he would never forget, "not merely because of the privations we were destined to suffer, but because of the grand team-work that helped us along the unknown road to freedom." For the remainder of the chapter in his book dealing with captivity, Bill concentrates on describing day-to-day life in the camps. You have to read carefully between the lines to discover the full horror of life as a POW. It is the comradeship that he wishes to convey to the reader. He explains that,

"There is an art in being a prisoner of war, at least, in being a successful one. It is a highly creative art; it is the art of living on one's wit and a not-too-full stomach… It is the story of how men in all walks of life, having been brought together behind barbed wire, learned in their captivity a degree of ingenuity and comradeship which defies adequate description."

Nevertheless, we do learn that day-to-day life was hard. On their removal from Tobruk and the frontline to the back area, at every stopping point, Italian guards carried out looting searches, which Bill described as "barefaced robbery of whatever valuables we possessed, notably our rings, watches and cigarette-cases." The worst aspect for

Bill was the lack of food. A cup of coffee at six a.m., a bowl of soup and fruit for lunch and a further bowl of soup at six p.m. was all that the soldiers had to sustain them for the first two months of captivity. When they were moved to more permanent bases at Bari and then, later, Chieti, it didn't get any better, an opinion supported by Bill losing four and a half stone in weight over the next three and a half years. Following the Italian Armistice of 1943, Bill hoped that he and his fellow 1700 captives would be freed from Chieti but the Germans arrived to take over. They were taken to Moosburg in Germany, a particularly squalid camp, where the men lived 300 to a bungalow. The conditions here were even worse and from here on the captives were moved at regular intervals, beginning with Mahrisch Trubau. For each move they "were herded eighteen at a time in a space equal to about a third of a cattle truck where we were fastened with barbed wire and handcuffed."

Despite these truly dreadful experiences, Bill writes more about the more bearable aspects of captivity. A shrewd chess player and solver of mathematical problems, as well as keen observer of his fellow men, perhaps Bill was better equipped than most to deal with life as a POW. He tells us how the prisoners tried to overcome the sheer boredom of camp life by forming organising committees to arrange activities in all manner of entertainment. Bill, unsurprisingly given his background, was given the job of sports officer. With 1700 POWs and no equipment this became quite a task. They managed to improvise and make some primitive equipment with whatever could be found, for example using shirts to make footballs, until the Red Cross discovered where they were and sent the genuine article. Bill describes baseball matches where the English prisoners beat the Americans at their own game; organising pantomimes and theatre as well as displays of musical talent whenever suitable instruments could be found. Nobody could ever accuse Bill and his colleagues of being defeatist.

However, making the best of the dreadful situations that POWs found themselves was not confined to those prisoners captured by the Nazis. The cricket journalist EW Swanton, a major captured by the Japanese, spent the last three and a half years of the war in camps on the Thai-

Burma railway where he organised cricket matches on flat, beaten earth pitches and equipment made from bamboo cane. When he was moved to camps at Tarsao and Chungkai and, finally at the hospital camp in Nakom Patom, Swanton continued to organise cricket matches. But perhaps his most remarkable achievement was to organise the rescue of 10,000 books from a library in Singapore. These books included work by Priestley, Galsworthy and Evelyn Waugh but the most popular book by far was the 1939 edition of *Wisden*. Swanton recalls that POWs talked for hours about cricket and resulted in him organising cricket quizzes and discussion about the game. Not that this should disguise the horrors of the Japanese war camps. But it does confirm the remarkable ability of some men to cope with the most horrendous of conditions, conditions that Swanton makes light of in his autobiography preferring to talk of cricket and comradery.

It was during sporting contests in Chieti that Bill met up once again with another England test cricketer, Freddie Brown, the Cambridge University and Surrey leg spinning all-rounder. Freddie had played with Bill on the latter's test debut against India in 1932. By that time, he had already played for England against New Zealand the previous year. Like Bill, he was selected for the 'Bodyline Tour' to Australia but did not play in any of the tests. He did play in the tests on the New Zealand leg of the tour but his test career was rather intermittent thereafter. As an amateur cricketer, he often had to put his business interests first so it was difficult for him to sustain his form. Following an appearance against New Zealand in 1937 it was thought that his test career was over.

With the outbreak of war, Freddie took a commission in the Royal Army Service Corps and helped to evacuate the British Army from Crete, for which he was awarded the MBE. Following his capture at Tobruk, Freddie spent the rest of the war with Bill organising sports activities. In case anybody thought that this was something of a relief or even an easy option it is worth noting that Freddie lost over four stones before his release in 1945. As we have seen, Bill suffered in a similar way and by the time the American soldiers liberated their camp he had lost a few pounds more than his cricketing colleague. In his autobiography Bill writes movingly of the day, 12th April 1945, when he and Freddie were liberated.

"I remember seeing men with tears of joy streaming down their faces. A few days later we climbed out of an aircraft on an airfield near Amersham, and I saw men actually falling on their knees to kiss the ground."

Tragically, before leaving the camp, Bill had heard through two recently arrived Canadian airmen, that his great friend and teammate Hedley Verity had died in Caserta. This was shattering news for Bill in particular, the one loss that he never really came to terms with.

But for Bill and Freddie, it was back to England with the possibility of reviving their cricket careers. Despite their loss of weight and dubious condition, both decided to continue with their careers. Bill was the more reluctant, fearing that he would not regain his pace and that his fielding, never a strength, would appear even more laborious. Freddie, like Bill, would not have been expected to achieve a great deal with many assuming his better days to be well behind him. Remarkably, after joining Northamptonshire in 1949, his test career revived and by the end of the summer, Freddie had been recalled to the test team as captain in the last two tests against New Zealand. Despite losing his place again the following summer, Freddie captained England on the 1950/51 tour to Australia and New Zealand and, despite losing the Ashes series 4–1, Freddie led the side against South Africa in 1951 before one last appearance, under Hutton, against Australia in 1953. Although Freddie was not popular with everybody — some, especially in Australia, saw him as a jovial character, fond of good food and a drink while enjoying lively company while others saw him as something of a snob and a bully, particularly in his dealings with young players — he became a test selector, an England tour manager, chairman of Northamptonshire and one of the first members of the Test Match Special radio commentary team. A remarkable career by any standards. Freddie died aged 80 in July 1991.

Freddie's successful reintegration to life back home and to his sport in particular was not the experience of every POW. Reg Allen was a very talented goalkeeper who had played a handful of games for Queens Park Rangers before the war, the first against Newport County in December 1938. He volunteered to serve at the very start of the war and joined the commandos who had been given the job of being an advanced striking force in German occupied Europe. Following vigorous training in Scotland, Reg was selected to be part of the Special Boat Service in six missions during 1941/42. Unfortunately, he was captured in North Africa while attempting to sabotage a German ship. As a result, Reg spent the next four and a half years as a POW when he met both Bill and Freddie. Not that he got to know these two particularly well as Reg proved to be quite a handful for his German guards, an attitude which resulted in him being moved from camp to camp. Reg was first of all taken to Capua camp near Naples and after three months was moved to Genoa where he helped one British and one South African prisoner to escape. For this Reg was given ten days hard labour and a severe beating. In the twenty-five months that he was at this camp, Reg survived on five ounces of bread and one bowl of soup a day. He was later moved to Stalag 344, where he attempted to escape by jumping from a moving train, before finally being moved to Vienna. By the time Reg was released in May 1945, both his physical and mental condition were very poor. In fact, he had become a manic depressive and was in need of a long convalescence.

Reg finally resumed his football career at QPR in 1947/48 when he played very well for a couple of seasons. So well indeed that Manchester United, starting to establish themselves under Matt Busby as one of the most powerful teams in English football, signed him for £11,000 in 1950. Reg proved to be worth the money as United won their first League title since 1911 in 1951/52. But by the autumn of 1952 Reg was a sick man. The war had taken its toll, in particular on his mental health. With talk of an England cap all over the newspapers, on October 4th, 1952, Reg took the field for an important league match against fellow footballing giants, Wolverhampton Wanderers. At half-time Reg, who had been described in one newspaper as being "frequently brilliant but periodically unwell", heard that Bert Williams, the Wolves goalkeeper, had been called up instead. The unstable Reg immediately disappeared and did not return for the second half. With no substitutions allowed, skipper Johnny Carey had to take his place in goal and United ended the match losing 6-2. Reg never played again.

After 80 appearances for United, Reg was given a testimonial in 1954 but he died, an unrecognised casualty of war, in 1976 at the age of 56.

Bill's life on his return to England was a good deal happier than that of Reg Allen, although he had needed some persuading to return to the cricket field. Following an appearance, and injury, in Hedley Verity's testimonial game, Bill decided to switch to bowling medium pace, relying on his cricketing intelligence and ability to swing the ball both ways to trouble batsmen. This he managed to do for two summers, including a final test appearance in England's first post-war Test match against India at Lord's, before concluding that Yorkshire would be better served if he left the arena to other, younger bowlers. He could do his bit by supporting their development, something he did to great effect when coaching the young Fred Truman. Besides his coaching role Bill also became a well-respected cricket journalist, with the *Yorkshire Post* who also wrote some highly regarded books on the sport, his *Express Deliveries*, published in 1949, being a particular success. In his later years, and despite his un-athletic, bespectacled appearance, Bill became something of a mentor to young Yorkshire cricketers like Truman, many of them, no doubt, unaware of the suffering which he had endured. This most kindly of men died in Otley on 4th September 1987 aged 79, a true sporting hero of World War Two.

Blair Mayne

CHAPTER 18
SURVIVORS 3: BLAIR MAYNE
"THE MOST DECORATED SOLDIER OF WORLD WAR TWO"

Not every international sportsman that survived the war was a test cricketer, although this sport has more than its fair share of war heroes. One of these was the seven times test batsman, Bryan Valentine. Valentine was a product of Repton School and Pembroke College, Cambridge and, like so many others, a gifted all-round sportsman. A serious tennis player, he had played with Davis Cup star and twice Wimbledon finalist 'Bunny' Austin. When he was at Cambridge, he won a soccer blue and became a 'scratch' golfer but cricket was always his first love. An attacking batsman with a particularly delightful on-drive, Valentine played for Kent between 1927 and 1948; one of those gifted players who saw cricket as a game rather than a profession. Nevertheless, he is one of the select band of England cricketers to score a century on his test debut, a feat that he accomplished in Bombay in December 1933 in the first test of that tour of India. In a period of strong England batsmen, he was unlucky not to play in more tests, especially given that he scored two centuries and one 97 in the nine times that he batted, figures which gave him an average of 64. His final test was the aforementioned 'timeless test' in Durban, March 1939. Indeed, Valentine was at the wicket with county colleague Les Ames when the game was called off with England 654/5, 42 runs short of a remarkable victory. It is quite conceivable that the Kent batsmen could have guided England to their target. With the onset of war, Bryan Valentine joined the Royal West Kent Regiment and was awarded the Military Cross "in recognition of gallant and distinguished services in North Africa." He returned to captain Kent until 1948 when he retired. He later served on the committee of Kent CC and in 1967 became its president. One of the many modest and somewhat unsung heroes of World War Two, Bryan Valentine died aged 75 in 1983.

Although Bryan Valentine is one of the most highly decorated survivors from the world of sport, he is not the most eminent. Possibly the most remarkable, certainly the most notorious, of our heroic survivors, was the Ireland rugby international Blair Mayne. Not only was his rugby career packed with incident and achievement but his army career saw him become possibly the most decorated soldier of the war and an early member of the fledgling Special Air Service, now known as the SAS. His life as rugby player, war hero and successful lawyer is a gripping story which can result both in great admiration and disapproval. Yet we can be in no doubt that when it comes to discussing genuine war heroes, the name Blair Mayne must be towards the top of the list, maybe even at the very top.

Robert Blair Mayne was born on 11th January 1915 in Newtownards, County Down, Ireland. He was the second youngest of seven children born to William and Margaret, a family of landowners who owned several retail businesses in the town. An experience of military action, however, was in the blood. Blair, later known as 'Paddy', was named after his mother's cousin, Captain Robert Blair who was killed in 1916 while serving in the 5th Battalion, Border Regiment and who was awarded a posthumous DSO for his action. Blair was also a descendant of Gordon Turnbull who led the famous 'Scotland Forever Charge' at the Battle of Waterloo. He was educated at Regent House Grammar School where it soon became clear that Blair was an exceptional sportsman playing rugby, cricket and golf to a high standard and also becoming a very good shot. Rugby in particular took his fancy and by the age of 16 the young Blair was playing regularly for Ards RFC. On gaining a place to study Law at Queen's University, Belfast, Blair took up boxing and was good enough to reach the final of the British University Heavyweight boxing championship. By this time, 1936, he had already won the Irish University title.

Despite this success on the sports field all was not well with Blair, even at this young age. His older brother Tom committed suicide while estranged from his father and this had a profound effect on the younger brother. Both boys had been heavy drinkers and, following Tom's death, Blair's drinking became worse. As if that in itself was not enough of a concern, excessive drinking had the usually quiet, reserved Blair take on a different, more unpredictable and often violent behaviour pattern. This was to become a recurring theme throughout both his rugby and army career.

Not that heavy drinking adversely affected Blair's rugby career in 1937 for in the April of that year, he made his debut at lock forward for Ireland in their final championship match of that season against Wales at Ravenhill, Belfast. In front of 20,000 Irish supporters the home side defeated Wales 5–3 to finish runners-up to England and confine Wales to the wooden spoon. The following year it was Ireland's turn to win the wooden spoon, losing all three matches against the other home countries. Despite scoring one of Ireland's four tries, directly from a lineout, against the seven tries run in by England, Blair was left out of the team to play Scotland, although he was back for the final defeat to Wales at Swansea.

Despite this disappointing season, 23-year-old Blair had done enough to impress the selectors of the British Isles team to tour South Africa in the summer of 1938. This tour of South Africa, the first since 1924, was the last tour where the British players wore the blue jersey but it was also the first where the team was known as the 'British Lions' rather than the British Isles. The press also covered the tour more fully than in previous years, although reports on the provincial matches still tended to be quite brief. County cricket was still receiving much more coverage than non-international rugby matches, with the notable exception of the annual varsity match, and the amateur status of the oval ball game was still very much to the fore. When the team were invited to South Africa House, London for a meal on the eve of their departure, the High Commissioner advised them to enjoy themselves and "not take even the Test matches too seriously." The aim, he said, "was to make friends for life." Although this attitude was rather typical of the time it was also partially a response to the Lions' inability to pick their strongest side. Unlike the dominion teams who tended to tour with all their best players, this did not apply to the Lions where many could not travel for business and professional reasons. These reservations apart, the British Lions, with Blair Mayne very much on board, set sail for South Africa on the 20th May 1938. The tour was to be the making of Blair as a rugby international.

That he was a key member of this Lions side is confirmed by the number of appearances he made in the famous blue jersey. Of the 20 provincial matches, Blair played in 17 as well as in all three tests. In the days before substitutions and the development of rugby as a 23-man game, this was a remarkable statistic. It did not take Blair long to make his mark and he performed brilliantly in the 21–6 victory over Orange Free State. He carried this form into the first test in Johannesburg where, despite losing 26–12 to an outstanding Springbok side, Blair caught the eye. Facing a much larger, heavier pack *The Times* reported that "Mayne was outstanding in a pack which gamely … stood up to a tremendous task." In front of 36,000 spectators, it had already become clear that Blair was the 'hard man' of the pack. By now he was capable of playing anywhere in the 'back five' of the pack, known for hard tackling, effective ball carrying and being particularly important when the going got rough. Another outstanding performance in the 6-5 victory over Eastern Province set him up nicely for the final two tests played over consecutive Saturdays in Port Elizabeth and Cape Town, respectively. The second test, played in almost unbearable heat, was lost convincingly 19–3 but the final encounter provided one of the great Test matches. Blair, as the press reported, "was outstanding both in the open and magnificent in defence", and, along with Bob Alexander who scored a try, set the standard for the Lions pack. These heroic efforts resulted in four tries and a 21–16 victory. The series had been lost 2–1 but Blair was now revered by his fellow tourists.

This being Blair, however, matters on the field were only part of the story. In their official history of the British and Irish Lions, Clem and Greg Thomas describe Blair as a "combination of hell raiser, rebel, combatant and hero, all it seems, in equal measure." Clem Thomas, who as a renowned player and distinguished journalist was in a position to know, wrote that he was the most charismatic and courageous man of action of all Lions who always made things happen both on and off the field. This included brawling in bars with locals on more than one occasion. Yet he also mixed well with his hosts and on one occasion went on a 'shoot' with local farmers. This might have gone relatively unnoticed until Blair turned up at the team hotel with the dead 'buck' slung over his shoulder.

His partner in crime on this tour was often fellow forward 'Bunner' Travers, son of George Travers, a member of the Wales team that defeated the 1905 All Blacks. Blair and Bunner frequented the bars together, sometimes even going to the docks in seamen's jerseys, waiting for somebody to pick a fight with them. Invariably this would come to pass and, also invariably our two heroic Lions would leave the bar having demolished their attackers. This, according to Harry Bowcott, a Lion of the 1930 vintage, was Blair and Bunner's idea of a night out. Bowcott, in the book *Behind the Lions*, thought Blair to be a very contradictory character, "a very quiet fellow you thought wouldn't hurt a fly until you saw him roused... Mad as a hatter." On one occasion Blair was said to have trashed a hotel room, Keith Moon style, because it was deemed to be not up to standard while he was known to leave a formal dinner given by his South African hosts in order to go hunting antelopes. Andy Bull, a sports journalist, wrote a fascinating and revealing article in 2013 which was published in *The Guardian* newspaper detailing some of the most extreme examples of behaviour on British Lions tours. He argues that Blair was without doubt the "hardest-drinking, freest swinging firebrand in the long history of the Lions." The management despaired of his behaviour to such an extent that they decided to make him share a room with George Cromey, a fellow Irishman, a fly half and, of greater relevance to the management, a Presbyterian minister. They, no doubt, hoped that the good Reverend would have a restraining influence on his teammate. It was to no avail. On the night of the renowned antelope hunt, Cromey was woken at three a.m. by Blair breaking down the door and announcing that he had "shot a springbok." It was with some relief that Cromey quickly realised that the victim was a poor animal and not a member of the opposition XV! Announcing that fellow Lion, the England winger Jimmy Unwin, had been complaining about the lack of fresh meat available to players on the tour, Blair proceeded to break down Unwin's door and toss the unfortunate beast on the bed, cutting his teammate's leg with the antelope's horn in the process. The poor animal ended the night dumped outside the room of the South Africa manager with an accompanying note which read "a gift of fresh meat from the British Isles touring team." Following this incident Andy Bull tells us that Blair, possibly concerned that there would be repercussions for this latest escapade, disappeared for three days, only reappearing in time for the journey home. There can be no doubt that, despite his obvious intelligence and outrageous sense of humour, Blair was a very difficult and complex character, particularly when he had been drinking.

On returning home from South Africa, Blair joined George MacLaine and Co (Solicitors) in his first role as a qualified lawyer. He also enlisted in the Territorial Army in his home town of Newtownards, County Down, thus beginning his career as a fearsome commando. There was still rugby to be played of course and Blair returned to Ireland with expectations of him greater than ever. He joined Malone RFC and continued where he had left off in South Africa. Newspaper reports confirm the improvement in his play saying that, despite not appearing to be the quickest around the field, he did in fact cover the ground at extraordinary speed given his build. The home international championship of 1939 saw Blair, now recognised by all as having improved following his Lions tour, play in all three matches. The championship ended in an unsatisfactory three-way tie with England, Ireland and Wales each winning two of their three games. Wales, who finished with the best points difference, prevented an Irish Triple Crown in Belfast as outside half Willie Davies scored all the points in a 7–0 victory. It was to be Blair's last appearance in an Irish jersey.

By the time that a new rugby season dawned, Britain was once again at war, and matters other than rugby were in the forefront of Blair's mind. In March 1939, he had joined the Supplementary Reserve in Newtownards and received a commission in the Royal Artillery. He was posted to 5 Light Anti-Aircraft Battery and then on to the 66th Light AA Regiment, Northern Ireland. By April 1940, Blair was serving in the Royal Ulster Rifles. The seemingly constant series of transfers between regiments serves to highlight both his restless nature and determination to experience some real action. He hadn't been with the Royal Ulster Rifles for very long before Blair volunteered for the newly formed No 11 (Scotland) Commandos, a move which gave him the action that he craved. In June 1941, Blair was heavily involved in the Syria-Lebanon campaign against the Vichy French Forces where he led his men during the Litany River operation. Such was Blair's reputation by this point that he had attracted the attention of Captain David Stirling who was in the process of recruiting for the newly formed Special Air Service, the forerunner of what is now called the SAS. As we have seen, Blair already had a reputation of being a heavy drinker and it is likely that some of his escapades were covered up. An incident with a revolver is one that has been referenced but details of any such event are hard to find. Indeed, at the time of Stirling's interest. Blair was under arrest for hitting his commanding officer, but the captain was determined to get his man. As a result, Blair was released to join this elite squad of eight to ten battle-hardened men known as 'L' Detachment. The chance to become involved in special operations, more of a commando than a regular soldier, suited him perfectly. Blair was far too difficult a character to be a regular soldier.

From here on until the end of the war, Blair's record as a soldier is astounding and almost defies belief. Between December 1941 and the end of 1942, he led numerous night raids in Egypt and Libya, causing chaos in the process. He pioneered the use of military jeeps and, through hit-and-run raids on enemy airfields, Blair and his colleagues were able to do immense damage. Reports tell us that he was personally responsible for the destruction of possibly up to 100 enemy aircraft.

It was during this early period of his time with the SAS, on 14th December 1941, that Blair gained his first Distinguished Service Order (DSO) when, at Wadi Tamet, he destroyed enemy aircraft along with bomb and petrol dumps. The citation tells us that during this raid he also killed many enemy soldiers in a "raid of a hazardous nature" where the success of the mission was mainly due to his action and leadership. The citation ends with the words "I cannot speak too highly of this officer's skill and devotion to duty." There was much more to come.

Following Stirling's capture in January 1943, Blair's role became even more crucial. Stirling, called 'The Phantom Major' by Field Marshall Rommel, managed to escape, was recaptured by the Italians and, following four more attempts at escape, was sent to the infamous Colditz Castle where he spent the rest of the war. The SAS was now divided into two distinct parts. Blair 'Paddy' Mayne now became the sole commander of the Special Raiding Squadron and led his men in mainland Italy and Sicily. It was here in Sicily that he won his second DSO when he and his men achieved the capture of a number of battalions, killing between 200-300 enemy soldiers and taking around 450 prisoners. The town of Augusta was captured and held; a particularly dangerous operation carried out in daylight. The citation referred to Blair's courage and the personal example which he set and which resulted in the success of the operation.

In January 1944, Blair was promoted to the post of Lieutenant Colonel and became the commanding officer of the first SAS Regiment. There had been other rugby footballers who had been part of the 1938 British Lions. The Irish wing, Vesey Boyle, had earned the Distinguished Flying Cross while both Wales wing WH Clement (later Secretary of the Welsh Rugby Union) and Scottish centre DJ McCrae won the Military Cross. England centre Basil Nicolson also made Lieutenant Colonel and played a major role in planning the Normandy landings but none achieved the heights reached by Blair Mayne. Following his second DSO, he went on to lead the SAS in France, the Netherlands, Belgium, Germany and Norway, gaining a third DSO following successful penetration of German lines while leading parties of re-enforcements. The fourth DSO was not long in coming as Blair became one of only 7 British Servicemen to win four such awards. This was a particularly notable award presented by Field Marshall Montgomery himself. Blair had successfully led two armoured jeep squadrons through the frontline to Oldenburg and cleared a path for the 4th Canadian (Armoured) Division which completely disorganised and confused the enemy. Initially it was intended that this action would result in the awarding of a Victoria Cross but, perhaps due to Blair's reputation as something of a troublemaker, this didn't materialise. Others thought that his Irish nationality counted against him. Whatever the reason Blair had to make do with four DSOs and the recognition bestowed on him by the French allies, namely the "Croix de Guerre" and the "Légion d'honneur." Meanwhile the campaign to award a VC still goes on. At the last count 100 MPs had called for the fourth DSO to be upgraded and the Blair Mayne Association continues the fight to this day, showing a determination that he would surely recognise.

Following the end of the war, Blair was reluctant to return to a mundane civilian life. Very much in keeping with his adventurous personality, he worked for the British Antarctic Survey in the Falkland Islands. However, a reoccurrence of a back injury sustained in action led him to bow to the inevitable and return home. Here Blair worked as a solicitor in Newtownards, County Down, his childhood home, before being appointed as the Secretary to the Law Society of Northern Ireland. Tragically, on the night of Tuesday 13th December 1955, Blair attended a meeting of the Friendship Lodge with fellow masons in Bangor, Northern Ireland. In the early hours of the following morning, while driving home, he collided with a farmer's vehicle only a few hundred yards from his destination and was killed. He was forty years old. Hundreds attended his funeral and the community quickly recognised his importance and huge contribution to the military. A statue was erected in Conway Square, Newtownards and a bypass has been named after him. Meanwhile his masonic jewel remains on display in the Mayoral Chamber in the Council Offices. As late as 2003, a temporary Royal Irish Regimental camp in Kuwait was named 'Camp Blair Mayne', the very camp that Lieutenant Colonel Tim Collins, the commanding officer of the Royal Irish Regiment, gave his address on the eve of the invasion of Iraq. Whenever the British military forces are deployed the bravery of Blair 'Paddy' Mayne is remembered.

Despite this, Blair remains a controversial figure in British military history. Some colleagues, certainly some senior officers, didn't know how to take him. They said that he had too high an opinion of himself and certainly didn't trust him when he'd had a drink. They respected his ability as a man of action but out of action he was something of a loose cannon. Even his relationship with the man who recognised his military talents more than anyone, Captain Stirling, had its difficulties. He later said that working with Blair "was like adopting a wolf." But most of the clashes between them consisted of more hot air than anything lasting as there was great mutual respect between them. On one occasion, Stirling ordered Blair to return from an operation after a falling-out. Blair returned to his tent and started drinking. Later Stirling approached the tent fully expecting a full-blown fight to develop between the two military heroes. Instead, he found Blair reading James Joyce and he was greeted with words "all I really want to do is write." This is very reminiscent of another incident, this time not involving Blair, when Stirling was heard to confide that "all I really want to do is paint." Such is the way that war, even for the bravest and most committed, changes men's priorities and even character.

The truth is that Blair Mayne was a legend both on the rugby field and in the arena of battle. Indeed, he is seen as true military hero whose ideas are still used today and form the basis of the SAS. It can be argued that in some crucial ways he revolutionised modern warfare. Much more modest than is generally recognised, (for example, he never much discussed his military exploits after 1945), Blair was a brilliant leader of men. He inspired confidence and trust followed by respect and even affection. Others were inspired in his company, honoured to work with him and had complete trust that all would, in the end, be well. Perhaps rugby historian Rob Cole sums Blair up best when he wrote the following in his book detailing the history of the British and Irish Lions,

"Myths and legend turned Mayne into a national hero for his acts of danger and derring-do… He became a cult hero, but among the men who knew him best, those who played rugby with him, and those who served alongside him, there appears to have been a strong bond of trust and belief in his principles, organisation and tactics as much as his gung-ho attitude …Wild maybe, but he was definitely someone you would want on your side."

As probably the best example of what qualities a sportsman can bring to the battlefield, nobody in this book so reflects the title, *Where Skill and Courage Count*, as well as Blair 'Paddy' Mayne, the most decorated British soldier of World War Two.

CONCLUSION
PICKING UP THE PIECES

World War Two finally ended in 1945, six long years after it began, with the unconditional surrender of the Axis powers. Victory in Europe was declared on May 8th following Germany's surrender. Japan fought on for a few more months before the dropping of the two atom bombs on Hiroshima and Nagasaki ensured their demise on 15th August. The formal surrender took place on 2nd September. To many, this moment must have seemed as if it would never come. The historian Stargardt wrote that to Germans waking up on May 9th,

"The stillness was remarkable. No shell bursts, no bombs, no blackout. It was neither the peace which had been so longed for, nor the annihilation that had been so dreaded."

Germans, he concluded, had a "rush of self-pity" as they tried to excuse their culpability by saying that "we did not deserve to be led into such a catastrophe." With the Russians in Berlin and the Allies about to determine their fate, the future must have looked very bleak.

As we saw in the Introduction, the global effect of this war was enormous and the cost in human life and suffering, in destruction and economic dislocation, was of unprecedented magnitude. But it is worth repeating some of these figures. World War Two demonstrated more than any other conflict the capacity of human beings for destroying each other and themselves. The Soviet Union puts its total deaths as around 20 million but recently historians have suggested that this figure might underestimate the true scale of their losses. Weinburg puts the number as nearer to 25 million. China have totalled their losses as around 15 million, Poland 6 million, Germany 4 million and Japan at 2 million. Total losses around the globe probably reached a staggering 60 million including, of course, the 6 million victims of the Holocaust. Add to this the chaos that resulted from migration, voluntary and forced, put at around 10 million by Weinburg, and we begin to see the enormity of those six long years of war.

Britain, with losses of around 400,000 armed forces and civilians, might at first glance appear to have suffered less. But Britain had suffered in ways that for the most part they had not experienced in the Great War, namely the damage done to towns and cities by the heavy German bombing. The need for rebuilding and reconstruction was to dominate post-war Britain as people tried to get back to 'normal' everyday living. For some troops 'getting back to normal' was still some way off as some took around a year to get home. On the whole, British prisoners of war were returned quickly but it still took time. Those soldiers crippled and disabled were now dependent on others for survival while those less obviously changed found that the post-war world was very different to the one that they had left as even rationing didn't fully end until 1954. As Churchill and the Royal Family stood on the balcony of Buckingham Palace waving in triumph, and undoubtedly some relief, at the crowds below some were already finding the future full of foreboding. Captain John MacAuslan, an intelligence officer, remembers the end of the war rather differently than the way he expected.

"After the war ended, I was surprised that I wasn't all that elated. I just felt a slightly lost feeling — relieved a little bit that one was safe now — but not very happy. I didn't know what to do. I knew that I'd have to be a solicitor but I didn't want to be a solicitor. What I knew about was all finished… what I'd known for such a long time vanished and there was nothing to take its place. It was all gone."

He was not alone.

But what about the returning sportsmen and their sport? How did they fare in this much changed world? The first problem that they faced in the first-class game, whatever the sport, was finding a suitable venue to display their hitherto redundant talents. Cricket had particular difficulties in this area. For example, the Oval had been used as a

270

searchlight site for part of the war before becoming a POW camp for German prisoners. It had been hit by seven high explosives during the war so some extensive reconstruction was necessary. This was carried out between November 1945 and February 1946 when around 40,000 turves were transported from Gravesend and laid in three months. It was May 1946 before the Oval was ready for first-class cricket. Bramall Lane in Sheffield and Old Trafford in Manchester had also suffered in the bombing while others had been used for military training. Clubs and counties had striven to keep afloat during the war years but it had proved to be a very difficult job. In the summer of 1945, only Oxford and Cambridge Universities were playing regular matches against other representative sides. Nevertheless, by spring 1946, the editor of *Wisden*, Hubert Preston was able to describe Lord's, the home of cricket, return to its full splendour,

"The turf looked superb — a real green carpet without a blemish, in as good order as ever could be wished — enriched by the stands receiving a new coat of white paint with 'Old Father Time' in position once more — a resplendent golden figure looking down with benign expectancy."

Cricket followers, starved of the game for so long, were impatient for the resumption. The cricket writer AA Thompson confirmed that "the desire of cricket's starved followers and frustrated lovers to see cricket again was over-whelming", although he recognised that the return of competition without so many of its former players was difficult for everybody in the game. The death-roll among club and school cricketers, wrote Thompson, "was sadly immense and immensely sad." It was also a different cricketing environment to which they returned. The emergence of a more egalitarian society changed the outlook of the sport with what Wodehouse called an "increase in professionalism and of professionalism." The appointment of a professional player as captain of England, Len Hutton, was still 8 years away but it was an inevitable development. The amateur player would soon almost completely disappear.

Some first class, international cricket did, however, take place before the summer of 1945 had come to an end. A series of Victory

Tests was arranged immediately that the war in Europe was over. Between the 19th May and 22nd August 1945, an English national side played a combined Australian Services XI in five matches, each spread over three days. The teams were captained by Wally Hammond and Lindsay Hassett and given first class, but not Test match, status. England appeared much the stronger on paper containing as it did a very strong batting line-up but the series was shared 2–2 with one match drawn.

The real significance however, was that first-class cricket was being played again and that some established sports stars were back on the field of play. Not that they all returned as they had left. Alf Gover, by now 38 years of age, opened the England bowling with his leg heavily strapped. A captain in the Surrey Regiment, Gover had been invalided out of the war but 'Plum' Warner insisted that he played. Len Hutton, who had recorded the highest ever Test match innings before the war played in three Victory Tests. Hutton, a sergeant-instructor in the Army Physical Training Corps, had fractured his left forearm and dislocated his ulna at the wrist in a training accident. Complications set in and Hutton was forced to have an operation which resulted in his left arm being two inches shorter than the right. He adapted well to his new circumstances, well enough to become England captain and greatest post-war batsman. A more moving return to the cricketing family was that of Graham Williams, the Australia fast-medium bowler and useful bat. Williams returned from a POW camp nearly five stone below his pre-war weight. When he realised that he was likely to survive and be released, Williams tried to improve his fitness by chopping down trees. Not that he had wasted time in the previous years and months. Williams had improved the lives of the blind POWs by teaching Braille and was rightly considered a hero on his release. On taking the field he was given a standing ovation that Keith Miller described as "almost orchestral in its sound and feeling... whenever I think of it tears come into my eyes." In later years, Keith Miller gave David Frith a more detailed memory of the occasion. Coming out to bat at the fall of the 7th wicket Miller tells him that Williams,

"...was given a great ovation that compares with anything given to Bradman, Lillee or Richards. But it was not the sort of clapping and cheering that greets a hundred. This was different. Everyone stood up. They all knew about Graham's captivity. He was a big fella, but he was gaunt from his experience, and he just walked around for a while as if in a trance."

Williams went on to score 53 from 56 balls but never played first-class cricket again. Keith Miller, who had countless photographs taken with royalty, prime ministers and film stars, had only one that hung in pride of place at his own home: the Australian Combined Services XI that played at Sheffield in 1945, a team that contained Williams. Later Graham Williams was awarded an MBE and died aged 67 in 1978.

Graham Williams, like so many others, might have been lost to the game but the sport, encouraged by the almost insatiable appetite of the public, did thrive in the post-war years. Crowds flocked to the Victory Tests bringing their own refreshments as the continued existence of rationing prevented their sale at the ground. Some first-class matches were played but the County Championship did not resume until 1946. Like so many before the war, it was won by Yorkshire. Test cricket in England resumed with a series against India, also in the wet summer of 1946, and by the following season Compton and Edrich, the Middlesex twins, were putting both counties and the touring South Africa to the sword in a glorious summer of cricket. Players had lost six summers to the war and were keen to make up for lost time. The tour 'down under' in the winter of 1946/47 had come to soon for an England team whose players were far from being in a condition to play test cricket on the other side of the world. Led by Wally Hammond, by now past his princely best, this ageing team lost the series 4–1. But the loss was to a great Australian team in the making. Led by Bradman, playing his last series, the tour of England in 1948 confirmed them as one of the greatest test teams of all time and they won the series 4–0. With players like Keith Miller and Bill Edrich on the field there was room for a more carefree attitude. As we have seen, these men had seen too much danger for them to lose a sense of proportion. England finally regained the Ashes, 1–0 in 1953, eight years after the cessation of hostilities, just like they had in 1926. Appropriately, Squadron Leader Bill Edrich was at the wicket as Sergeant-Instructor Denis Compton hit the winning runs with Flying Officer Keith Miller looking on.

Football too was not long in picking up where it had left off despite the death of just under 100 players and the loss of many more through injuries sustained in wartime. With appetites whetted by a tour of Britain by Moscow Dynamo, the 1945/6 season saw a resumption of the professional game. Despite the Moscow team being under strict supervision with no opportunity to socialise, and meals and accommodation being confined to the Soviet Embassy or consulates, the tour was a great success. It was agreed that competition could begin in England immediately. The forty-four clubs in the top two divisions before the war would compete in the Football League North and the Football League South. The FA Cup did resume that season with each round up to and including the quarter final played over two legs. In the final Derby County defeated Charlton Athletic 4-1 after extra time in front of 100,000 football-starved fans. The first post-war League title was won by Liverpool the following year. Crowds flocked to the grounds and by the 1948/49 season 41,000,000 fans were pouring through the gates. A crowd of 95,000 watched Bromley defeat Romford 1–0 in the Amateur Cup Final at Wembley that year, clear evidence of the thirst that the still mainly male sports-loving public had for live football.

And an exciting period of football it proved to be. In 1945 Company Sergeant Major Matt Busby, who had served in the 9th Battalion of the King's Liverpool Regiment and in the Army Physical Training Corps during the war, was appointed as the new manager of Manchester United. The club had been made homeless by the destruction of their Old Trafford home by German bombers, the grandstand left in ruin, the terraces overgrown with weeds and a thorny six-foot-high bush sprouted in the middle of the pitch. A few huts served as changing rooms and offices while the 'training pitch' was a pile of rubble behind the Stretford End. Hardly the modern 'Theatre of Dreams'. Busby was to turn this around as he established himself as the first great football manager of the modern era and set Manchester United on the path to becoming England's premier club. In the following years United won the FA Cup in 1948 and were runners-up in the top division on four occasions in five years before finally winning the title in 1952. They were captained by the great Johnny Carey, a native of Dublin and a citizen of the Republic of Ireland, who had served with distinction during the war. Being Irish, Carey was under no obligation to fight for his adopted country but he maintained that "any country giving me a living is worth fighting for." Carey served in the Middle East and in Italy where his football skills did not go unnoticed. He was offered the chance to join a number of Italian clubs after the war. Carey, a true 'gentleman' and highly respected by his teammates, proved to be a great leader, just the 'type' that Busby had in mind. These teams had set the standard and it wasn't long before Busby was introducing the 'Busby Babes' changing British football very much for the better. Another Army Physical Training Instructor, Stan Cullis, developed a team to rival Busby's. Wolverhampton Wanderers won the FA Cup in 1949, the year after Busby, and the League title three times in the 1950s. Cullis, a tough, rather abrasive character, had refused to join his teammates in performing a Nazi salute prior to the England game against Germany in Berlin in May 1938. He was the only player so to do and was promptly withdrawn from the team, although later he did win back his place. In May 1939, he was made England captain aged only 22 but like many others his best years were lost to the war.

Football players themselves were now household names. The quest for Stanley Matthews, who was to become football's first knight, to finally win a winner's FA Cup medal took on national importance. A corporal in the RAF during the war and a losing finalist in 1948 and 1951, Matthews finally achieved his goal in 1953 in what became known as 'The Matthews Final', despite Stan Mortensen scoring a hat-trick in the 4–3 victory over Bolton Wanderers. Jackie Milburn, 'Wor Jackie' to the Newcastle United faithful and cousin of Bobby and Jackie Charlton, was idolised on Tyneside, somebody locals could identify with far more easily than they can the modern player. Milburn denied Matthews his FA Cup winners medal in 1951 scoring both goals in a 2–0 win and played a key role in two further FA Cup triumphs in 1952 and 1955. The player most respected by football men was 'The

Preston Plumber', Tom Finney, a one-club man. Also later made a knight, Finny was idolised by fans and players alike. Bill Shankly, a former teammate at Preston, once described Finney as being able to torture opposition full backs while "playing in a concrete overcoat." Finney, unlike some, had seen active service in World War Two. He served in Monty's 8th Army in Egypt and later in Italy where he was involved in the Battle of the Argenta Gap as a Stuart tank driver with the 9th Lancers. Matthews might have received more plaudits but Finney remained 'the player's player', despite a lack of domestic medals to accompany his 76 England caps.

Rugby Union too experienced the surge of interest resulting from six years of war. Club rugby saw unprecedented crowds with 48,000 witnessing a clash between great rivals Cardiff and Newport at the Arms Park in 1948. The fact that it was still an amateur game with only expenses as a reward (at least in theory) did nothing to quell the enthusiasm. Quite the contrary. Players remained at the heart of their communities, especially in South Wales where the rugby club was the heart and soul of every village, particularly as attendance at the chapels declined. International rugby became more popular than ever. Touring sides were more frequent in the post-war era and the Rugby Five Nations was enhanced by the improvement in the French contribution. Banned for much of the 1930s, the French were readmitted to the tournament in 1947 when the fixtures resumed. In 1954, they shared the title with England and Wales, finally winning it outright in 1959. Ireland won their first Grand Slam in 1948 inspired by the great fly half Jackie Kyle while Wales had a 'mini golden era' in the early 1950s, winning grand slams in 1950 and 1952 as well as defeating New Zealand for the third and, as I write, for the last time, in 1953. Popular British Lions tours to New Zealand in 1950 and to South Africa in 1955 confirmed rugby union as a thriving sport.

Perhaps the event that signified more than any other the recovery of sport in post-war Britain was the decision to stage the 1948 Olympics in London. Helsinki had been the original choice of venue but so badly damaged was the Finnish capital that they would be forced to delay their hosting of the Olympics for a further four years. As in 1908, London stepped into the breach. Not that London was in very much better shape, damaged as it was by the German Luftwaffe, bankrupt and trying to cope with rationing. Even the new Labour Government of Clement Attlee were lukewarm at best on the idea. The promise of a boom to tourism finally convinced them to go ahead. There was no 'Olympic minister' and the organising committee ran the Games without any Government interference. The intention was for this Olympics to be a low-key event, thus avoiding the hyper nationalism of Hitler's Games twelve years earlier. The result was a triumph of British sporting values, the last Olympics, argued Mihir Bose, which could be claimed to have been a pure sporting festival. Stadiums were packed as the British public satisfied their hunger for top-class sport. There was not even a hint of controversy or scandal, a precedent which was not followed in the Olympics of the second half of the twentieth century. This London Olympics had clearly led the way in moving sport forward following the horrors experienced in six years of war.

But, just as in 1919, moving forward was easier said than done for many of those who had taken part. Sportsmen, like all the combatants, had to come to terms with their experiences. Some, like Keith Miller, gained a greater perspective on life following the war. Others, like Bill Edrich or Blair Mayne, ever after searched for excitement, made restless by the dangers that they had faced on a daily, even hourly, basis. The mundane life that followed was, for many ex-soldiers, difficult to handle. Moreover, as the war began to slide back into history the contribution that our sporting heroes made was often forgotten. Whereas the Great War, with its 'Pal's' battalions and war poets, regained a prominent place in the nation's psyche, the history of World War Two went through a different experience. During the less traumatic years, at least for the Western world, of the second half of the twentieth century memories of World War Two began to fade, taking on a nostalgic form to many. In Britain there developed a rather one-dimensional view of this worldwide conflict and Britain's part in it. As AA Thompson wrote, "Nostalgia, although a pleasant companion, is a bad master." As the years went on, and the events of the war faded or took on a mythic quality, sport itself took on an importance that sometimes lacked a true sense of proportion. The great cricket writer and commentator, John Arlott, on his retirement from the commentary box in 1981, reflected on his long and distinguished career as cricket's greatest commentator, to ex England cricket captain, Mike Brearley. Clutching his usual glass of fine claret, he mused "sometimes I feel that we take sport far too seriously and life not seriously enough." Arlott himself had suffered the death of his twenty-year-old son in a tragic car accident so knew well the meaning of loss.

It is unlikely however, that those sportsmen and women who played an active role in the dreadful events of 1939–1945 ever lacked a proper sense of perspective. What has become clear in this study is that the efforts and commitments shown by our sportsmen over two world wars should never be forgotten. The selection of 'Where Skill and Courage Count', taken from a 1942 USA Army poster, as the title of this book was not accidental or random. Our sportsmen and women, along with their comrades, showed plenty of both skill and courage. In 1940, along with the whole country, our British sportsmen were in the thick of the action whether it be at Dunkirk, in the Battle of Britain or in resisting the Blitz. Throughout the remaining years they helped to turn the tide in the efforts to overcome fascism, fighting in the deserts of North Africa, the mountains of Italy, in the Far East and on the beaches of Normandy. Those that survived played an important part in the reconstruction of society as Britain strove to recover from the turmoil of the war years. That Britain succeeded in resisting the threat of fascism and was able to move towards a more peaceful second half of the twentieth century, owes much to our sportsmen and women. They played their part and are deserving of our recognition and respect as well as our eternal gratitude.

BIBLIOGRAPHY

NEWSPAPERS
The Times (1919–1950)
South Wales Argus (1919–1945)

FOOTBALL:
Patrick Barclay: The Life and Times of Herbert Chapman, Weidenfield and
    Nicholson 2014
Patrick Barclay: The Man Who Made a Football Club, Ebury Press 2017
Norman Barrett (ed): Daily Telegraph Football Chronicle, Carlton 1993
Andy Dougan: Dynamo: Defending the Honour of Kiev, Fourth Estate 2001
Eamon Dunphy: A Strange Kind of Glory: Sir Matt Busby and Manchester
    United, William Heinemann Ltd 1991
Simon Kuper: Ajax The Dutch, The War: Football in Europe During World
    War Two, Orion 2003
Chris Nawrat & Steve Hutchins: Sunday Times Illustrated History of
    Football, Hamlyn 1994

RUGBY FOOTBALL:
Stephen Jones, Tom English, Nick Cain and David Barnes: Behind the
    Lions, Polaris 2012
Steve Lewis and John Griffiths, The Essential History of Rugby Union:
    Wales, Headline Books 2003
David Parry-Jones: Out of the Ruck: A Selection of Rugby Writing, Pelham
    Books 1986
David Smith and Gareth Williams: Fields of Praise: Official History of the
    Welsh Rugby Union 1881–1981, University of Wales Press 1980
Clem Thomas and Greg Thomas: 125 Years of the British and Irish Lions,
    Mainstream Publishing 2013
JBG Thomas: Great Rugger Clubs, Stanley Paul and Co 1962

CRICKET:

Norman Barrett (ed): Daily Telegraph Chronicle of Cricket, Guinness
  Publishing 1994

Bill Bowes: Express Deliveries, Sportsman's Book Club 1958

Neville Cardus: Cardus on Cricket, Souvenir Press 1997

Neville Cardus: Cardus on the Ashes, Souvenir Press 1989

Dudley Carew: To the Wicket, Chapman and Hill 1950

Bill Frindall (ed): Wisden Book of Test Cricket Vol 1 1877-1977,
  Macdonald, Queen Anne Press 1979

Bill Frindall: English Test Cricketers, Willow Books 1989

Benny Green (ed): Wisden Anthology 1900–1940, Guild Publishing 1988

Benny Green (ed): Wisden Anthology 1940–1963, Guild Publishing 1985

Benny Green: Wisden Book of Obituaries, Macdonald Queen Anne Press
  1986

Benny Green (ed): The Wisden Papers 1888–1946, Guild Publishing 1989

Ramachandra Guha (ed): The Picador Book of Cricket, Picador 2001

Duncan Hamilton: The Great Romantic: Cricket and the Golden Age of
  Neville Cardus, Hodder and Stoughton 2019

Duncan Hamilton: Harold Larwood, Quereus 2009

Andrew Hignell: Turnbull: A Welsh Sporting Hero, Tempus 2001

Andrew Hignell: A Who's Who of Glamorgan County Cricket Club,
  Breeden Books 1992

Andrew Hignell: The History of Glamorgan County Cricket Club,
  Christopher Helm 1988

Alan Hill: Herbert Sutcliffe: Cricket Maestro, Simon and Schuster 1991

Alan Hill: Bill Edrich: A Biography, Andre Deutsch 1994

Gerald Howat: Cricket's Second Golden Age, Hodder and Stoughton 1989

Laurence Le Quesne: The Bodyline Controversy, Union Paperbacks 1985

Derek Lodge: The Test Match Career of Walter Hammond, Nutshell
  Publishing Co Ltd 1990

Christopher Martin Jenkins: The Complete Who's Who of Test Cricketers,
  Orbus Publishing 1980

Clive W Porter: The Test Match Career of Sir Jack Hobbs, Spellmount Ltd
  1988

AA Thompson: Cricket: The Great Captains, Sportsman's Book Club 1967

AA Thompson: Cricket: The Wars of the Roses, Sportsman's Book Club 1968

Simon Wilde: England The Biography, Simon and Schuster 2018

Anthony Woodhouse: The History of Yorkshire Cricket Club, Chistopher Helm 1989

MISCELLANEOUS SPORTS BOOKS:

Mihir Bose: The Spirit of the Game, Constable 2011

Duncan Hamilton: For the Glory: The Life of Eric Liddell, Doubleday 2016

HISTORY BOOKS:

Max Arthur: Forgotten Voices of World War Two, Ebuey Press 2004

John Campbell (ed): World War Two: History of the 20th Century Vol 5 1939–1945, BCA 1993

Niall Ferguson: War of the World: History's Age of Hatred, Allen Lane 2006

Niall Ferguson: Kissinger: The Idealist 1923–1968, Allen Lane 2015

Martin Gilbert: Never Again: A History of the Holocaust, Harper Collins 2000

Nicholas Stargardt: The German War: A Nation Under Arms 1939–1945, Bodley Head 2015

Gerhard L Weinberg: A World At Arms: A Global History of World War Two, Cambridge University Press 1994

WEBSITES:

http://cwgc:Commonwealth War Graves Commission;

http://espnscrum.com online rugby database;

http://www.footballersunited.co.uk;

Forces War Records;